#				
1 STONE DRAB	2 LIGHT DRAB	3 DRAB	4 RED DRAB	5 MAZARINE BLUE
6 LIGHT DRAB	7 DRAB	8 CRIMSON	9 BROWN OLIVE	10 YELLOW
11 YELLOW	12 ORANGE	13 ORANGE	14 FAST RED	15 GREEN
16 LILACH	17 LILACH	18 CLOTHIER'S DRAB	19 CLARET	20 LAVENDER
21 BROWN	22 GREEN OLIVE	23 DEEP LILACH OR LIGHT PURPLE	24 DARK PRUNE	25 PEACHWOOD RED
26 DARK SLATE	27 MAZARINE BLUE	28 MILK CHOCOLATE	29 PINK	30 PINK
31 PINK	32 BROWN OLIVE	33 (MISSING) CRIMSON	34 YELLOW	35 LIGHT BLUE
36 COMMON PINK	37 BEET ROOT	38 LAC SCARLET	39 LIGHT BLUE	40 DARK BROWN OR DAMSON COLOUR
41 SCARLET	42 SAGE DRAB	43 CLARET	RECIPE MISSING	

NATURAL DYES
AND HOME DYEING

(formerly titled: Natural Dyes in the United States)

RITA J. ADROSKO

Associate Curator, Division of Textiles
Museum of History and Technology

DOVER PUBLICATIONS, INC.
NEW YORK

This Dover edition, first published in 1971, is
an unabridged and corrected republication of the
work originally published in 1968 as United States
National Museum Bulletin 281 under the title
Natural Dyes in the United States.
The work is reprinted by permission of the author
and the Smithsonian Institution Press, publisher
of the original edition.

International Standard Book Number: 0-486-22688-3
Library of Congress Catalog Card Number: 70-140228

Manufactured in the United States of America
Dover Publications, Inc.
180 Varick Street
New York, N. Y. 10014

Contents

PREFACE

Hopefully the first part of this publication, a discussion of dyes used in America during the 18th and 19th centuries, will draw students and craftsmen into further exploration of this many-sided subject which encompasses chemistry, botany, textile technology, and fashion.

The second part, devoted to dye recipes, is a revision of the United States Department of Agriculture Miscellaneous Publication No. 230 "Home Dyeing with Natural Dyes" by Margaret S. Furry and Bess M. Viemont. Although this publication was issued in December 1935, the information gained through the research remains pertinent and useful for today's dyers.

I wish to express my appreciation to Mr. Dieter C. Wasshausen of the Department of Botany, Smithsonian Institution, for assigning contemporary equivalents to all the early botanical sources of dyes mentioned.

The illustrations reproduced on the part title pages (pages 1 and 55) are from Pierre Pomet's Histoire générale des drogues, book III, part I: Paris, 1694.

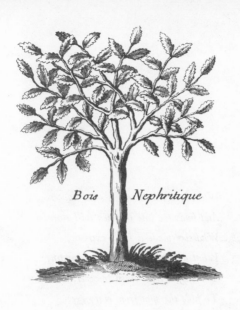

Bois Nephritique

PART ONE

Dyestuffs Used in America During the 18th and 19th Centuries

Santeaux

When lovely woman tilt's her saucer,
And finds too late that tea will stain,
Whatever made a Lady crosser,
What art can wash all white again;
The only art the stain to cover,
To hide the spot from every eye;
And wear an unsoiled dress above her,
The proper colour is to DYE.

From (Swartz, 1841, p. 36)

HISTORICAL BACKGROUND

Coloring is one of the most delightful arts, also a most responsible branch of manufacture; and a good dyer makes a manufacturer wealthy, happy, and renowned, while
a poor one brings ruin, bankruptcy, and misery; and not considering the fineness of the
cloth or the faultless weaver, the color sells the goods.

This statement, by a dyer who started working a hundred years ago
(Haserick, 1869, p. 2), echoes a sentiment well understood by today's
colorists.

It is difficult to imagine that before the mid-19th century professional
dyers of fine silks and woolens had to rely on such homely substances as
dried insects, roots and leaves of plants, and chamber lye for carrying on
their work. The accidental discovery in 1856 by William Henry Perkin of
a lavender dye artificially produced from a constituent of coal tar marked
the first step in the decline of the use of natural dyestuffs and the rise of
the synthetic dye industry throughout the world. Today natural dyestuffs
have practically no economic importance.

A fairly simple explanation for this almost complete rejection of materials
that had played such an important part in commercial and industrial life
during centuries past is that the quality and effectiveness of natural dyestuffs depended upon a great many factors. The dyestuffs were difficult to
store, and much time was spent in extracting color from these raw materials
and imparting it in cloth. Dyes made in the laboratory do not depend
upon growing seasons and do not have to be ground or chipped before they
are ready for use. Many, such as indigo, are chemically identical to natural
dyes; since they are manufactured pure, their colors are unaffected by the
impurities that dim dyes of vegetable origin. Before synthetic indigo was
introduced to the market in 1897 natural indigo had been considered of
excellent quality if it yielded 48 percent of its weight in pure coloring matter.

Today natural dyes are used in limited quantities by craftsmen in various
parts of the world. Although difficult to obtain commercially, dyes are
readily obtained from plant materials gathered in gardens, woods, and
along roadsides. Craftsmen are becoming increasingly enthusiastic about
this out-dated and time-consuming process for one of the reasons that
manufacturers rejected it: difficulty of standardization. Natural dyestuffs
produce offbeat, one-of-a-kind colors. No two dye lots are identical, each
having subtle differences due to impurities peculiar to the particular plant

3

material used. Thus the very characteristics of natural dyes that often made them the despair of earlier dyers appeal to today's craftsmen searching for the unique.

Textile Dyeing Before the Discovery of America

The first western dyers were probably the Swiss Lake Dwellers who lived about 2000 B.C.; in the East a Chinese chronology dated a thousand years earlier mentioned dye workshops, so the craft must have originated in China some time before 3000 B.C. Among other ancient peoples, the Egyptians of the Middle Kingdom not only dyed textiles but also understood the use of mordants (metallic salts with an affinity for both fibers and dyestuffs that improved the colorfastness of certain dyes). The Phoenician dye industry, begun in the 15th century B.C., was renowned for its purples obtained from a species of shellfish processed in the city of Tyre until 638 A.D. when the Tyrian industry was destroyed by conquering armies.

India, the country whose dyeing practices have exercised the greatest influence on European dyers from the 16th century, appears to have had a dye industry long before its transactions were recorded in writing, perhaps extending to the period of the Indus Valley civilization ca. 2500 B.C. Marco Polo described in detail its indigo manufacture during the 13th century A.D., about three hundred years before the Portugese introduced it to Europe.

European dye techniques improved slowly before the 18th century— mainly through trial-and-error. During the second quarter of the 18th century a number of French chemists began to organize contemporary information on textile dyeing and through experimentation gradually developed an understanding of the chemical and physical mechanisms of dyeing. Application of these theories gave impetus to the French textile industry and encouraged dyers in other parts of Europe and the United States to apply scientific methods to their own work.

The American Indian contributed comparatively little to the European settlers' knowledge of textile dyes. Scattered references suggest that while the Indians obtained some coloring materials from their natural surroundings which abounded in dye plants, the colonists generally depended on traditional methods and imported dyes whenever they could be obtained.

Textile Dyeing Among European Colonists and Their Descendants

No matter how seriously the subject of textile dyeing is discussed, one must inevitably acknowledge that the basis of the whole business is a

4

FIGURE 1.—Dyeing silk yarn. The interior of a French dye workshop showing main procedures and implements used in yarn dyeing (Encyclopédie . . . , 1772).

singularly powerful but frivolous one, fashion, and that the center of the fashion world around 1800 was Europe. Thus Americans still looked to Europe for the latest fashion colors and, to a great extent, for dye materials that produced them. Elijah Bemiss was keenly aware of this situation when he remarked:

Europeans apprised of our increasing manufactures, attempt to baffle our attempts by imposing on us mixed cloth as fashionable; they are sensible that the younger look to the older nations for the patterns of their garments, and for fashionable colours of their cloths; for this reason the Europeans frequently change or mix their colours to retain our adherence to their markets (1815, p. 262).

Almost all the professional dyers who practiced their trade in America until the mid-19th century either were trained in Europe or employed by men who had such a background. Evidence of this can be found by studying dye manuals printed in America during this period. It was natural that dyers would prefer ingredients they had learned to use in Europe. Thus

FIGURE 2.—The earliest known illustration of the interior of an American dye house (Hazen, 1836). Left: A worker lifting a dye bucket from a vat heated by a furnace that encases the vat. Right: Workers bent over various vats. The cloths draped on overhead beams indicate that finished cloth was being piece-dyed here.

it is not surprising that a table of "Goods and Produce imported into the several Provinces in North America . . . ." in 1770 included 70 tons of imported dyewoods (Sheffield, 1784, table 4), even though these were expensive and their availability fluctuated.

Imported dyes were generally superior to the domestic product due to lack of knowledgeable American technicians. Even when high quality raw materials were produced here lack of experience in preparing them reduced their market value. Only indigo succeeded for a span of about thirty years, boosted by a sixpence-per-pound bounty payment which was finally cut off at the start of the Revolutionary War. In producing good quality indigo it was important to pick the leaves and process them at their peak of maturity—just before the plant flowered. Some South Carolina planters, unable to ferment the leaves all at once after they matured, allowed them to remain in the fields two to three weeks after they ripened. This indigo had to be marketed as a second-rate product, since it could not yield the maximum quantity of dye. Planters in Bengal, India, avoided such a situation by simply staggering plantings. Thus indigo, successfully marketed before the Revolutionary War, could not compete in price with the East Indian product after the conflict. When southern planters learned that rice and cotton were more profitable, these superseded indigo as their cash crops.

Certainly many attempts had been made to exploit the natural resources of the colonies since the first colonists' arrival. English naturalists recorded in illustrated volumes their observations on the flora and fauna of the new land and their possible uses, while colonial governors sent specimens to England for study. These efforts showed the great interest in natural curiosities typical of the 17th and 18th centuries, and also the desire of the English to find new sources of cheap raw materials. All efforts toward using dye drugs to this latter end eventually failed. Then because other crops proved more profitable, dye plants were not cultivated in the United States on a commercial scale during the 19th century.

Before the Revolutionary War high import duties added to the prices of dyes. The post-war situation found dyers still suffering the hardships of high tariffs imposed on dyes imported from European countries and their colonies. Asa Ellis clearly expressed the Americans' problems and their possible solutions in these remarks:

For a great proportion of the ingredients employed in dyes, we depend on Europe to furnish . . . As we attempt an independence of their markets, they increase their duties on dyestuffs which we import. Not one cask, of Cochineal, can we obtain from our sister continent, South-America; from thence it must pop through the hands of Spain and England. From England we receive it, at an extravagant price . . . Foreign nations receive a large revenue from this country, for the dyestuffs we import. Does it become an independent nation, to be thus dependent on others, for articles, which, perhaps, may abound in our own country? Or shall we, without enquiry conclude that nature has denied us these articles; being partial in the distribution of her favours? . . .

If our government should consider it worthy of their attention, to encourage some able chemist to explore the qualities of our fossils, woods, barks, shrubs, plants, roots, weeds and minerals, perhaps, the advantages, our rising nation might derive, would soon indemnify us for the extra expense (1798, p. 137–139).

The following list of dye prices from an 1831 dye manual shows the price relationship of the six principal dyestuffs; the list also indicates that cochineal maintained its luxury price long after the wars with Britain:

quercitron, per lb.	$ .06
fustic " "	.06
logwood " "	.06
madder " "	.18¾
indigo " "	2.25
cochineal per oz.	.31 a 37½ (Lynde, p. 8).

Lack of funds for luxury dyes like cochineal, plus distance to cities where such items were obtainable, forced many rural inhabitants to explore their surroundings for dyes for the wool and linen yarns of their own manufacture.

Unfortunately the full extent of home dyeing and its importance in the overall view of colonial American textile manufacture may never be assessed accurately because written records on the subject are scanty. One exception is an excerpt from *An examination of Lord Sheffield's observations on the commerce of the United States*, on the state of American dyeing, published in 1791:

The implements hitherto used in household manufactures, have been of the most ancient kinds. The art of dyeing has been advanced in families little further than what was communicated by a recipe as brief as those in a book of culinary instructions; the colouring ingredients have generally been such as nature handed to the thrifty housewife. The operations, from the raw to the manufactured state, have often been the simplest that can be conceived. Under circumstances like these, it will not be too sanguine to expect the dissemination of useful instruction in the practice of dyeing, in the nature of colours, and concerning other parts of the business . . . ([Coxe], 1791, p. 120).

The sense of nationalism and desire for self-sufficiency on a national scale boosted American manufactures after the Revolution. Unfortunately the voices of influential individuals, such as Thomas Jefferson and Dolley Madison, raised in favor of home-grown dyestuffs, could not persuade farmers to raise madder, indigo, woad, or weld crops on a commercial scale. During this same period, however, the dyer's profession here advanced with sound chemical practice, gradually replacing former trial-and-error methods.

We must depend mainly on personal papers, regional and family traditions, and books of miscellaneous household recipes for home dyeing infor-

8

mation. Among the latter were volumes such as *Mackenzie's five thousand receipts in all the useful and domestic arts*, assembled by the Englishman Colin Mackenzie and adapted for use in this country by "an American Physician." This particular book went through numerous printings throughout the 19th century. One edition, printed in 1831 in Philadelphia and Pittsburgh, provided many good ideas on the subject of coloring textiles. It seems strange that such a volume, meant for the use of novices, often left so much to the imagination and judgment of the dyer. For example, in explaining the use of alum as a mordant the author states:

Alum, to make a mordant, is dissolved in water, and very frequently, a quantity of tartrate of potass is dissolved with it. Into this solution WOOLLEN cloth is put, and kept in it till it has absorbed as much alumine as is necessary. It is then taken out, and for the most part washed and dried. It is now a good deal heavier than it was before, owing to the alum which has combined with it (p. 81).

Important sources of information on raw materials used in 18th and 19th century American dye houses are the manuals written by dyers and printed in the United States between 1797 and 1869. Very few of these publications are the original works of Americans, since many were printed first in England, while others are merely collections of recipes assembled from earlier French, English, and German books. Frequently authors lifted whole sections of earlier works without crediting the original sources. When such volumes were printed in the United States, however, they were sometimes adapted for American use, with plants found in America added to the others. Even when no attempt was made to adapt recipes, the fact that these books were printed and sold here suggests that the foreign methods and dyes described were utilized by American dyers and clothiers.

Other sources, more difficult to ferret out, are dyers' and apothecaries' newspaper advertisements and patents. Dated apothecary advertisements often revealed partial stocks of these shops, which usually included some dye drugs and chemicals. Patents related to dyeing and dyestuff processing are virtually untapped sources of information, particularly interesting because they show the relationship between dyers and other craftsmen of the period.

Dyeing After 1850

Perkin's discovery in 1856 of a lavender dye made from aniline, a coal-tar product, marked the beginning of the end of the natural dyestuff era. It created considerable excitement in England and soon became popular in France, where the new color was known as mauve. "Queen Victoria wore a mauve dress at the Great Exhibition of 1862, penny postage stamps were

FIGURE 3.—Commercial piece-dyeing in England (Tomlinson, 1854).

A. Logwood-cutting machine—reduces blocks of logwood to usable chips.

B. Logwood sawdust dye tubs—logwood is soaked before put into dye-beck.

C. Mordanting: an alum cistern. At left center the unmordanted cloth is drawn into the cistern on the left, rolled overhead, drawn through a wringer, then stacked on the right.

D. Dye-beck (dye vat). A worker winds the cloth over and under a series of rollers, keeping the cloth moving continuously through the dyebath to promote even dyeing.

E. Water extractor on the right, finished cloth being rolled on the left.

A.

B.

C.

D.

E.

dyed with mauve, and according to *Punch,* the London policemen directed loiterers to 'get a mauve on' " (Holmyard, 1958, vol. 5, p. 272).

Although news of the new dye reached the United States soon after its appearance, a number of years passed before it was in general use—partly due to the political upheavals that were taking place in America during that period. For decades after aniline dyeing became standard procedure, the old natural dyes continued to be used side by side with the latest manufactured dyestuffs. But by the end of the 19th century all but a few natural dyes such as logwood, indigo, catechu, and cochineal had been replaced by the more dependable manufactured dyes. At that time American professional dyers depended almost entirely on Germany for supplies.

World War I cut off supplies of dyestuffs, causing a "dye famine" that jolted American chemical manufacturers into the business of large-scale dye manufacture. During the war there had been a temporary upsurge in demands for natural dyes. As soon as American manufacturers could supply the textile industries with a wide range of colors, however, natural dyes became obsolete. Only in mountainous and rural areas of the southeastern quarter of the country, traditional methods of weaving and dyeing survived among home dyers unaware of developments in large-scale chemical dyeing. These country dyers, working far from the mainstream of American life, did not follow the trends toward standardization of dyes and dyeing procedures generally accepted in the northern industrial areas. They are unique in this respect and preserved traditions of home dyeing with natural materials longer than any other group of dyers in the United States.

During the first quarter of the 20th century a revival of interest in arts and crafts led to experimentation with old methods of spinning, weaving, and dyeing. This movement, plus efforts to encourage the continuation of southern mountain folk crafts, inspired textile craftsmen throughout the country to explore the field of natural dyes once more. During the same time the Navajo Indians almost entirely ceased working with the generally poor quality commercial dyes they had used since the late 19th century, replacing them with natural dyes. Today the Indians are once again turning to chemical dyes in which improved color range and fastness and ease of application permit users to color yarns more quickly and efficiently than heretofore.

Many contemporary textile craftsmen, working professionally or as hobbyists, however, turn to natural dyes for color ideas. Although fine, dependable commercial dyes are on the market, devotees of natural coloring materials derive a nostalgic pleasure from handling vegetable materials and extracting uniquely "impure" colors from them. It is this latter group who would find that experimentation with untried plants might turn up unexpectedly interesting results.

THE DYESTUFFS

There are, no doubt, a great number of dying drugs in this country, which, if known, might become valuable. It is much to be regretted, that some institution does not exist in this country to test and bring to notice its native colouring matters. In the hands of a practical and theoretical dyer, many valuable discoveries might be made of new dyes now lying dormant. Many of them might be used to advantage by the dyers of this country, and also become objects of some magnitude, as exports.

In spite of this notion, expressed by William Partridge in 1847 (pp. 37–38) and subscribed to by many others since his time, we know that the American dye industry never could rely on home-grown raw materials.

The most important and most frequently used dyes of the United States in the 18th and 19th centuries were indigo for blue, madder and cochineal for red, and fustic and quercitron for yellow. Logwood was the most commonly used black dyeing ingredient, and sumach, though not strictly a dye, so often was used in neutrals and blacks that it deserves a special mention along with the other six coloring materials. Of these only quercitron and sumach were native to the United States. To complete the picture of dyes used in this country during the 18th and 19th centuries and to suggest plants for further experimentation, appendixes B, C, and D have been included. Appendix B is a list of dyes occasionally mentioned in dyers' publications printed in America between 1797 and 1869; Appendix C provides a list of South Carolina dye plants compiled during the first decade of the 19th century; and Appendix D is a list of dye plants which Thomas Cooper translated and borrowed from the work of D'Ambourney and included in his 1815 dye manual.

Most of the dyestuffs which were regarded as basic stock in dye houses are discussed in detail below. The remainder are native materials less frequently mentioned in dye manuals but very likely used by home dyers because of their availability.

BLUE DYES

*INDIGO [1] (*Indigofera tinctoria*) also known as anil (Fr.)
WILD INDIGO (*Baptisia tinctoria*, formerly known as *Sophora tinctoria*)

Indigo, the dyestuff most widely used in America during the 18th and 19th centuries, is not a native of this country. It is a blue dye derived from the leaves of a leguminous plant which grew in India and Egypt long before the Christian era and later was used by the Romans in making an ink they called indicum. In the 16th century it was brought to Europe from India by Portuguese, Dutch, and English traders.

---

[1] Recipes for dyes marked with an asterisk (*) are given in Section 2.

Goußes de l'Anil

Anil

FIGURE 4.—Indigo plant (Pomet, 1694).

The earliest known attempt to grow indigo in America is revealed in a tract dated 1649 (Force, 1838, p. 4).[2] From it we learn that indigo was planted with the notion that it would eventually prove ten times more

[2] This excerpt from an anonymous letter included in Peter Force's collection of early documents appears in a section entitled "A Perfect Description of Virginia: Being a full and true Relation of the present State of the Plantation, their Health, Peace, and Plenty . . . certified by diverse men . . ."

profitable than tobacco, and that the planters hoped to grow enough indigo to take over India's profitable indigo trade. Since no more is heard of indigo cultivation in the colonies until about ninety years later, one assumes that the project failed. This indigo may have been the plant sometimes called wild indigo or yellow wild indigo (*Baptisia tinctoria*) mentioned by John Clayton, who supplied information for an 18th-century book on the flora of Virginia (Gronovius, 1762, p. 64).

Dutch settlers also attempted to grow wild indigo in New York City and Albany as early as 1650 (Bishop, 1866, vol. 1, p. 348). Other scattered references to wild indigo appeared throughout the colonial period and in the later 19th century. One informs us that as late as 1873 some South Carolina planters still cultivated it, contending that in spite of indigo's low price—75 cents per pound—it was still more profitable than cotton ("Baptisia Tinctoria," 1895, p. 81).

Introduction of a species of *Indigofera* to South Carolina in 1739 and its subsequent commercial success must be credited mainly to the intelligent and persistent efforts of Eliza Lucas Pinckney. Her father, Governor of Antigua at the time, sent her seeds of various plants that might be suited to growing conditions in Carolina. After many trials she managed to produce enough indigo in 1747 to make up a shipment for England. It met with approval in England and remained the staple crop of the colony from the late 1740s until the war, reaching its peak in 1773, when 1,107,660 pounds were exported to England (Sheffield, 1784, table 1).

During the war this crop was neglected in favor of rice; after the conflict it could no longer compete with the cheaper but better quality East Indian variety. Thus toward the turn of the 18th century cotton took over from indigo as Carolina's important crop. Georgia and Louisiana cultivated some indigo but never succeeded in making a large-scale commercial success of it.

The French had introduced indigo to Louisiana in 1718, and 10 years later its export began. With the help of French bounties, indigo production and exportation continued until later in the century when it was learned that cotton could be produced more profitably (Bishop, 1866, vol. 1, p. 348).

Natural indigo was used throughout the 19th century, for it was not synthesized until the 1870s, and more than 20 years passed before methods were devised for producing it in quantities and at prices suitable for marketing. Synthetic indigo has replaced that of natural origin to such an extent that natural indigo is now practically impossible to obtain in this country.

Indigotin, the main constituent of indigo, is prepared from the leaves of various species of *Indigofera*. Only about four ounces of indigotin are extracted from 100 pounds of plant material, according to a 20th century

15

FIGURE 5.—Indigo processing—a Frenchman's interpretation of indigo preparation in India during the late 17th century. Steps include cutting the plant, placing the stalks in a water-filled vat, agitating the soaking indigo stalks, and carrying the precipitated dye material to dry (Pomet, 1694).

source. Preparation for market requires many steps: First the plants are cut just as they mature, then steeped and allowed to ferment; next the solution containing indigotin is drawn off and the plants are disposed of; the indigotin solution is then subjected to another series of steps. The solution is beaten with paddles to incorporate air into it and to promote oxidation. When oxidation is complete, the indigo material is allowed to settle, the liquid is drawn off, and the mass of indigo, pressed, cut, and dried, is ready for market.

Early in the 19th century, indigo was often sold in the form of dark blue cubes or cakes called "junks." The quality of these "junks" was a matter of great concern to the professional dyer, for indigo was an expensive dye. If, as one dyer stated, 6½ pounds of indigo would dye 100 pounds of cloth a full deep blue, the cost of indigo alone per pound of cloth dyed would be more than 14¢, based on the 1831 price of $2.25 per pound (Lynde, p. 8). The cost of indigo and other indigo dye ingredients such as potash, bran, and madder, plus labor costs, added up to a very costly dye operation.

Opinions differed greatly on which country exported the best grade of indigo. Some dyers considered Bengal (India) indigo the best, claiming that it would color at least 10 percent more cloth than the best Spanish Flote indigo, imported from the Spanish dominions in central America. The criteria by which the 19th-century dyer judged the quality of indigo included: light weight in relation to bulk, smoothness in the fracture, and a bright violet, purple, or bronze hue.

There was general agreement that the price paid for the indigo should be in proportion to its yield. Thus sometimes buying low-priced indigo with moderate yield could be more profitable than purchasing the highest priced article with proportionately lower yield.

Since the indigo vat is described in detail in the Dye Recipe section it is only necessary to make some general remarks about indigo dyeing practices in America.

One learns from early dye manuals that many kinds of blue vats were worked. The main ingredient in all of these was either woad, indigo, or a combination of both. Dyers' opinions differed on the relative merits of woad and indigo; however, it is now known that although the dyeing ingredient indigotin is common to both dyes, it is present in indigo in much greater quantity.

Indigo is insoluble in water before dyeing, but it is made soluble in the blue vat. Dipping textile material in the dye solution deposits dye in the fibers. When the textile is removed from the dye vat, the air oxidizes the indigo, returning it to its original insoluble form.

Several combinations of ingredients will help to put indigo into solution. These account for the variety of instructions for making up blue vats that

17

one encounters in 19th century dyers' books. The main purpose of these ingredients was to combine them with indigo to reduce it and make it soluble in alkali solutions; in this dissolved state indigo could be absorbed by textile material.

Bran and madder, by inducing fermentation, act as reducing agents. Other chemical compounds (such as copperas) which also act as reducing agents were frequently used. Indigo, in its reduced state, then is dissolved in an alkali solution—usually made up of lime, potash, or soda in water.

A typical and comparatively uncomplicated vat that Thomas Cooper said was used by wool dyers of Pennsylvania and American back-country dyers (1815, p. 45) is basically similar to the "Blue-Pot" recipe given in the Dye Recipe section. Another dyer of the same period commented that urine used as a fermentation-inducing ingredient in indigo dyeing had been used with great success. Each individual dyer's procedures were adapted to the amount of cloth dyed, frequency of dyeing, and the available ingredients. Thus though the blue vat was often worked under primitive conditions, 18th and 19th century professionals and home dyers alike considered the complicated indigo-dyeing process as the basic method of coloring textiles.

Other Blue Dyes

Although indigo was by far the most important dyestuff used throughout 18th- and 19th-century America, a few other blue dyestuffs were employed by professional clothiers and dyers. Among these were woad, chemic, and Prussian blue.

WOAD (Isatis tinctoria)
Also known as pastel (Fr.); der (Färber) Waid (Ger.)

Woad was well known long before traders introduced East Indian indigo into Europe early in the 16th century. During the 17th century, indigo's value became more and more recognized in spite of determined efforts by the guilds of the woad processors to limit its use. Woad was probably the first blue dyestuff used in America, carried from their mother country by the earliest colonizers. By 1700, however, indigo could be obtained from the West Indies, and from that time woad's importance diminished as indigo became more and more widely used.

The woad vat was basically similar to the indigo vat, requiring care in controlling the fermentation process by which the coloring agent was reduced to its soluble form. According to many 19th-century American dyers, great skill was required to develop the correct degree of fermentation in the woad vat due to great quality differences in the raw material. Often the experienced woad dyer's most valuable asset was his sensitive nose,

18

with which he could detect changes in the fermenting activity, the changes in turn signaling when more lime or bran should be added or the vat stirred.

Perhaps early dyers were not aware that indigo and woad contained a common dye principle, indigotin, and that indigotin was present in greater concentration in indigo; however, they gradually realized that woad was definitely the less potent of the two substances. Long after dyers discovered the true value of indigo it was still being used in combination with woad, because it was supposed to promote fermentation and to "render the colour brighter." Regarding the latter, some dyers felt that only with the addition of woad could certain fine blue tones be produced. This notion may have been true, or it may have simply indicated the dyers' lack of skill in working indigo vats to produce these hues.

Very little woad was grown in the United States. Some was grown in Britain, but most of the woad used here was imported from France and Holland. William Partridge in 1847 remarked that an inferior quality of woad had been grown and marketed by a number of farmers located in the Hartford, Connecticut, area. He felt that the inferior quality was the result of poor processing. Homegrown woad, also mentioned by other dyers of that period, was probably raised on a small scale in various parts of Northeastern United States, since growing conditions were quite suitable for its cultivation. Processing was a far greater problem than growing, for even before it could be used woad required long, complicated fermentation and drying procedures. It was sold in the form of 150- to 200-pound bails and also in balls that resembled clods of dried earth interlaced with plant fibers.

Although its use continued throughout the 19th century, its importance diminished gradually until the end of the century when it was practically obsolete. Woad is last mentioned as a dye ingredient in early 20th-century English dye literature; by that time its use was certainly very limited.

CHEMIC (a popular name for indigo sulfate) or Saxon blue

Chemic, frequently mentioned by 19th-century dyers, is a product of the treatment of powdered indigo with concentrated sulfuric acid. Its properties were totally different from those of indigo, for chemic had poor fastness to light and washing, contrasted to the indigo vat dye's excellent colorfastness. It was applied to some silks and coarse wools and even cotton because of its relatively simple application (mordanting and immersion of cloth in dye solution) and characteristic, though short-lived, blue coloring.

According to one story chemic was discovered by a certain Mr. Seidelman who lived in Altenburg, Saxony, during the mid-18th century. He combined sulfuric acid with powdered indigo, which made a black paste. This black paste was then set aside in the dye house where he was employed, and after a while, thinking it was useless, the dyer threw the compound out the window onto the snow. As the snow melted Mr. Seidelman "saw . . . the beautiful blue veins of the dissolved indigo. He at once took part of it in a tumbler of hot water, added some alum and dipped some wool yarn into it; the result was a new color" (Haserick, 1869, p. 17). Supposedly he later sold his secret in England for $6,000.

Apparently this rather inferior dye was used by professional dyers on coarse goods throughout the 19th century; with improved methods of application, its use continued until the early 20th century.

PRUSSIAN BLUE
Also known as bleu de Prusse (Fr.); das Berlinerblau (Ger.)

One of the earliest chemical dyes used in America, Prussian blue is made by combining prussiate of potash with an iron salt in which the prussiate acts as a dye and the iron salt as a mordant. They combine to form a white solution that turns blue when oxidized.

Its discovery is credited to a German chemist of the first decade of the 18th century, but its practical application was delayed for about a hundred years until a method of fixing it on fabrics was developed. The first use of Prussian blue in this country appears to have been in 1832, when F. Tassard of Philadelphia dyed broadcloth "Lafayette" blue. Specimens of this cloth, made in Dedham, Massachusetts, were exhibited at the Fair in the American Institute in New York in 1833 (Bishop, 1866, vol. 2, p. 372).

Prussian blue-dyed cotton is extremely fast to light; however, the same coloring agent darkens on wool and decomposes in boiling soap solutions. In applying Prussian blue to silk, only the prussiate of potash needs to be applied if the silk has been weighted previously with iron salts. Weighting eliminates the need for an extra mordanting step, and thus simplifies the dyeing procedure.

Prussian blue was used until the early 20th century when improved means of achieving the same color made it obsolete.

RED DYES

*MADDER (Rubia tinctorum)
Also known as common madder; garance (Fr.); der Krapp (Ger.)

It is well known that Madder is so essential to dyers and callico-printers, that neither business can be carried on without it. The consumption of it is so great in England, that, upon a moderate computation, more than 180,000 sterling, is annually paid for what is imported from Holland, exclusive of their supplies from other parts; and as in a little time, manufacturers of these kinds, must of necessity, progress in America, the sooner some attention is paid to this article, the better.

20

This opinion was expressed by Bernard McMahon of Philadelphia, author of one of the most important American garden books of the early 19th century (1806, p. 322).[3]

Doubtless many of McMahon's contemporaries agreed with him on the importance of madder. It was a staple red wool, silk, and cotton dye by the 18th century, although it had probably been brought to America a century earlier by immigrating colonists. Madder dye was obtained from the roots of *Rubia tinctorum* until the last quarter of the 19th century when alizarin, its main constituent, was synthesized.

The perennial madder, a native of Asia Minor, was cultivated in Italy, then France and Holland. Most madder imported to America came from the latter two countries. It seems strange that it was never cultivated to any great extent in America though growing conditions were considered quite suitable. In 1785, the Society for the Promotion of Agriculture in South Carolina offered a premium for growing madder. Many prominent citizens, among them Thomas Jefferson and Dolley Madison, strongly urged farmers to raise this useful plant. Evidently Jefferson was personally interested in madder cultivation, for an 1811 entry in his garden book reveals that he imported madder seeds from France and planted them in the southeast corner of his garden. This madder, *Galium mollugo*, was known as wild madder, and although its roots also contain red dye, it is a member of the lady's bedstraw family and not the true madder, *Rubia tinctorum*. Jefferson, in replying to a Boston gentleman's query about madder, recalled that it had been cultivated in Virginia for household use since before the Revolution (Jefferson, 1944, p. 452).

The American Philosophical Society in 1802 offered a $150 premium for the "best experimental essay on the native red dies of the United States." Mrs. Madison was to have made a report to the society on specimens dyed with madder raised under her direction; however, this paper never appeared in the society's transactions. Thomas Cooper, in his account of madder cultivation in the settlement of Harmony, about 20 miles from Pittsburgh, Pennsylvania, reported that 8 or 10 acres of madder were planted annually for local consumption.

Homegrown madder was very simply prepared. It took 3 years for the roots to reach their peak yield. Then, according to Jefferson, the fresh root was beaten into a paste 12 hours after it was washed. He claimed that fresh madder was twice as potent as the dried root. Commercial madder

---

[3] This entry does not appear in the 1857 edition. Thomas Jefferson's letter to William Coolidge on the cultivation of madder refers to the 1806 edition (see Jefferson, 1944, p. 452).

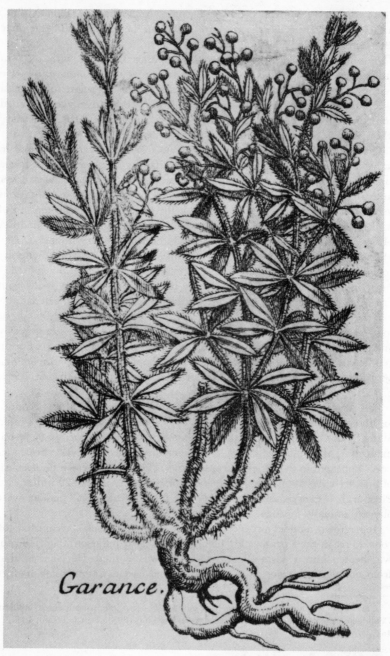

Garance.

FIGURE 6.—Madder plant. An illustration based on one in Gerard's *Herbal* of 1597 (Pomet, 1694).

imported from Holland went through many more complicated preparatory steps. First it was oven-dried then pounded into powder. The husks removed in this first pounding were sifted out and sold at a low price. The second pounding resulted in separating out one-third of the remaining roots and, after sifting, this material was sold as an intermediate quality. The final pounding left only the "interior, pure and bright part of the roots" and made up the first quality "Kor Kraps" or crop madder. Packed in casks, madder's potency would increase with aging for 1 to 2 years. During this aging period and during shipping, it tended to pick up moisture that could, in excess, deteriorate the madder. Besides overaging, buyers had to contend with the possibility of adulteration with brick dust, sand, mahogany wood, almond shells, and many other mineral and vegetable substances. Mineral substances were generally less harmful because they would simply reduce the quantity of dye as they settled to the bottom of the vat; however, vegetable substances could sadden bright red hues.

Madder dyeing of cotton, called Turkey red dyeing, originated in India, from there it was transmitted to other parts of the East (including Turkey, from which the process derived its name) and eventually was carried to Europe by the French. Turkey or Adrianople red became one of the most sought-after colors of the 19th century. In 1840 the Merrimac and Hamilton Mills in Lowell, Massachusetts, alone produced more than a quarter-million yards of cotton fabrics dyed or printed in madder colors "of a price and quality that rivalled the foreign" (Bishop, 1866, vol. 2, p. 421).

The whole process was, according to one dyer, the most complicated application of mordant in the whole art of dyeing, requiring, in addition to madder, an oil, galls, alum, dung and—in one recipe—the intestinal liquor of a ruminating animal and the blood of oxen or sheep.

John Rauch, whose dyebook gives complete directions for Turkey red dyeing, believed that the dyer of such yarn had to have his whole dye house geared to that purpose only. He felt it was necessary to have 4,500 or 5,000 pounds of yarn on hand, so that with the assistance of 8 or 10 helpers the dyer could finish 100 pounds per day (1815, p. 34).

Rauch stated that it took 16 actual working days with one drying day allowed after each day's work. A total of 40 to 50 days were required to complete the process. Basically cotton was prepared by soaking in soda, after which the cloth went through several days' dippings in oil and sheep-dung solutions. Then it was dipped in soda and nitric acid, later in nut gall solution, and finally in alum solution. The first three-fourths of the processing mordanted and prepared the yarn. The actual dyeing in madder solution took only 3 hours. The remaining dips were in oil and soda solutions, concluding with a final alum, nitric acid, and water bath, rinse, and shade-drying.

The rich red color that resulted from this process was permanently fixed on the cotton yarn or cloth used in shawls, ginghams, and table coverings.

*COCHINEAL (*Dactylopius coccus*, formerly known as *Coccus cacti*).
Also known as cochenille (Fr.); die Cochenille (Ger.)

When the Spaniards entered Mexico in 1518 they found the natives dyeing with cochineal. This red dyestuff which the Spaniards mistook for tiny seeds was actually the dried bodies of the insect *Dactylopius coccus*. Soon the Spaniards shipped the dye back to Spain for export to various parts of Europe; later some cochineal was sent back across the ocean to the English colonies. Guatemala and Mexico were at first the two main sources of this dye, because the insects' food *Opuntia cochenillifera* (sometimes called "nopal" or "cactus opuntia") grew in these countries.

Opuntia also flourished in Georgia and South Carolina, thus there were great hopes that cochineal could also be produced in this country. In 1762 the Society of Arts offered a premium of £40 for the largest quantity imported from the colonies (Bishop, 1866, vol. 1, p. 350); however, there seems to be little further reference to its production here.

Although it was high priced, after 1793 cochineal was considered a staple red dye along with the cheaper madder. Coarse woolen stuffs were dyed with madder or orchil, but fine cloth was almost exclusively dyed with cochineal, according to an 1831 source. Its coloring principle, carminic acid, produced beautiful crimsons, pinks, and scarlets on wool and silk when mordanted with tin or alum.

Cochineal-producing insects, either wild or domesticated, yielded equally good color but the wild variety, yielding only one-fourth the amount of dye, was considered less desirable. As the insect matured, the wingless dye-yielding females were swept off the leaves to which they were attached and killed in hot water, then dried in the sun, or placed in a bag and stove-dried. The latter method yielded silver cochineal, so-called because of its silver ash-gray color. The other type was blacker and drier, and called "negra." It takes 70,000 dried insects to produce one pound of cochineal and an acre planted with *Opuntia* yielded 250 to 300 pounds of the insects.

Cochineal powder could be damaged by sea air and adulterated very easily, sometimes with "stones large as a fly." Thus the wary buyer was warned to examine each sample carefully. The home dyer probably relied to a great extent on less expensive madder for her reds; however, if cochineal was purchased for home use it could be ground to a powder in a coffee mill or mortar.

To dye woolen cloth, it was recommended that the cloth be finished— milled, napped, and sheared—before dyeing, since subsequent dressing would "tarnish the color." Dyeing was comparatively simple, with tin combined with tartar or an alum mordant used either in a separate bath or in the dyebath. The color could be blued by adding a little alkali— ammonia or sodium carbonate—to the dyebath.

Sometimes professional dyers reduced costs by using part cochineal and part brazilwood or a yellow dye to stretch the cochineal. It was not always considered legitimate, but one dyer cautioned that it was better to complement the cochineal with red dyewood than to overboil pure cochineal in attempting to extract the maximum amount of color.

Cochineal was used even on a commercial scale until the turn of the 19th century when azo-scarlet dyes were introduced. None of the new synthetic dyes offered a perfect substitute, for as late as 1910 azo reds tended to bleed and stain neighboring colors. Because of more predictable quality, supply, and lower costs, azo reds eventually superseded natural cochineal red.

Other Red Dyes

Madder and cochineal were the most important red dyestuffs used in 18th- and 19th-century America. Next in importance were brazilwood and other red dyewoods. Although the colors they produced were fugitive these woods were known and used by most professional dyers, probably because they were cheap and readily available. The remainder of the reds were extracted from alkanet, annatto, lac, safflower, and local plants such as pokeberries.

BRAZILWOOD (mainly *Caesalpinia echinata*)
Also known as Pernambuco; Fernambouc; Santa Martha wood; Bois de Bresil (Fr.);
Peach wood; Queen's wood; redwood; das Rotholz (Ger.)

The general term brazilwood refers to the wood of several different trees from which red dye was obtained. The common names listed usually denote the trees' place of origin. The South American country, Brazil, received its name from the forests of red dyewood trees encountered by its discoverers when they landed about 1500. These trees were a Western Hemisphere species similar to the sappan (*C. sappan*) that grew in the East and had been known in Europe for over two-hundred years. The Brazilian dyewood yielded a commercial quality of red dye that became a profitable article of trade throughout the American colonial period. By the beginning of the 19th century the supply of these trees had diminished considerably, and other available dyewoods of equal quality took their place.

Caesalpinia sappan

During the Middle Ages this brazilwood (*C. sappan*) was an important article of European commerce obtained from India, Malaya, and Ceylon. Eventually it became known in Europe and America as "sapan," its Malay name, and was thus distinguished from other brazilwood. One

25

source incorrectly ascribes the origin of its name "sapan" to a misinterpretation of "Japan," one of its countries of origin. Sapan, the most ancient source of brazilwood, remained in common use until some time after the middle of the 19th century.

Haematoxylon brasiletto

The third important source of brazilwood dyes was a shrub grown in Nicaragua, Colombia, and Venezuela (*Haematoxylon brasiletto*). Its export began about 1848, and its trade continued into the early 20th century when the First World War caused a brief revival of interest in natural dyes. The heartwood of this tree produced hues that ranged from reds to purples. Since the dye was fugitive, it was replaced by synthetic dyes soon after the war. Besides being called by the other common names for brazilwood, braziletto was also known as Nicaragua wood and hypernick.

All brazilwoods that contained the basic dye ingredient brasilin were processed in the same manner. The reddish heartwood, shipped in log or stick form, was rasped or chipped before it could be used. It was treated like logwood: placed in a sack, immersed in a water bath until the dye was released, then the sack of chips removed before the wool, silk, or cotton material was entered. Different mordants such as nutgalls and alum with tartar produced a variety of red hues, values, and intensities, but none were as fast to light and washing as madder and cochineal. These mordants could be applied to a textile before, during, or after dyeing.

Brazilwood which gives textiles pink and claret hues was often used in calico printing and as a finishing dye in combination with other more stable but less brilliant hues. In this way it could be combined with logwood to produce violet or brown or used to brighten madder scarlets; it was frequently one of the many ingredients used in black dyeing.

CAMWOOD or BARWOOD (mainly *Baphia nitida* and varieties of *Pterocarpus*) and Sanders or Red saunders (*Pterocarpus santalinus*)
Also known as das Kamholz (Ger.)

Dye manuals of the 18th and 19th centuries distinguish between camwood, barwood, and sanders wood; however, all three can be discussed as a group since they all share a common dye principle, santalin, and the same botanical genus, *Pterocarpus*. Each has a different place of origin: camwood from the West Coast of Africa, barwood from Sierra Leone, and sanders (also spelled saunders, red sanders, santal, or sandal) from India, Ceylon and other parts of tropical Asia, and the Coromandel Coast (many 19th century works mention the latter as the source of sanders).

These woods superficially resemble brazilwood in their red coloration (under certain conditions) and in imparting in textiles similar fugitive red hues. Their dyes were more lasting but much more time-consuming to process because of the hardness and fine grain of the woods. The same basic dyeing technique, however, was still used for both dye groups.

Camwood, barwood, and sanders were known but seldom used in America before the 19th century. The British had used barwood for dark red printed imitations of East Indian bandanas before 1814 (Bancroft, 1814, vol. 2, p. 251), yet while it was fairly durable on wool, the color was not permanent when applied to cotton. An American dyer of 1798 said that this reddish-brown dyestuff was imported in casks and ground fine like flour. The powder was far more convenient for the dyer than the stick form which had to be chipped very fine and required much boiling, yet it too had its drawbacks for, the same dyer continued, if the floury dye material was agitated a hot dust would arise to irritate the nose and throat glands.

Another dyer 40 years later expressed the opinion that camwood injured the quality of (woolen) goods more than twice the value of the cost of dyeing. This harmful effect on wool is not mentioned in later scientific dye manuals. This raises the question of whether prolonged boiling or other processing could have been more responsible for injuries to cloth than were the dyestuff's harmful properties.

Most dye manuals emphasize the distinctive characteristics of the three woods grouped together here. The quality of the trees, care in packing and shipping, and variations in dyeing methods and mordants, however, probably influenced the color and degree of fastness obtained far more than variations between camwood, barwood, and sanders woods.

These woods continued in use until the early 20th century when they were at last completely replaced by synthetic dyestuffs. The latest applications of these woods were in combination with other dyes, producing compound shades such as browns, and in giving a bottom to woolens before indigo dyeing.

ALKANET (*Alkanna tinctoria* or *Anchusa tinctoria*)
Also known as alkanna, alkanea, orcanette, orcanète (Fr.)

Englishmen who landed along the southeastern coast of America probably found *Alkanna tinctoria* soon after they settled in their new homeland. Another variety of this plant was cultivated in England and France where it had been used as a dye for many years, thus it was undoubtedly quite familiar to many early dyers. In America the dye was probably much more important to the Indians than to European settlers who had access to more stable red-coloring agents such as madder. Hollberg in 1763 mentioned *Anchusa virginiana* as the source of puccoon, a yellow dye employed by the Indians for painting body designs. Since it is not found in the United States, it may have been mistaken for the European plant. Catesby and Ramsay gave the name puccoon to bloodroot (*Sanguinaria canadensis*) which yields a yellowish-red dye used by the Indians.

27

Home dyers undoubtedly used alkanet in areas where it was locally available. Red color is extracted from alkanet roots by immersing them in various solvents. The coloring material was placed in a water bath into which the textile material—usually wool or silk—was immersed. This processing imparted a fugitive red color. An 1869 source also mentioned that limited amounts of cotton and thread were also alkanet-dyed a bluish lilac by using alum and iron mordants.

ANNATTO (*Bixa orellana*)
Also known as annotta; arnotta; roucou (Fr.); racourt; orlean; and otter

Apparently annatto was commonly used during the 18th and 19th centuries, producing pink, reddish, and orange hues on cotton and silk, and yellow-orange colors in butter and cheese.

The dye is derived from the orange-red outer covering of the seeds of a tropical shrub, *Bixa orellana*. Specific preparatory techniques differed; however, in general the seeds were soaked, fermented, macerated, and washed, then pressed into small cakes or sold as a paste. The shrub that bears this fruit thrives in tropical areas all over the world; however, annatto was imported to America mainly from South America.

The knowledge that bixin, annatto's dye principle, could be dissolved readily in alkali was applied in 1814 and later when an alkaline annatto solution was sold in London as "Scott's Nankeen Dye."

All 19th century annatto-dyeing procedures employed potash and often used an alum mordant with a variety of recommendations for combining these ingredients. One early 20th century cotton-dyeing procedure required two steps: the cloth was first immersed in a warm alkaline dye bath (sodium carbonate), followed by a dilute sulfuric acid bath in which the red coloring matter developed.

Because of its fugitive nature this dye was used often in combination with weld, brazilwood, or other dyestuffs. Authors of a number of dye manuals cautioned users that soap and wind "carried off" its colors.

GUM-LAC (*Laccifer lacca*, formerly known as *Coccus lacca*)
Also known as gomme-laque (Fr.); der Gummilack (Ger.)

This dye was known for centuries in India before it was finally exported to England in 1796 (Bancroft, 1814, vol. 2, p. 13). A few years later it was imported into the United States, where it found a ready market throughout the remainder of the 19th century. Its popularity was due to reasonable price (half the cost of cochineal for which it substituted) and dull but very fast red colors.

Lac dye was derived from the dried bodies of East Indian insects related to the cochineal-producing insect, *Dactylopius coccus*. These attached them-

Roucou

Negres fabriquant le Roucou

Gousses de Roucou

FIGURE 7.—Annatto (roucou) processing as interpreted during the late 17th century. The seed pod is on the left; soaking vat is shown in center, with natives in foreground reducing the fermented seed coverings to a pulp; whole plant is on the right (Pomet, 1694).

selves to twigs of trees of the genus *Ficus* on which they reproduced rapidly. After the insect bodies had formed a thick gummy red coating on the twigs, the twigs were broken off and sun-dried to kill the insects. Until about 1810 lac could not be purchased in any other form. It was a laborious task to grind the sticks and pound them into a powder, put the powder into water to dissolve the coloring matter, and then dispose of the remainder of the material (90 percent of the whole). An addition of alum precipitated the dyestuff that could then be filtered out and dried.

Before 1810 a cake form of lac came on the market (Bancroft, 1814, vol. 2, p. 15), however, the quality of the cakes proved so erratic that dyers were discouraged from using them, usually preferring to process the dye themselves.

The scarlet, crimson, and orange shades dyed with lac were not as brilliant as those produced by cochineal; therefore, brilliant cochineal was often combined with durable lac to make a very attractive, permanent dye, with the added advantage of being considerably less expensive than cochineal alone.

SAFFLOWER (*Carthamus tinctorius*)
Also known as carthamus; bastard saffron; carthame (Fr.); der Saflor (Ger.)

The safflower plant, a native of Egypt and some parts of India, was cultivated in Europe for the clear pinkish-red colors it imparted to cottons and silks. Although probably used much more in Europe than in the United States, safflower is mentioned in various 19th-century dye manuals. Professional dyers acquainted with its attractive colors may have applied it here. Unfortunately the clear reds extracted from safflower were not long-lasting due to its sensitivity to acids, alkalis, and light. These latter qualities greatly limited its usefulness.

The flower head of this annual of the thistle family contains two coloring matters; water-soluble yellow that is unsatisfactory for dyeing and the alkali-soluble reddish dye. To extract the red dye the flower heads were first placed in a sack, crushed and washed in a stream of cold water until all soluble yellow color was removed. Then the reddish dye was extracted from the remaining mass of safflower heads by placing them in a weak alkali solution into which the cloth was also immersed.

The most important application of this dye was in coloring cotton tapes used to tie together legal documents—the source of the original "red tape" so familiar to bureaucrats.

POKEBERRY (*Phytolacca decandra*)

The dye extracted from pokeberries seems to have been used a great deal by home dyers; however, comments by professional dyers on the dye source always mentioned its short-lived color.

It was used as early as 1749, but even then Peter Kalm [4] expressed regret that no method had been found to fix the color on woolen and linen cloth (1772, vol. 1, p. 153). Many of the families who own old handwoven coverlets tell the story of grandmother gathering pokeberries and extracting their juice to dye coverlet wool deep jewel-toned reds. This is a rather unlikely possibility, unless our home-dyeing ancestors possessed some well-guarded secret methods of fixing the dye.

Kermes and mungeet (or munjeet) are two other red dyestuffs worthy of passing recognition. These were frequently mentioned but apparently little used by dyers in America.

Kermes (the genus *Kermes*) is a red dye of very ancient origin that, like cochineal, was derived from the dried bodies of insects related to cochineal-producing *Dactylopius coccus*. Its color was durable, but not as bright as cochineal's. The kermes insects fed on a certain type of oak (*Quercus coccifera*) and were raised in Southern France, Spain, and along other sections of the Mediterranean coast.

Mungeet (*Rubia cordifolia*), referred to as "R. munjista" by Bancroft and other 19th-century authors, is related to madder and produces a similar color. It was a very important dye in India for many centuries but only occasionally used in America, since madder could be obtained readily.

YELLOW DYES

*FUSTIC (*Morus tinctoria* or *Chlorophora tinctoria*)
Also known as old fustic; yellow wood; dyers' mulberry; mora; bois jaune (Fr.); das Gelbholz (Ger.)

Thomas Cooper's opinion, expressed in his 1815 publication, was that fustic, although cheap enough to be commonly used, should not be employed in dyeing fine cloths. His contemporary Joseph Swartz agreed that it was a dull color yet in spite of it felt that fustic made a "good standing" dye. No two 19th-century dyers agreed exactly on the value of fustic as a dye for woolens, silks, and cottons, yet all included it among their stocks. The dye was used both for yellows and for compound hues made by combining yellow with other colors. It was frequently mentioned in recipes for snuffs, drabs, greens, oranges, and red oranges.

An English navigation statute of 1661 lists fustic as one of the English colonial products that could be shipped from their place of origin only to other lands under English rule (Bishop, 1866, vol. 1, p. 87). Another indication of its early use here is the inclusion of 230 pounds of fustic among

---

[4] Peter Kalm, a Swedish natural historian, in his *Travels in North America* recorded his observations on many dye plants used by colonists in the Middle Atlantic colonies and Southeastern Canada.

31

dyestuffs recorded in the inventory of a Boston dyer who expired in 1695 (Haynes, 1954, vol. 1, p. 46).[5] The "stockfish wood" referred to by Captain William Dampier, the adventurer who wrote a diary in 1676, was also fustic. Throughout the 18th century, apothecaries imported it from Brazil and a number of West Indian islands such as Jamaica, Tampico, and Cuba. The tree that yielded the dye is a member of the mulberry family, and for that reason fustic was known as dyers' mulberry.

Asa Ellis, writing in 1798, gives a fine description:

Fustick is much used in this country . . . It should appear when split of a bright yellow, tinged with the orange colour. The wood is close and hard; generally hard to split and full of splinters. The root and that part of the wood which is knoty is the best. It comes to us in large logs from six inches to one foot and a half through; if it be rotten, or otherwise injuried it will not answer well for Saxon greens; however, it may be employed in dark drabs (p. 20).

Although generally purchased as logs or sections of logs, it was prepared for dyeing by first rasping or chipping into small fragments. The fustic then could be placed in the dyebath; however, it was often soaked in water for two or three days before being used, since the dye was released more readily if the wood was premoistened. Fustic and other dyewood chips were tied in sacks before being immersed in the dyebath so they would not splinter and tear the textile material and could be removed easily after dyeing.

Alum was the standard mordant and was used often with cream of tartar. Some early dyers claimed that fustic would not impart a lasting color. This may have been due to improper mordanting or other unscientific dyeing techniques. Potassium bichromate, the mordant used in fustic dyeing today, was known but not used as a mordant until later in the 19th century.

At least one 20th-century authority, a dye chemist writing in 1910, said that fustic combined with a chrome mordant was at that time still regarded by some as the best yellow coloring matter the dyer possessed. He further stated that it was fast to milling and soaping and stood light well. On exposure to light the shade became browner, but in many compound shades the change was not readily noticeable (Knecht, 1910, vol. 1, pp. 351–352).

Fustic has been superseded by other yellow dyes, but not until after it provided several generations of dyers with an economical and reliable source of color.

*QUERCITRON (*Quercus velutina*)

Also known as black oak; yellow oak or American oak; and known earlier as *Q. nigra* or *Q. tinctoria*

---

[5] Original source is Suffolk County Probate Records, XIII, p. 743.

Mark Catesby, a mid-18th century English naturalist, described the black-oak tree as one whose wood was "of little use but to burn" (1771, vol. 1, p. 19). This erroneous judgment was corrected later in the same century by a fellow Englishman, Dr. Edward Bancroft, who returned from a journey to America with quite a different opinion. He had learned that black-oak bark yielded an excellent yellow dyestuff (he named it quercitron) that he believed could become a cheap substitute for weld. In 1785 the British Parliament thought highly enough of Bancroft's idea to award him the exclusive right to use and apply it to dyeing and calico printing for several years.

Black-oak bark ". . . was first sent to England before the Revolution from Wilmington, Delaware, where an export trade in the article was established soon after the Peace by one of the discoverers of its valuable dyeing properties" (Bishop, 1866, vol. 1, p. 461).

Even before Bancroft published his discovery, American home dyers probably used the bark of this locally grown tree for dyeing bright yellow woolens, cottons, linens, and silks. Only after it was introduced to Europe, however, did this indigenous American dyestuff take its place among the important vegetable dyes. It remained in commercial use until the second quarter of the 20th century.

In his complete description of the preparation of quercitron bark, Bancroft stated that the greatest amount of coloring matter is found in the inner bark or cellular coat of the tree trunk. This and the cortical sections were ground by millstones to a fine powder. Apparently this method was not entirely satisfactory for in 1810, 1812, and 1822 patents were issued to Americans who had developed improved methods of preparing quercitron and its extract. Numerous other patents were issued during the 19th century to inventors of bark crushers, grinders, packers, etc., indicating continuous efforts to improve quercitron and other dyewood processing.

Usually the bark was mordanted with alum and cream of tartar and dyed according to the individual dyer's recipe. A wide range of proportions of bark to wool were used—from 1½ pounds of bark per 20 pounds of wool to 6 to 8 ounces of bark per 1 pound of wool.

Bronson, in 1817, stated that the quercitron bark priced in New York for export was valued at $45 to $60 per ton (p. 192). Apothecaries and druggists in the York, Pennsylvania, area sold it at 12½ cents per pound. Quercitron contained much tannin and was used by tanners as well as dyers, thus home dyers whose apothecaries could not supply them were able to purchase quercitron from tanners for as little as 1½ cents per pound. Although quercitron was sold for a wide range of prices, it was still inexpensive compared to other purchased dyes (Lynde, 1831, p. 8).

Black oaks grow throughout Eastern United States, with Georgia, Pennsylvania, and the Carolinas supplying the greatest quantity. Although mainly used in wool dyeing, it was also applied to cottons and to a lesser degree, to silks. Recipes for drabs, smoke, olive, snuff, oranges, yellowed reds, cinnamon brown, and a range of yellow called for quercitron alone or combined with other dyestuffs.

Other Yellow Dyes

Yellow-dyeing plants are everywhere. A complete palette of yellows, golds, and browns can be created from products of roadsides, forests, and gardens. From this wide range of possibilities only a few of the most widely used plants are mentioned here. Local supplies of dyes varied with the location of the dyer, the season, and the effects the dyer wished to achieve.

ARSEMART (*Polygonum persicaria*)
Also known as smartweed

This weed, a member of the buckwheat family, grows along roadsides in many parts of the Northeast. During the 18th and early 19th centuries it was recommended by professional dyers because of the durable yellow color it imparted to woolens, cottons, and linens. Thomas Jefferson made no record of its intended uses, but he did list a species of arsemart (*P. sagittatum*) among the plants grown at his home in Charlottsville, Virginia (Jefferson, 1944, p. 644).

Plants were cut while in bloom, then dried, and soaked for several days to induce fermentation. The dye liquid was then heated and alum-mordanted cloth immersed in it. One 19th-century dyer suggested its use in compound colors such as black, smoke, snuff, and green.

ASH, WHITE (*Fraxinus americana*)
Also known as frêne (Fr.); die Esche (Ger.)

The bark of the white ash produced a dye valued for the beauty of its clear yellows and tans and for its colorfastness. It could be prepared "green or dry, boiled or simmered" and was especially useful when nut-galls were unavailable.

BARBERRY TREE (*Berberis vulgaris*)
Also known as epine-vinette (Fr.); die Berberitze (Ger.)

Thomas Cooper mentioned that barberry root was imported to Pennsylvania from Boston, and that its fruit made "an excellent tart, and a beautiful pickle" (1815, p. 20). Besides these valuable properties, barberry supposedly produced a fugitive but rich, bright yellow dye without mordants. It was used by leather dyers and in textile dyeing when combined with other more permanent coloring agents.

34

CHROME YELLOW (Lead chromate)
Also known as das Chromgelb (Ger.)

Chrome yellow dye was probably introduced into America in the 1830s after it became known in Europe. This mineral dye was fast when applied to cotton; however, it was very fugitive to light, soap, and acids when applied to wool. It was considered the best yellow cotton dye throughout the second half of the 19th century and continued in use in the 20th century.

The dyeing technique required two steps: First, successive steeping in basic lead acetate, followed by squeezing off; and second, immersion in potassium bichromate to develop the mineral color. By the latter step insoluble lead chromate or chrome yellow was developed on the fiber.

Chrome mordant (potassium bichromate) was first patented in 1840 by a Leeds, England, cloth manufacturer (Fierz-David, 1953, p. 3633). After its introduction to American dyers in the 1840s it became a staple mordant.

DOCK (*Rumex* sp.)
Also called Peterswort; patience (Fr.); der Ampfer (Ger.)

Like smartweed, this member of the buckwheat family produced a yellow dye commonly used by home dyers. Within the last one-hundred years a variety of dock native to the American Southwest has also been used by Navajo Indian weavers and dyers for coloring their rug and blanket yarns. The roots and leaves of this plant afforded a yellow color that made a "good duck's wing green" when combined with other dyestuffs. It is mentioned in a number of late 18th and 19th century dye manuals.

DYER'S BROOM (*Genista tinctoria*)
Also known as dyer's weed; greenweed; woodwax; woodwaxen; genestrolle (Fr.); der Färberginster (Ger.)

Dyer's broom is not indigenous to the United States; however, it could have been cultivated here had there been a sufficient demand for it during the late 18th and early 19th centuries. It was imported ground and packed in casks. The greenish-yellow color it imparted to woolens was fast; because its natural greenish cast combined so well with blue, it was frequently used to top blues in green dyeing. An entry in a 17th-century English volume mentioned it among the three yellows used in England at that time; the other yellows were weld and old fustic (Sprat, 1667, p. 296).

GOLDENROD (*Solidago* species, mainly *S. virgaurea*)
Also known as verge d'or (Fr.); die Goldrute (Ger.) and called *S. canadensis* by Hollberg (1763, p. 5) and other early botanists

Many professional dyers acknowledged the clarity and fastness of golden-rod yellows, but for some unknown reason this native American plant was used mainly by home dyers. Its abundance and reliable colors should have made it popular with professionals, yet they paid comparatively little attention to this excellent source of yellow.

35

Goldenrod was applied to alum-mordanted wool and was suggested as a substitute for weld in calico printing as well. It is mentioned by the naturalist Peter Kalm in his mid-18th-century publication, but it was certainly used by American colonists before that time. Home dyers throughout the 19th century used goldenrod in areas where it grew. Goldenrod was gathered just as it was beginning to bloom; its flowers could be dried and stored until needed.

*HICKORY (*Carya tomentosa* or *Hicoria tomentosa*)
Also known as hiccory; mockernut; white hickory; das Hickoryholz (Ger.)

Although the color of hickory bark was strong and stable it was apparently of little interest to commercial dyers of yellow woolen textiles. It is mentioned several times in home dyeing manuals, sometimes as a substitute for turmeric or fustic. This tree, common along the entire east coast of America, was first noted here by a 17th-century observer, later mentioned by Mark Catesby, and in 1749 referred to specifically as a yellow dye by Peter Kalm. Bancroft in the late 18th century thought enough of its dyeing possibilities to have it patented as a greenish yellow dye (Bancroft, 1814, vol. 2, p. 164). Bancroft derived no profits from his patent though for a number of reasons: The yellows it produced were duller than those made from other dyes; its bark was tough and difficult to grind; the more concentrated quercitron was already successful commercially and there was no need to add hickory bark to the long list of available yellow dyestuffs. Hickory bark is not mentioned by professional dyers writing after the mid-19th century.

PEACH (*Prunus persica*, known earlier as *Amygdalus persica*)
Also known as pêche (Fr.); der Pfirsich (Ger.)

A yellow dye was prepared from peach (and pear) tree leaves and bark during the 18th and 19th centuries. It was applied mainly by home dyers to alum-mordanted wool. Bronson believed the dye was more durable than fustic and recommended in his recipe that as much as could be crowded into a kettle should be used for each dye lot, indicating that its color was not too concentrated.

*PERSIAN BERRIES (*Rhamnus* species, including *R. infectoria* and *R. tinctorius*)
Also known as berries or grains of Avignon; French berries; dyer's buckthorn; der Kreuzdorn (Ger.)

Persian berries were well known in France during the 17th century; in America they were probably used by professional dyers during the 18th century and the first half of the 19th century. This dye never achieved great popularity here because so many less expensive yellow dyes were readily available, including the excellent quercitron, native to America.

Various common names of this dye were derived from its places of origin. For example, some *Rhamnus* species were grown in Persia (and Turkey)—

thus the name Persian berries. They also grew in southern Europe—"grains of Avignon" is derived from the town of Avignon in southern France.

The shriveled yellowish-green berries were gathered before ripening, then dried, and when ready for use were ground into a powder. Tin mordant gave woolens colored with this dye bright yellow and orange shades, which turned brown when exposed to light. Copper mordants produced lightfast yellow-olive shades. Persian berries were used in wool and calico printing, in addition to their use as a cloth dye.

*SASSAFRAS (Sassafras albidum, called Laurus sassafras by P. Kalm)

While visiting the Philadelphia area in 1748 Peter Kalm learned that local residents used the bark of the sassafras tree as a dye and its leaves as a tea. The bark was used for dyeing worsted a fine lasting orange color, which was sunfast. The wool was dyed in a brass boiler, with urine used in place of the usual alum mordant (Kalm, 1772, vol. 1, pp. 114–115). Later Asa Ellis told of the light brown and ash colors it produced and of its ability to leave cloth soft and pliable. He also believed that this bark was profitable to country dyers when they did not have a supply of nutgalls.

Only one 19th-century dye manual lists sassafras among its dye ingredients, implying that, although it was readily available along the east coast of America, professional dyers of the time did not rely on it because similar results were obtained with other substances. There is a strong possibility, however, that home dyers continued to use sassafras during the 19th century when they lived near a source of supply.

TURMERIC (Curcuma longa)
Also known as turmerick; turmerech; curcuma; terre merité (Fr.); das Kurkumagelb (Ger.)

Yellow dyes were extracted from the ground root of the turmeric or Indian saffron plant. This bright orange powder was a rich but fugitive dye, considered the finest yellow by many professional dyers and used frequently throughout the 18th and 19th centuries. Turmeric was the only yellow dye that did not require a mordant to fix it on wool, cotton, or silk; but its sensitivity to light, soap, and alkali reduced its value considerably. It was used principally in combination with other dyes to make browns and olive greens.

WELD (Reseda lutea)
Also known as wold; dyer's weed and dyer's mignonette; réséda des teinturiers (Fr.); der Wau (Ger.)

This excellent dye may have been the most common yellow dye used in England until the advent of synthetic dyes. Although it was employed by

1 *Coggygria Theophrasti*
Venice Sumach.

FIGURE 8.—Young fustic plant (Gerard, 1597). Library of Congress photograph (LC–25901).

American dyers during the 18th century it was never used a great deal in America. Its cultivation here is mentioned briefly and hopefully by a few dyers; however, limited demands appear to have been met by importation of weld from England. Besides being expensive, great quantities of the dried branches and stems were needed and its bulk added to the difficulty of shipping.

Gilroy, in 1859, criticized a fellow dyer, William Partridge, for his lavish praise of weld, remarking that Partridge

is completely in love with weld as a tinctorial substance. This dyewood is indeed, as every practical man knows of great value; but nevertheless, we are not prepared to go to the same extent in its praise, that Mr. P. has: "(its) . . . color . . . (is) more permanent . . . than any other *yellow dye* . . . but its chief superiority consists in . . . a very superior degree, of imparting a great degree of softness to the woolens dyed with it" (Gilroy, 1859, p. 127).

Weld was cultivated in France and also grew wild in Italy at one time. The upper part of this herbaceous plant, especially the leaves and seeds, were chopped for dyeing, along with the stem that contained less coloring matter. Large amounts of weld were required, since its coloring matter was not concentrated. Processing was generally similar to that of fustic and quercitron bark.

Although weld is best known for its bright yellow hues, various mordants and different fibers combined to create hues ranging from yellow to yellow olive. Wool and cotton will dye olive-yellow with chrome; copper mordant dyes wool yellow-olive; alum, yellow; and a very bright yellow could be achieved in silk using a titanium mordant. Most early 19th-century dyers' mixed results were caused by their almost universal use of the alum mordant. By 1920 weld was no longer used in England and had not been in common use in the United States for a number of years.

YOUNG FUSTIC (*Cotinus coggygria*, also known as *Rhus cotinus*)
Also known as Venice sumach; fustel or fustet (Fr.)

This dye, obtained from a small tree of the sumach family, is botanically unrelated to fustic, the well-known tropical dyewood. Both impart yellow-orange colors to textiles, but young fustic is so fugitive to light that its usefulness has always been limited. The stems and trunk of the tree *Cotinus coggygria*, native to the West Indian islands and southern Europe, were cut and gathered into small bundles for export. Dyers rasped or cut and boiled young fustic to extract its dye. Usually it was combined with other, more permanent dyes to heighten their hues, leaving behind a fast color when its temporary hue had vanished.

Brown Dyes

BUTTERNUT or *WHITE WALNUT* (*Juglans cinerea*) and
BLACK WALNUT (*J. nigra*)

Butternut and black-walnut trees belong to the same botanical genus and have common dyeing properties. Although certain color differences may be noted, methods of extracting the dyes are similar, thus both varieties are discussed together.

Americans knew the art of extracting rich and durable browns from the roots and nuts of native walnut trees as early as 1669, when Governor Winthrop of Connecticut sent the following report with samples of butternut dyeing to the Royal Society of London:

Shreds of stuff made by the English planters of cotton and wool, put up to shew the colour, which was only dyed with the bark of a kind of walnut-tree, called by the planters the butter-nut-tree, the kernel of that sort of walnut being very oily, whence they are called butter-nuts. They dyed it only with the decoction of that bark, without allum or copperas, as they said (Birch, 1756, vol. 2, p. 418).

In the mid-18th century Peter Kalm observed that women in Pennsylvania and New Jersey used black-walnut bark and nut husks to dye wool a lasting brown. Thomas Cooper, in 1815, stated that usually the green hulls or rinds of the walnut were used for dyeing browns. The roots' inner bark—sometimes referred to as walnut bark—was also used, even though it was less potent than the rind. Since no mordants were needed for walnut and butternut dyeing, the vegetable material could be boiled for a certain period and the wetted cloth dipped until the desired color had been achieved.

Besides producing browns, walnut dye was often used to ground fabric in preparation for black dyeing, or for black dyeing as explained in an anonymously written 1811 dye manual:

> Black is sometimes dyed without having given it a blue ground, but this ought to be only for stuffs of inferior quality . . . butternut bark put in an iron kettle, if (allowed) to remain long enough will dissolve enough of the iron to make a tolerable black, as the experience of many women has demonstrated, in coloring stockings (p. 39).

CATECHU; also known as cutch; cachou (Fr.); das Katechu (Ger.)
   from *Acacia catechu*, sometimes called Bengal catechu
   from *Areca catechu*, sometimes called Bombay catechu
GAMBIER (*Uncaria gambir*); also known as gambier catechu and gambia

Catechu, the last important vegetable coloring agent added to the professional dyer's repertoire, was used in Indian calico printing long before its advantages were realized in Europe and America. This brown dye was first applied to European printed cottons around 1800 in Augsburg, Germany (Persoz, 1846, vol. 3, pp. 98–99). One American scientist who compared the properties of catechu and chestnut bark in 1819 mentioned that catechu was discovered "12 or 15 years" earlier (Sheldon, 1819, p. 148). It is difficult to ascertain how widely it was used in America during this early period. Thomas Cooper mentioned its use as a substitute for galls in 1814. The process apparently was little used in France until 1829, however, when M. Barbet of Jouy exploited this secret process to great commercial advantage for three years. During the 1830s catechu came into general use in Great Britain and America, where rapid strides were made in improving methods of application.

The name "terra japonica" was sometimes applied mistakenly to this brown dye because it was believed to be an earth found in Japan. Actually three different Mideastern plants produced this excellent dyestuff. Bengal catechu was an extract from the heartwood and pods of *Acacia catechu*, a leguminous East Indian tree. Bombay catechu was produced mainly by areca or betel nuts, the fruits of the tropical Asian betel-nut palm, *Areca catechu*. Gambier was an extract made from the leaves and twigs of a vine that grew in India and the Malacca Islands, *Uncaria gambir*.

40

The following excerpt from an 1846 dyer manual clearly describes the processing of *Acacia catechu* and would also apply generally to the other types:

As soon as the trees are felled, all the exterior white wood is carefully cut away, the interior or colored wood is then cut into chips; narrow mouthed unglazed pots are nearly filled with these, and water is added to cover them and reach to the top of the vessel. When this is half evaporated by boiling, the decoction without straining is poured into a shallow earthen vessel, and further reduced two-thirds by boiling. It is then set in a cool place for one day, and afterwards evaporated by the heat of the sun, being stirred several times during that process. When it is reduced to a considerable thickness it is spread upon a mat or cloth, which has been previously covered with the ashes of cow-dung. This mass is divided with a string into quadrangular pieces, which are completely dried by being turned frequently in the sun, and are then fit for sale. It is a brittle compact solid, of a dark brown or chocolate color . . . ([Parnell], 1846, pp. 59–60).

Catechu and gambier were applied to cotton, silk, and, to a lesser extent, wool. Its natural brown color could be modified with various compounds to produce olive, drab, and gray tones. Since catechu and gambier extracts were soluble in boiling water, the application of this dye was comparatively simple. In coloring cotton and wool the dye was boiled with the cloth and a copper salt added. This bath was allowed to stand for several hours, then the cloth was removed, washed, and dried. In order to assure lightfastness and deeper shades, copper salts were recommended by early 20th-century dye chemists.

Gambier was used in black-silk dyeing as late as the first quarter of the 20th century mainly because it could be applied along with metallic salts in weighting silk. A U.S. Tariff Commission report on natural dyestuffs imported into the United States between 1910 and 1917 reveals that gambier was by far the most important dye brought into this country, both in terms of quantity and monetary value (1918, p. 56). Although such a survey, recording pounds of extract along with pounds of raw materials (such as woods), cannot be considered a completely valid basis of comparison, it does suggest strongly that gambier far outranked in importance any of the other dyes surveyed. By 1917 the quantity of most natural dyes, including gambier, had diminished considerably, yet they were still used in amounts great enough to be recorded. Between the First and Second World Wars the dye industry made such strides that this natural dye, along with all others, has become obsolete.

Other Brown Dyes

BARKS OF VARIOUS TREES
ALDER (Alnus sp.)
Also known as oler or owler; aune (Fr.); die Erle (Ger.)

It was natural for home dyers living in a heavily forested country like America to search for coloring materials among the barks of trees which surrounded them. The most frequently mentioned brown-coloring barks were tannin-rich alder, hemlock, and maple. Use of these probably depended to a great extent on availability. A New York State dyer said that alder bark was not much used in America, except in the small domestic dye; yet other dyers of the period mentioned it frequently enough to suggest that it was generally known, either as a dye or as a substitute for sumach or galls in black dyeing.

William Partridge, the New York dye merchant, described the gathering and use of alder bark in this way:

. . . The sticks are cut in the month of April, or the beginning of the month of May, when the sap runs; the bark is stripped off as soon as cut, (which is easily done by children) and is dried in the shade, when it is fit for use. The poles make good bean sticks, or excellent firewood. This bark, when the colouring matter is strong, produces a brownish drab with alum, and a light forest drab when only a small quantity is used. When employed in the black dye, it increases the body of the colour even more than sumach, and is equally durable (1847, pp. 38–39).

According to various other dyers it imparted brownish and fawn colors, yellow oranges or drabs to silk, wool, or cotton, depending on dyeing procedures and mordants used.

Dye potentials of the native alder tree were never fully exploited in America. Alder bark (from *Alnus glutinosa*) was much used by European dyers because of its high tannin content. According to William Tucker, however, the dyeing quality of the alder grown in this country was equal to the imported variety. It was noted by Bancroft after his late 18th-century journey to America and was also mentioned by Asa Ellis in 1798 as a good and durable dye, "useful in almost all dark colors." Although professional dyers working in the second half of the 19th century may have found other brown dyes more valuable, it was still mentioned by O'Neill as late as 1869. Probably its principal users later in the century were home dyers.

*HEMLOCK (Tsuga canadensis)
Also called spruce pine or hemlock spruce; ciguë (Fr.); die Hemlocktanne (Ger.)

Hemlock bark provided settlers of Eastern United States with another good source of reddish-brown dye. Peter Kalm and Joseph Bancroft both applied the scientific name *Pinus abies* to this tree, known as *Tsuga canadensis* to today's botanists. This dye was applied to both wool and cotton and employed in tanning leather in Nova Scotia. When combined with an alum mordant it resulted in a durable bright reddish-brown hue on wool and an impermanent nankeen (brownish yellow) on cotton. Copperas mordant produced dark drab and slate colors.

RED MAPLE (Acer rubrum)
Also known as swamp or scarlet flowering maple

O'Neill dismissed red maple in his *Dictionary of dyeing and calico printing* as not having been mentioned in recent works on dyeing, and he stated that it probably never had been used. This statement may indicate that by 1869 red-maple dye was obsolete; however, it definitely was known and used in America during the 18th century, as indicated by Peter Kalm's description of its application in the Philadelphia area in 1748:

With the bark they dye both worsted and linen, giving it a dark blue colour. For that purpose it is first boiled in water, and some copperas, such as the hat-makers and shoe-makers commonly make use of, is added, before the stuff (which is to be dyed) is put into the boiler. This bark likewise affords a good black ink (1772, vol. 1, pp. 131–132).

Certainly maple bark would have been an uncommon source of blue dye; in fact one suspects that its "blue" was closer to the "slate" color mentioned by other authors who combined maple bark with copperas (ferrous sulfate). In addition it was used in black dyeing, sometimes substituted for white-oak sawdust or sumach, and was also known to give "lasting" cinnamon-brown tones to wool and cotton when used with an alum mordant.

PURPLE DYES

ORCHIL (originally from *Rocella* sp., esp. *R. tinctoria*)
Also known as archil; orchille; orseille (Fr.)

Orchil is an ancient dyestuff derived from several different varieties of the lichen *Rocella*, which grew on rocks along the Mediterranean coast. During the early 18th century a new source of *Rocella* was discovered in the Canaries; a few years later it was found in the Cape Verde Islands. These areas supplied most of the orchil used in Europe and probably America until the 19th century. India and Ceylon supplied England with *Rocella* in the 19th century, mainly due to decrease in quality of *Rocella* supplied by island sources (Kok, 1966, p. 259).[6] American dyers imported the dye processed and ready for use. It may have been used here for dyeing wool and silks during the 18th century, however, it is not mentioned in American dyers' manuals or advertisements until the early 19th century.

One of the few substantive dyes, orchil produced beautiful but light-sensitive colors which included the whole range of hues between red and blue. One American dyer writing in 1869 stated:

It is seldom used by itself for dyeing, but usually to help or top other colors; when used alone it can give very agreeable shades of violet, peach, and lilac, which colors are very loose in air, fading almost visibly in sunlight; in combination with other coloring matters it usually darkens them, giving chocolate colored shades; but archil is chiefly valued for a peculiar softness and velvet bloom it communicates to colors (O'Neill, pp. 68–69).

In processing orchil, whole lichens were first steeped in an alkali such as fermented urine or slaked lime which were used often during the late 18th and early 19th centuries. This mixture was allowed to set for about a week until it turned deep purple. After three more weeks, without the

---

[6] This article gives a complete history of orchil dyeing.

addition of urine or lime, the "urinous volatile spirit" of the dye was replaced by a violet scent and the liquid had turned crimson. Then blue or red orchil could be made by simply adjusting the solution's alkalinity. This material was dried and sold in paste or cake form. After the mid-19th century it could be purchased in America as a liquid as well as a paste (O'Neill, 1869, p. 68).

The basic technique of dyeing with orchil was very simple. Requiring no mordant, the dye was added to lukewarm water, slowly heated to the boiling point, and the textile material added. The dyebath was then reheated slowly to just below the boiling point to obtain the brightest colors. The whole dyeing process was repeated as many times as was necessary to obtain the depth of color desired. Alum or iron salts added to the dye would not improve its fastness, however, they modified its hues; iron salts turned orchil-dyed cloth rich reddish purple, while acids and alum had a reddening effect (Kok, 1966, pp. 264–265).

After the advent of coal-tar dyes, orchil's use gradually declined, but in spite of this dye's sensitivity to light and milling it did not become obsolete as a textile dye until the first half of the 20th century. The soft, rich tones it imparted to wools kept it commercially useful until manufacturers could produce dyes that gave the same effects.

A number of 19th century dye manuals mentioned another type of orchil made from the "lichen parellus" (*Ochrolechia parella*) that grew in the Auvergne region of France. Its processing and dyeing methods were essentially the same as orchil's and apparently it was used along with the aforementioned and more durable orchil; however, its use was probably less general.

CUDBEAR (a compound consisting of *Ochrolechia tartarea* [later *Umbilicaria pustulata*], *Urceolaria calcarea* and *Cladonia pyxidata*)
Also spelled "cut bear" and "cudbierd"; teinture d'orseille (Fr.)

Cudbear is a dye closely related to orchil, since both are derived from lichens and contain the same coloring principle. Cudbear consists of a combination of lichens; it was patented in 1758 by a Scottish merchant named Cuthbert Gordon, who named it for his mother whose maiden name was Cuthbert (Kok, 1966, p. 257). It became popular with British dyers because, besides being made entirely from lichens found in the British Isles (these grew in Norway and Sweden also), it was sold in powdered form, which simplified application and storage. Some American dyers of the 19th century considered cudbear too fugitive to be important; others suggested it might even be sought for possible commercial exploitation in this country.

Litmus and turnsole, infrequently mentioned in American dyers' manuals, were made from lichens also. Litmus, still used as an indicator of alkalinity or acidity (red for acids, blue for alkalis), was made first from *O. tartarea*, the chief ingredient of cudbear, and later from *Rocella* and other lichens. Turnsole was another kind of litmus, sometimes used for coloring Dutch cheese (Kok, 1966, p. 264).

BLACK DYES

*LOGWOOD (*Haematoxylon campechianum*)
Also called Campeachy wood or blackwood in English; bois d'Inde and bois bleu (Fr.); das Blauholz (Ger.)

The bloody disputes which this useful Tree has occasioned between the Spaniards and the English, are too well known to say much of here . . . (I wish) . . . that the inhabitants of our Southern plantations could be induced to propagate it, as well for their own advantage, as that we may be supplied by them, when wholly deprived of getting it from the Spaniards, as we have hitherto done, either by force or stealth.

This statement written by Mark Catesby in a volume first published in 1731 suggests that conflicts over logwood trade were fairly common during the early years of the 18th century (1771, vol. 2, p. 66).[7]

Probably logwood was introduced to England soon after Queen Elizabeth ascended the throne. A few years later, about 1581, a law was passed prohibiting the use of logwood because the colors it produced were so fugitive. The truth is that too little was known about mordanting procedures to fix the dyes on the fibers properly at that time. The logwood prohibition laws were repealed nearly a hundred years later during the reign of Charles II.

The earliest English settlers must have brought it with them to the American colonies for it seems to have been known here during the 17th century (otherwise it would not have been referred to in the Navigation Acts of 1660 and 1671). Although logwood is not named specifically in these acts, the "other dyeing woods" mentioned very probably refer to logwood. The wording of the acts strongly suggests that logwood was used in the colonies as early as the third quarter of the 17th century (Bishop, 1866, vol. 1, p. 87). At that time American ship owners began to carry on an active trade with non-British ports even though the Navigation Acts expressly forbade such dealings. Currency was needed and this valuable dyestuff which was easily sold in foreign ports brought in needed currency.

Logwood grew naturally in Central America, Mexico, and parts of northern South America. From Spanish-controlled Campeachy and British-owned Honduras it was brought to Jamaica and other West Indian

---

[7] The third edition of a publication that first appeared in 1731 (vol. 1) and 1743 (vol. 2). These volumes were based on Catesby's observations made between 1712 and 1726.

islands where it was successfully propagated. The trees, which attain a merchantable size in 12 years, were shipped in the form of logs 3 to 12 feet long. This cargo proved valuable not only for the good price it brought but also because it could be taken on as ballast.

According to William Partridge, writing in the 1840s, the best logwood came from Campeachy, with lesser grades coming from Santo Domingo, Honduras, and Jamaica, in that order. Jamaica was the distribution point from which New England-based ships sailed for Atlantic ports all along the east coast between Charleston and Boston, and then on to English (and continental) ports. Privateers of the period were often spared the efforts of logging by capturing Spanish vessels laden with this valuable commodity.

Logwood was sold by apothecaries and in general stores, as evidenced by frequent advertisements in 18th-century newspapers which list logwood among their various other wares. It was generally sold in the form of logs that had to be rasped or broken down in some other manner before they could be used. This process could have been carried on in mills, either before or after purchase. Since buyers always feared adulteration, however, logwood was frequently purchased in log form and then rasped or chipped later by the consumer. One Pennsylvania newspaper advertisement of 1798 informed its readers that, among other items produced by inmates of the Philadelphia prison, chipped logwood could be had on reasonable terms.

Dyeing with logwood was a comparatively simple matter. Only the reddish heartwood was used, with the outer parts chopped away before shipping. First the rasped or chipped wood was dampened with water and allowed to "mature" or ferment slightly for a few days. This fermented wood was then gathered in a sack and immersed in the dye kettle. After being boiled for 20 minutes or more the bag containing logwood chips was removed and the textile material was submerged in the clear coloring liquid. Mordanting could take place either before, during, or after dyeing. Logwood was used on cotton, silk, and wool, with the hues produced depending on the particular mordants chosen.

Logwood was most important in black and blue dyeing; although it produces other colors, such as silvery grays and purples, they are extremely fugitive in light. A good navy blue could be made when the textile had been mordanted with potassium bichromate; however, although this compound was known around 1800, it does not appear to have been used as a mordant until much later in the 19th century. Instead, copperas, blue vitriol, and verdigris were frequently utilized in dyeing navy blues that contemporary dyers considered beautiful and which were definitely cheaper than indigo blues.

In 1798, Asa Ellis said that woolen yarn for coverlets and stockings could be advantageously colored with logwood. He did not fully explain whether logwood-dyed textiles would prove more profitable to the dyer or the consumer. Other 18th- and 19th-century dyers considered logwood blues poor substitutes for indigo, because although they were lower in price they faded when exposed to light. In France at that time logwood was frequently added to indigo dyebaths for fuller and richer blues.

The most important application of logwood was in dyeing blacks, which continued throughout the first third of the 20th century. Since black was considered a compound color many dyers felt that it required a combination of dyes, each of which yielded a different tone. Thus a black recipe might use logwood and sumach for their black tones, fustic for yellow, and a metallic oxide such as copperas which in the process of oxidation fixed the black. Sometimes 18th- and 19th-century dyers used so many ingredients and such great quantities of them to reinforce the effects of logwood that even without it the dye solutions might have yielded the desired deep black tone.

Now logwood is no longer commercially valuable; however, it has certainly proved to be history's most tenacious natural dyestuff, defying substitution almost until the beginning of the Second World War.

Neutral Dyes

Most of the dye materials included in this grouping imparted color to textiles; however, their main value lay in their mordanting power. For this reason tannin-rich nutgalls and sumach, the most widely used among these substances, were considered essentials in every dyer's shop.

BARKS OF VARIOUS TREES
BIRCHES, known as bouleau (Fr.); die Birke (Ger.)
Yellow birch (*Betula lutea*)
Cherry or black birch (*B. lenta*)
White, paper, or canoe birch (*B. papyrifera*)

The barks of several varieties of birch trees were utilized in dyeing, mainly in light browns, blacks, or other drab colors. Peter Kalm mentioned *Betula alnus*, which referred to a variety of birch used in the mid-18th century. In 1869, O'Neill informed his readers that birch bark was "employed in dyeing, but principally by the peasantry" (p. 77).

OAKS, known as chêne (Fr.); die Eiche (Ger.)
White oak (*Quercus alba*)
Red oak (*Q. rubra*)
Chestnut oak (*Q. prinus*)

Quercitron or black oak was most famous for the fast and bright yellows it imparted to textiles. Other native oaks, however, were also utilized by

47

18th- and 19th-century dyers, for they too contained tannins and other dyeing agents which would give woolens stable colors.

Peter Kalm mentioned three different oaks that were used in mid-18th-century dyeing. Red oak produced yellows, chestnut oak was used in reds, and white oak was utilized by New York dyers to color wool brown or "Thée bou" (muddy tea) color. The latter dye was not bleached by the sunshine (Hollberg, 1763, p. 3).[8]

Standard procedures for dyeing with bark called for stripping it from the trees, chopping it into fine pieces, and boiling it. Alum-mordanted cloth was usually immersed in the dye liquid when the barks were used for plain yellows, drabs, or browns. Compound shades or black dyeing involved complicated recipes which included the bark plus many other ingredients. One such compound black recipe designed to color 16 pounds of cloth (probably cotton) called for the following: 12 oz. argol, 6 oz. verdigris, 6 lbs. logwood, 2½ lbs. sumach, ¼ lb. fustic, 7 lbs. white-oak sawdust, and 3 lbs. copperas (Partridge, 1847, p. 57). Swamp-maple bark could be substituted for the oak sawdust and sumach. For an unusually rich and full-bodied color, the black cloth could then be put into liquid in which alder bark and black-walnut hulls had been soaked.

The various oak barks were certainly used by professional dyers during the first decades of the 19th century; however, there is little indication that they were in common use by any but home dyers after the 1850s and 1860s.

*IRON BUFF

Each of the metals . . . is capable, when dissolved, of becoming a basis or mordant, for fixing and modifying some at least of the different adjective animal or vegetable colouring matters, with more or less advantage, by dyeing. But besides this property . . . several metals . . . afford coloured solutions or oxides, which are capable of being united and fixed directly in the fibres of linen, cotton, silk, or wool, and of thereby producing various permanent substantive colours (Bancroft, 1814, vol. 1, p. 233).

Of the above-mentioned compounds iron oxides were most important for both mordanting and dyeing. They were a very common, albeit dull, source of color in household dyeing throughout the 18th and 19th centuries. Often bits of old iron, such as nails, were soaked in acid, such as vinegar, before a buff dyeing session was planned. An 1811 source suggested that iron liquor could be made by filling casks with scraps of iron and filings on which vinegar or sour beer was poured and left to stand for several weeks.

---

[8] Hollberg's publication, a Master's thesis, was based mainly on the observations of his major professor, Peter Kalm.

48

Professional dyers, although generally more sophisticated in their methods, utilized the same raw materials for dyeing buff-colored cottons. A typical recipe, by Thomas Cooper in his 1815 manual, stated that buffs could be made by dipping textile material in a hot copperas solution, taking them out, wringing, opening and airing them, then raising the color in lime water. This procedure was repeated until the desired depth of color was reached (p. 309).

The above directions for iron buff dyeing are typical of those found in dyers' books until after the middle of the 19th century, when the buffs seem to have become unfashionable with the advent of the rainbow of clear, fresh colors and new methods introduced by scientifically oriented dyers.

Copperas (ferrous sulfate) was the main ingredient in dyeing cotton buff color. Hazael Warfield, in his *Clothier's guide*, explains the composition of copperas in this way:

Copperas is an extract of Iron corroded with acid, or for a substitute for copperas, take the filings of iron put it in vinegar, let it stand one month and you will have a much better darkening substance; the best copperas is the brown or that which appears to be mouldy, deep green copperas will make the brightest blue but it is not so strong as the other, and will not make so good a black, that of a pale green colour is worth but little. Copperas ought to be kept in a cellar where it is not very damp nor open that the acid may evaporate (1832, pp. 27–28).

While one might deduce correctly that iron buff would not necessarily produce a lively color, it was expected to last for the life of the textile. Many times this was true, but with faulty dyeing procedures, the textiles themselves were sometimes rather short-lived. Iron salts, especially those applied in large concentrations, caused textiles to become brittle and tender. Bancroft noted that most people had observed examples of iron spotting (then called iron-mould) on linens which produced holes long before any occurred in the body of the cloth. This effect can be noted in some early printed textiles in which one colored figure, usually brown or black, has been completely disintegrated because of the corroding effects of its iron mordant. Thus a well-dyed buff-colored cotton retained not only its color but also its strength throughout a reasonable period of use.

Regarding the color itself, buff seems to have covered a considerable range of values and intensities of red-yellows. The generally accepted version is a somewhat brownish yellow, originally the color of oil-tanned calf or goatskin "buff" leather. Although buff was originally derived from the Italian word "bufalo" it referred to the common European ox, rather than the buffalo that roamed our Western Plains.

GALLS
Also known as nut-galls or gallnuts, noix de galle (Fr.); der Gallapfel (Ger.)

The galls used in dyeing are nutlike in appearance and are actually infections on trees caused by certain insects. They are formed when female gall-wasps (*Cynips gallaetinctoriae*) puncture the young buds on small branches of certain species of oaks (especially *Quercus lusitanica*) and deposit their eggs within these punctures. This action stimulates surrounding plant tissue to grow, eventually enveloping the gall larvae which continue to develop. If allowed to reach maturity, the insect punctures the gall and escapes.

The bluish or greenish-colored galls collected before the insects leave them were richest in tannic acid. Other factors affecting tannic acid content of galls were the region in which they were grown and their harvesting season (August and September were best). The finest blue galls were imported from Aleppo, Syria; slightly inferior qualities were those from Smyrna, Turkey, and Tripoli, Libya. Galls of the same type were also found in southern Europe on the *Q. sessiliflora* and *Q. pubescens* oak species (Thorpe, 1912, vol. 2, p. 647). Although several 19th-century dyers voiced the opinion that galls could be cultivated on American oak species, no commercial amounts were ever produced here. Galls were purchased either in powder or nut form; however, since there was always great danger of adulteration when one purchased dye materials already ground, whole galls were preferred.

Galls dyed only grays, and in compound colors, grayed yellows such as drabs. Their most important use was in mordanting, rather than dyeing, and they were most valuable in mordanting cottons that would later be dyed dark neutrals or black tones. With few exceptions most natural dyestuffs would not produce fast, deep colors on cottons without preparatory treatment by tannin-rich substances such as galls. Since tannin is the principal component of galls, making up 25 to 70 percent of the chemical composition of the nuts, it is obvious that galls held an important place among dyers' supplies.

O'Neill reminded dyers of still another property of galls—an ability to weight silks, giving them body without the aid of metallic salts:

In the better class of blacks upon silks, galls are still much used; they give a very durable but somewhat grayish shade of color, and possess a property, very much esteemed in certain trades, of weighting, i.e., accumulating on the fibre in such quantity as to add very materially to the weight of the silk (1869, p. 231).

Generally black dyers combined galls with iron salts and logwood, adding madder and any other coloring material that would attain the tone of black the customer or fashion dictated.

One 18th-century recipe for dyeing 20 yards of fulled cloth an ash color called for 3 or 4 tablespoonfuls of the "flour of Nut-galls" to a piece of alum about the size of "a quail's egg" and a teaspoonful of copperas. Such recipes, typical of those employing galls around 1800, suggest how unscientifically some American dyers approached their craft, even when they urged their colleagues to consider dyeing as a scientific application of chemical principles.

Bronson, recognizing the plight of the small-scale dyer in having to purchase galls at high prices, suggested that, if used in sufficient quantity, sumach could be used as a substitute. Other dyers suggested substituting catechu, myrobalans (the fruit of trees of the East Indian *Terminalia* species), valonia nuts, and certain tree barks such as alder, chestnut, and oak. All of these substances contained varying percentages of tannin, and if used alone or in combination with galls could save the dyer considerable amounts of money.

Galls were used until the early part of the 20th century. Tannic acid today still has applications in certain dye processes, as well as in medicine.

SOOT
Also known as Suie (Fr.); das Sott (Ger.)

Soot certainly could not be considered among the most important coloring agents used by early dyers. Its use does, however, illustrate the ingenuity of our ancestors in finding dye materials among the most unlikely substances.

This material, consisting chiefly of carbon, was used by Indians to tattoo designs on their bodies; it was also employed in textile dyes to sadden yellows, and in fawn and black tones. Thomas Cooper, the chemist who recommended the use of soot, gave this rather extensive explanation of its use:

Soot is so far from being a despicable ingredient in dyeing, that when it balls well in handling it, you may be sure it will give out an useful colour. The colours of tapestry borders cannot receive their golden tint without soot. The colour of ozier (willow) and wicker baskets require soot, so do all the landscape colours in tapestry.

Although the colour produced from soot is very solid, it must never be used in conjunction with the mineral acids, which degrade it.

In a boiler of thirty buckets of water, put from ten to twenty buckets of soot. Boil it for two hours, till the soot no longer rises up on boiling: fill the boiler with water, and let it remain for an hour, that the soot may subside. In this liquor pass the yellow cloth which has been already dyed with three or four pounds of weld to one pound of cloth. The colour is browned in proportion as the cloth is permitted to remain in the liquor; which may be from half an hour to two hours, at a pretty high degree of heat, not boiling . . .

(The use of soot is too little known in England and this country; but it is of more use as it seems to me in drabs, olives, and browns, than in yellows) (1815, pp. 170–171).

51

FIGURE 9.—Sumach plant
(Pomet, 1694).

Cooper's fellow dyers had somewhat different experiences in using this material. One claimed that soot hardened wool, another that it gave "a disagreeable smell to the stuffs" and that it was better not to make use of it for "dyeing stuffs that bear a price," since all its shades could be achieved by other ingredients which were more lasting and also left the wool with a softer hand.

This ingredient therefore was probably seldom used except where other better choices were not available.

SUMACH (chiefly *Rhus glabra*—smooth or red sumach and *R. coriaria*—Sicilian sumach)
Also spelled sumac (Fr.)

Even before sumach became important to the earliest American colonists, native American varieties of this shrub were used by a number of American Indian tribes. Among them the Ojibas utilized sumach's fruits in a cool summertime beverage and drank it warmed and sweetened with maple sugar during the winter months; the Kiowa Indians smoked a mixture of tobacco and dried sumach leaves (Uphof, 1959, p. 312). Until after the mid-19th century American dyers considered it a necessity among their stocks of drugs. Besides being a valuable mordant, it was used as a local dye and also could be collected and processed for trade within and outside the colonies.

Mark Catesby, the Englishman who recorded American flora and fauna during the 1720s, noted the presence here of *Rhus glabrum* and *R. virginianum*. Thirty years later Peter Kalm mentioned its use as a dye in the Philadelphia area. Irascible Thomas Cooper remarked in 1815: "It grows in Syria, Spain, Portugal, Montpelier; and plentifully in Pennsylvania, where want of population, or want of industry, prevents its being gathered" (p. 14).

Bronson used the stalks in a yellow, with alum mordant. The shoots and leaves with coloring matter similar to that of nutgalls yielded drab and slate colors on woolens and cotton. Sumach was also used in black dyeing (1817, p. 193).

The finest imported sumach was prepared for market in the following way: Just before the plants flowered, younger twigs were removed, sun-dried, and beaten to remove leaves and flower panicles. The leaves were then exported or, as happened more frequently, the dye was shipped in powdered form. Dyers had to be wary of the latter, for adulteration with sand, ground branches, and other useless or inferior materials was quite common and difficult to discover.

During the second half of the 19th century, O'Neill stated that Sicilian sumach was the most esteemed and brought the highest prices. He described it as having a greenish-yellow color, bitter astringent taste, "and, when good, a smell reminding of tea, or sometimes of new hay." At that time the author admitted there were no reliable methods of determining the quantity of sumach's various components. Research around 1900 revealed that European sumach (*R. coriaria*) and the native American variety (*R. glabra*) both contained about 25 percent tannin, along with small amounts of other substances.

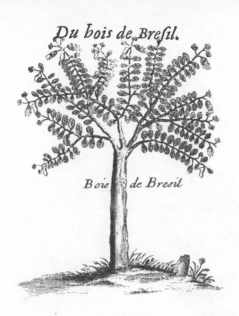

Du bois de Bresil.

Bois de Bresil

PART TWO

Home Dyeing With Natural Dyes (Revised)

Saxafras

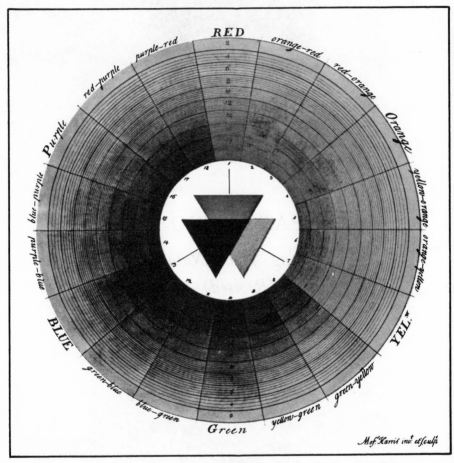

FIGURE 10.—Color wheel. The first known arrangement of colors in wheel form (Harris, 1766).

(*This illustration is reproduced in full color on the inside back cover.*)

WORKING WITH COLOR

"This art is so useful, and the practice of it is at the same time so enter-taining, that he ventures to say, when once a lady has perfected one colour, she will not rest satisfied till she has acquired a further knowledge of colours in general."
These are the words of William Tucker, author of *The Family Dyer and Scourer*, published in 1831 (p. v), which perfectly express the purpose of the discussion that follows.

Seeing Color

Close your eyes for a few seconds. After you open them again you will realize that shutting out all light results in total absence of color. You may conclude then that color perception depends upon the presence of light. This fact was long recognized but not clearly understood until the 17th century when Isaac Newton discovered that the "white" light of the sun is a mixture of all colors.

Newton proved this by allowing a beam of light to pass through a glass prism. As the light, composed of a range of light waves of different lengths, passed from air through the denser medium of the prism its components, the colors of the visible spectrum, traveling at different speeds were refracted or bent at different angles. Since each color had a definite wave length, each was separated out at a slightly different angle, resulting in a fan-shaped series of hues within the prism. Performing this experiment yourself you will see that the colors are arranged in a definite order. Red with the longest wave length is always followed by orange, yellow, green, blue, and indigo. Violet with the shortest wave length is at the opposite end of the visible spectrum from red.

It was further learned that red, green, and violet are the basic or primary colors of the visible spectrum. This can be proved by directing beams containing equal amounts of red, green, and violet light to one point on a wall. This combination of the three primaries results in a spot of "white" light.

When daylight strikes a colored object such as a red cloth, all the various wave lengths in light except the red ones are absorbed. Thus the eye, focused

57

upon the red cloth, sees the color red because red wave lengths are not absorbed but reflected and perceived by the viewer. Exactly how this sensation is received and transmitted by the human nervous system is not known, although there are a number of theories on this aspect of color perception. The classic theory of the nature of color was more fully interpreted for the layman by Sargent (1964). Land's interesting new concept of color vision is also recommended for those who wish to pursue the subject further (1964).

The relationship of light to colored objects is of great concern to the dyer to whom a colored textile will appear quite different under varying light conditions. For example, the red of the cloth in question may appear clear and pure in daylight, yellow red in yellowish incandescent light, and bluish red under blued fluorescent lighting. These effects can be predicted since substances can only reflect rays present in the light that falls on them. We know that daylight, being white light, contains all wave lengths, so all wave lengths except red will be absorbed. Only red will be reflected, thus we will perceive the cloth as pure red. Incandescent light is a weak yellow light; thus the light waves of yellow red will be reflected from the surface of the cloth. The same will be true of the slightly blued fluorescent light which will allow the blue-red light waves to be reflected. If a strong blue-green light almost devoid of red were turned on the red cloth, the object could reflect almost no red and would appear black under the new light. This would explain why two "perfectly matched" colors will appear different under differing light conditions. It also suggests that colors can be modified by clever use of lighting.

Mixing Colors

Most of the dyer's everyday problems will concern colored textiles, rather than colored light. Although identifying and describing color is as elusive as trying to describe musical sound, color theorists have succeeded in developing systems which enable dyers to communicate their ideas.

The systems vary greatly, but most have in common the notion that all colors possess three qualities: hue, value, intensity. To illustrate this point, you might try painting or dyeing a green swatch, roughly matching a green I am thinking of. If you dye a *dark, dull yellowed* green it will be incorrect. A *dark, bright yellow* green will also be incorrect. My green is *light, bright* and close to *blue* green. Your next comment would be that you were not supplied with an adequate description of the particular color requested. This is true because the hue or color name alone did not give us any idea of the value and intensity of this special green. Any color description omitting these two qualities would be too vague to be useful.

Value refers to a hue's lightness or darkness—its nearness to black or white on the value scale (figure 11). Intensity or saturation indicates the purity or brightness of a hue. At one end of the saturation scale a hue is most pure and bright. At the opposite end are the dulled or neutralized hues.

FIGURE 11.—Value chart showing the range of grays between black and white.

The first-known use of a wheel arrangement of hues is shown in figure 10. Moses Harris devised this system in about 1766, and since his time many color theorists including Chevreul, Munsell, Ostwald, and others have developed and modified this theme.

Red, yellow, and blue are the basic or primary hues on this color wheel, since no mixture of colored pigments will produce either red, yellow, or blue, but mixing varying quantities of the primaries will theoretically produce all other hues. Pairs of primaries make the secondary hues: orange from red and yellow; green from yellow and blue; purple from blue and red. Between the primaries and secondaries on the Harris color wheel are hues which combine a primary with its adjacent secondary. These include red purple, purple red, orange red, red orange, etc., with the second part of the color name indicating the predominating hue. Thus by mixing pigments one can theoretically achieve the following results:

Primary	Secondary	Tertiary		
RED		less purple	+ more red	= purple red
	= Purple	less red	+ more purple	= red purple
+		less purple	+ more blue	= purple blue
BLUE		less blue	+ more purple	= blue purple
BLUE		less green	+ more blue	= green blue
	= Green	less blue	+ more green	= blue green
+		less green	+ more yellow	= green yellow
YELLOW		less yellow	+ more green	= yellow green
YELLOW		less orange	+ more yellow	= orange yellow
	= Orange	less yellow	+ more orange	= yellow orange
+		less orange	+ more red	= orange red
RED		less red	+ more orange	= red orange

59

Because concentrations of dye solutions vary, one must experiment to learn the exact proportions needed to obtain specific colors. For example, one drop of blue in a cup of yellow dye solution could result in a satisfactory green. One drop of the same yellow in a cup of the same blue may not make any noticeable change in the appearance of the blue dye. Thus the above chart is only a guide suggesting which hues may be combined to form new hues or to modify existing ones. The individual who mixes dyes will become acquainted with the infinite range of colors possible once he knows the color wheel and the character of his own dyes or pigments.

Of the neutrals, only black is included on Moses Harris' color wheel. As Harris has indicated, all three primary pigments mixed together will make black. Dyers have known this for centuries; in fact, this combination was used during the 18th and 19th centuries to dye tapestry yarn black at the Gobelins factory in Paris. Dipping wool into a blue vat first, then into a red and a yellow dyebath was very expensive and time-consuming, but the resulting dye was rich and durable. Even more important, yarns dyed black in this way did not require iron mordants that after a few years would corrode the wool fibers.

White, another of the neutrals, is the absence of colored pigment and can only be achieved in textiles by bleaching. Bleaching is necessary to provide a clean background when dyeing a pure, light color.

Grays are obtained in several ways. Black and white pigments can be mixed together to make gray; additions of white result in light grays, additions of black darken them. Another way of mixing gray is by combining hues directly opposite each other on the color wheel. Each pair of these complementary hues will make an individual gray. For example, mixtures of red and green, orange and blue, and yellow and purple will produce three noticeably different grays. Grays made by combining complements can also be lightened or darkened by addition of white or black.

All the hues shown along the outer edge of the color wheel are meant to be at their highest intensity. Because of the age and quality of the colors used by Mr. Harris, several of these hues appear dulled. Let us assume, however, that they are as bright as the hues in the spectrum. How can one of these colored pigments be neutralized? There are two possibilities: black and white can be added; also, addition of the hue's complement will accomplish the same general effect. Two complements will usually make a "livelier" gray than will a black plus white combination. Regardless of the neutralizing pigment, if the addition is lighter than the original pigment, it will lighten as well as neutralize. If the addition is darker than the original, its effect will be that of darkening and neutralizing.

The above information can only be considered a brief introduction to the subject of color systems. Fuller discussions may be found in Itten, 1961; Minnaert, 1954; Munsell, 1941; and Sargent, 1964.

Color Variation in Home-Dyed Textiles

Even the most methodical home dyer will find that it is practically impossible to duplicate the colors of textiles dyed with natural dyestuffs. The dye material itself makes variation the rule since so many factors influence the growth and development of vegetable materials. The subject is far too broad to be explored in detail here, however, the causes of color variation in natural dyes are worth mentioning. They include differences in growing conditions, the area in which the plants are grown, climatic conditions, and quality of soil. Different members of plant families may contain varying amounts and qualities of dye principles. Usually the greatest quantity of dye is extracted from plants when they are ready to mature, although timing would differ with each plant. Often flowers can be used fresh or dried, but even the manner in which they are dried could affect the quality of dye extracted.

Aside from care in selecting and handling the plants, one key to successful dyeing is a supply of soft water. Writers of early 19th-century dyebooks never failed to mention this point. There are very few dyestuffs that work most effectively in hard water; where hard water is needed, chemicals can be added to harden the water. Although the calcium, magnesium, and iron salts and other minerals which make water hard may not change color radically, they can cause spotting and irregular distribution of dyes in textiles.

Since mordants are discussed more fully in a later section, it is only necessary to mention here that the mordant used often affects the hue as well as colorfastness of the dyed textile. A notable illustration is that of cochineal-dyed wool. White wool becomes purple when dyed with cochineal mordanted with chrome. It takes on a red hue when mordanted with a tin compound. The same mordants will produce very slight differences in hue or intensity when combined with other dyestuffs. Each dye recipe specifies the mordant needed to obtain stated colors. If you decide to experiment with mordants, remember that the primary purpose of a mordant is to unite dyestuffs to fibers. A beautiful color achieved by combining a dye with an incompatible mordant will result in a color that may fade soon after washing or exposure to sunlight, or it may adversely affect the wool's texture or wearing qualities.

61

Limited Color Range of Natural Dyes

At first glance the range of hues made with natural dyestuffs may seem disappointingly narrow. More than half the dye recipes in this book produce yellows—from light and bright to dark and dull—with the emphasis on the neutral end of the saturation scale. Beyond these, a few browns, grays, oranges, and reds are included, with one each of purple and blue. Some 18th- and 19th-century textile dyers who were keenly aware of the color limitations of native natural dye materials searched the world for new sources of permanent dyes. Others with little concern for lasting results, and with an eye on profits, lowered their standards of colorfastness to broaden their stock of salable colors by using dyes they knew would fade in sunlight and washing.

Most color names listed with the dye recipes are descriptive and should be self-explanatory, e.g., light greenish yellow, dark brown, etc. If they seem general, they are deliberately so, because of the above-mentioned variations inherent in natural dyes. Even though there is seldom a direct reference to saturation in these color names, the purest colors result from using fresh, carefully selected flowers or other plant material and strict adherence to mordanting and dyeing time and temperature requirements. The color names not found in any color chart, such as brass and khaki, can be checked in the "Dictionary of Color" by Maerz and Paul. Because the color plates in that book were printed in 1930 and the paper on which they were printed has changed color, these now only roughly approximate the authors' original color swatches. Flag red, the only color not included in the color dictionary, can be interpreted as a pure red of medium value.

Fiber, Yarn, and Piece Dyeing

We have just noted the color limitations imposed by natural dyestuffs. Working with textile materials, however, the craftsman has an unusual opportunity to mix colors to achieve unique effects. Top-dyeing (see p. 107), the most obvious way of expanding the range of colors, consists of dipping a textile into several different dyebaths in succession. Thus, dipping a cloth into a blue vat then a yellow dyebath will make green; red and yellow dippings will result in orange, etc. The technique can be applied to any combination of colors, although generally the dyes producing the clearest colors are best for top-dyeing.

The way a textile is processed—starting with very fine individual raw fibers, combining these into lengths of yarn, and finally weaving the yarn into sheets of cloth—makes it possible for the dyer to color textile material while in the fiber, yarn, or cloth stage. Fiber-dyeing, most frequently applied to raw wool, refers to wool that is sheared from the sheep, scoured, and then dyed. If the fibers are then divided among several different colored dyebaths and mixed and carded together, the fine colored fibers will be so thoroughly blended that yarn spun with them will appear solid-colored from a distance. A close-up view will reveal subtle variations in hue. Tweeds are often fiber-dyed or "dyed-in-the-wool."

Many home dyers color yarns for weaving or knitting into solid-colored textiles; however, yarn dyeing can present other creative opportunities to the imaginative colorist. For example, a textile can appear solid-colored, yet may actually be a blend of two tones alternating in the warp and weft, or two colored strands knitted or woven as one. Another way of achieving this effect is by combining one color in the warp with another color in the weft. These treatments add depth to a "solid" hue. Other more traditional uses of yarn-dyed materials are in checks, plaids, stripes, or irregular patterns. Some optical tricks are played by placing controlled amounts of contrasting hues adjacent to each other. Yarns can also be tie-dyed and top-dyed to achieve patterns.

Most piece-dyed cloths are dyed as solid colors. However, patterns can be introduced into sheer fabrics by tie-dyeing them or by resist-dyeing techniques such as batik. Since all of these specialized patterning techniques require skills beyond the scope of this book, we recommend that you consult Pellew's book (1913) for information on "Tied and Dyed Work" and Krevetsky (1964), Mijer (1920) or other more recent publications for a detailed explanation of batik.

Finally certain factors outside the dyestuffs and their union with cloth affect the appearance of colored textiles. These include the effect of light on colored materials and the effect that adjacent hues have on each other. Texture, which has not been mentioned previously, greatly influences the distribution of light on the surface of fabrics. Folding a fabric emphasizes its textural qualities. For example, light playing on a sleek red satin causes it to appear much lighter than a thick, rough tweed having the same red hue. Drape the satin, and there will be a distinct difference in value between the outermost and innermost parts of the folds. These effects can be exploited only when they are thoroughly understood. Thus the home dyer who develops a sensitive eye, understanding of color, and an experimental attitude will derive the greatest enjoyment from working with this challenging color medium.

PLANNING A HOME DYEING PROJECT

The revision of *Home dyeing with natural dyes* presented here reports the results of tests on about 65 natural materials used for dyeing cotton and wool cloth. Most of the dyes studied are of vegetable origin. In fact the terms "natural" and "vegetable" dyes are often used interchangeably though a few, such as cochineal, are of animal origin, and iron buff and others are developed from mineral pigments.

Samples of all the dyes used in these experiments were given standard tests for colorfastness. Many were discarded as unsatisfactory, and recipes are included only for those that produced attractive colors fast to both light and washing. Since the common names of trees and plants differ from place to place, the scientific names are given. The college of agriculture in any state will help in identifying plant materials. In each locality there are many natural dye materials that by one dye method or another will give satisfactory colors. This publication is intended merely as a guide for such work.

Colorfastness

A dyer writing ca. 1830 remarked: "As to garments whose colours are changed every year, if the colour preserves its full brightness during the season, it is as much as can be required . . ." Most contemporary craftsmen have neither the time nor inclination to exert the effort required to dye textiles unless they can be reasonably sure that their efforts will not be lost within a short time; thus the fastness or permanence of a dye is an important consideration.

While fastness is of great concern, the home dyer should be aware that no dye is absolutely fast under all conditions. It may be fast to light, or to perspiration, or to washing, but seldom fast under all three conditions. Futhermore, a dye may be fast on one fiber and not on another; or it may be fast when dyed by one method and not another. Of all the textile fibers, wool can be dyed most easily, and the resulting colors change the least. Cotton does not combine easily with dyes, and fast colors are produced on it only by complicated processes.

The need for a particular kind of fastness depends on the nature of the color change and the use to be made of the dyed fabric. For example, a fabric dyed brown with tree bark may darken on exposure to light. While this color change might be satisfactory in a hooked rug, it would be unacceptable in window draperies.

To make sure that these recipes produce colors permanent enough to be useful for most purposes, the dyed fabrics were tested for their fastness to light and washing. The results are included in the dye recipes.

For the light test, samples of the dyed fabrics were cut and exposed for 40 hours to the rays of a carbon-arc lamp. Throughout the test period half of each piece was shielded while the rays of the lamp shone directly on the other half. Then the two parts were compared and the fastness to light rated as follows: Good—no appreciable change of color; fair—appreciable but not objectionable change of color; poor—objectionable change of color.

Though these light tests were run in a standard fading apparatus, the same method can be followed at home by exposing samples to sunlight. Cut 2-inch-square openings in each of two pieces of heavy cardboard, fasten a swatch of dyed cloth to one piece of cardboard and lay the other cardboard over the swatch, sandwich fashion. It is important that the light come through the fabric. Then place this sample in its frame out of doors in the direct sunlight and tilted toward the sun. After a few days remove and compare the section exposed to the sun with the covered portion.

This test cannot be considered absolutely conclusive, since the exposure, strength of sunlight at the particular season, and other factors modify results. Such a test will, however, suggest whether a dyed fabric may be satisfactory as a curtain or decorative fabric that would be exposed to sunlight.

To determine whether a dye will bleed, stain or fade in washing, samples were prepared by sewing a 2″ x 4″ piece of dyed fabric to a similar piece of undyed material. Each sample was placed in a half-pint jar partly filled with neutral soap solution (0.5 percent for wool and 0.1 percent for cotton) at 120° F. and agitated in a shaking machine for 30 minutes. The sample was removed, squeezed through a wringer, and rinsed by agitating in water for 10 minutes. Rinsing was repeated five times and the temperature of each rinse gradually dropped to lukewarm. The samples were dried quickly, then compared with the original unwashed fabric, and rated as in the light test. A similar test could be devised for wash testing under home washing conditions.

Equipment and Supplies

Simple equipment and a few easily obtainable supplies are needed to dye textile materials at home. These include:

Scales that will weight accurately in fractions of an ounce.

Kettles of enamel or copper, large enough to immerse the material completely. Because iron darkens colors and tin makes colors harsh, kettles made of these materials should be avoided if possible.

Large pails or tubs for rinsing dyed materials.

Measuring equipment: gallon, peck, and quart measures, tablespoons and dippers.

Cheesecloth for straining dye liquor.

Sticks or glass rods for stirring and turning material in the dyebath. These should be made of smooth, splinter-free wood or very thick glass. Glass towel rods are useful. Most plastics melt or bend when subjected to high temperatures, thus most plastic rods could not be used.

Stove: if possible, have it set lower than usual so that lifting pots of water and stirring the dyebath will be easier.

Thermometer for testing temperature of the dyebath and rinse water.

Rubber gloves for protecting the hands from chemicals used in dyeing.

Drying rack or clothesline sheltered from the sun.

Soft water supply: filtered rain water or chemically softened water will help to prevent spotting caused by minerals in water.

Neutral soap: mild soap such as recommended for lingerie and fine woolens is satisfactory.

Dye materials and chemicals which cannot be found in nature may be purchased from drugstores and botanical-drug suppliers. See appendix A for list of common names of dye chemicals.

Preparation for Dyeing

A NOTE OF CAUTION: *Keep dye material out of children's reach. Some of these substances are poisonous, and may cause skin irritation.*

1. Collecting and storing plant materials

It is difficult to make general statements on this subject beyond an old-time dyer's warning: "In collecting die-stuffs, be particular to get the best kind of every sort; for in having one (specimen) that is poor, it may be a great injury to the color . . ." (Waite, 1815, p. 80). The most concentrated dyes are usually found in material that is harvested just as it is reaching maturity. Often it is used immediately; in certain cases, the plant material can be spread out and dried carefully, avoiding the danger of mold caused by trapping plant moisture.

2. Weighing

The dry weight of the fiber, yarn, or cloth to be dyed determines the quantity of soap to use in washing it before dyeing; it also determines the quantity of chemicals and dyestuffs to use in the mordanting and dyeing processes. All recipes are based on 1 pound of wool or cotton weighed dry before mordanting.

3. Washing

Dye solutions penetrate textile materials more thoroughly and evenly if the yarn or fabric to be dyed is washed in soap and water and well rinsed before dyeing. Starch and sizing which prevent fibers from readily

66

absorbing dyestuffs should be removed by washing. Spots and stains cause uneven dyeing and should also be removed before washing.

4. Washing Wool

Before dyeing wool, use the following washing procedure. Dissolve neutral soap in 5 gallons of lukewarm (95° F.), soft water. Wash the material thoroughly and squeeze out suds. Repeat the washing procedure. After the second washing squeeze out the suds, rinse the material three or four times, or until all traces of soap have been rinsed away.

Felting and shrinkage can be avoided if wool is handled quickly and gently throughout the washing and dyeing processes. Always squeeze excess moisture out of materials. Never wring or twist wool. Also, since sudden temperature changes will cause wool to shrink and become harsh, the following measures should be taken to avoid these conditions. First, keep the temperature of the material as even as possible by transferring it directly from suds to rinses without delay; second, keep the water at a lukewarm temperature for all suds and rinses.

If unspun wool is to be used for dyeing, the raw wool must be thoroughly scoured and cleaned first. The natural wax and grease in raw wool tend to make the fiber water repellent, thus the dye solution cannot penetrate. After scouring (Davenport, 1964, p. 117) and dyeing, wool is carded and spun into yarn. When wool from different dye lots is blended together in carding, interesting tweed color effects can be achieved.

5. Washing Cotton

Before dyeing cotton, use the following washing procedure. Dissolve neutral soap in 5 gallons of hot (140° F.), soft water. Wash the material thoroughly and squeeze out suds. Repeat the washing procedure, then rinse. The second rinse water should be hotter than the first one, and the material should be allowed to soak in it for at least a half hour. This should be followed by two or three cooler rinses.

Mordants

Many natural dyes will fade and "bleed" badly unless the yarn or fabric is first treated with a chemical called a mordant, a metallic salt that helps to fix the color to the fiber. The mordants commonly used with the natural dyestuffs are alum (aluminum potassium sulfate), chrome (potassium dichromate), copperas (ferrous sulfate), and tannic acid or some other source of tannin such as oak galls or sumach leaves. Commercial dyers use oils and other substances too difficult for the home dyer to apply.

By using different mordants, a variety of shades and sometimes even different colors may be obtained from a single dyestuff. For example, on wool, dahlia flowers used with a chrome mordant give an orange color

67

and with alum, a light yellow. Cochineal mordanted with alum gives a red and with chrome, a purple.

Both wool and silk have the property of holding chemicals in their fibers. For example, when wool is boiled in a solution of potassium dichromate (chrome mordant) a certain amount of chromium oxide is held in the fiber, and the dyestuff then combines with this mordanted wool to form a permanent color.

Cotton and the other vegetable fibers do not absorb mordants as readily as wool. Vegetable fibers, however, combine well with tannic acid, which is used either as a mordant or as an agent for fixing mordants in the fiber.

Mordanting Wool

Alum Mordant

For 1 pound of dry wool, use
    4 ounces potash alum (aluminum potassium sulfate)
    1 ounce cream of tartar

Dissolve the alum and cream of tartar in 4 to 4½ gallons of cold soft water. Immerse the wool after first wetting it thoroughly and squeezing out excess moisture. Gradually heat the mordant bath to boiling; boil it gently for 1 hour. While the wool is in the solution, it should be turned and stirred to insure complete penetration of the mordant. As liquid boils away, add more water to maintain the original level of the bath. Allow the wool to stand overnight in the mordant. The following morning squeeze out excess moisture, roll the wool in a dry towel, and store it in a cool place. Rinse the mordanted material well just before immersing it in the dyebath.

Chrome Mordant

For 1 pound of dry wool, use
    ½ ounce potassium dichromate

Dissolve the potassium dichromate in 4 to 4½ gallons of cold soft water and follow directions for mordanting wool with alum.

Mordanting Cotton

Alum Mordant

For 1 pound of dry cotton, use
    4 ounces potash alum (aluminum potassium sulfate)
    1 ounce washing soda (sodium carbonate)

Dissolve the alum and washing soda in 4 to 4½ gallons of cold water. Immerse the cotton, after first wetting it thoroughly in clear water and squeezing out excess moisture. Stir while gradually heating to boiling, then boil for 1 hour. Allow the yarn to remain in the bath overnight. The following morning remove the cotton from the mordant solution, squeeze out excess moisture, roll the material in a dry towel and store it in a cool place. Rinse the mordanted cotton well before immersing it in the dyebath.

Alum-Tannin-Alum Mordant (process takes three days)

For one pound of dry cotton, use
    8 ounces potash alum (aluminum potassium sulfate)
    2 ounces sodium carbonate
    10 ounces powdered oak galls, or one ounce tannic acid, or extract from 4 to 6 ounces dry sumach leaves

Dissolve half of the alum (4 oz.) and half of the washing soda (1 oz.) in 4 to 4½ gallons of cold soft water. Immerse the cotton, after first wetting it thoroughly and squeezing out excess moisture. Stir while gradually heating to boiling, then boil for one hour. Allow the material to remain in the bath overnight.* The following morning squeeze excess moisture from the material, rinse and put it into a bath of oak galls, tannic acid, or sumach leaves heated to 140° to 160° F. Work the yarn in this bath for one hour and allow it to stay in the bath overnight. The following day rinse it briefly. Then dissolve the remainder of the alum and washing soda in 4 to 4½ gallons of water and repeat the mordanting process to* above. The following morning squeeze excess moisture out of the cotton and rinse thoroughly just before dyeing.

To prepare the extract of sumach leaves, soak the dry leaves in water for half an hour, boil them for 30 minutes, strain the liquid, and allow the bath to cool to 140° to 160° F.

DYE RECIPES
General Instructions

Dye recipes are arranged alphabetically by the name of the flower, bark, or other dye material. The heading "barks" includes directions for the four basic methods of dyeing with tree barks and is followed by an alphabetical listing of many tree barks that were tested; special information about dyeing with these barks is found in this listing.

Read complete instructions for mordanting and dyeing before undertaking any project. It is also helpful to assemble all chemicals, dye materials, and equipment before starting the dyeing process.

All dyebaths require a plentiful supply of soft water—at least 4 to 4½ gallons for each pound of yarn or cloth dyed. Crowding textiles or using water that contains certain mineral deposits may result in streaked or spotted colors.

Although there are specific instructions for extracting dyes from each type of plant or animal material listed, certain general procedures apply to all dyeing:

1. When textile materials are immersed in mordanting and dye liquors they should be opened out and turned over gently in the liquid from time to time to allow maximum, even penetration of the dye or mordant. This process is sometimes referred to as "working" the material.
2. Sudden temperature changes should be avoided in all stages of dyeing and mordanting, particularly when handling wool. Temperature of the dyebath should be lukewarm (95° F.) for wool; hot (140° F.) for cotton. Dyebaths are then heated gradually to boiling and simmered or boiled according to the specific recipe.
3. If the dye liquid boils down, lift out the fibers, yarn, or cloth and add boiling water, thus keeping the water level of the dyebath constant throughout the dye process.
4. After dyeing, the first rinse water should be the same temperature as the dyebath. Temperature can be cooled gradually until finally arriving at the last cool, clear rinse water. Insufficient rinsing often causes dye to rub off or crock later.
5. When squeezing excess moisture from materials after mordanting, dyeing or rinsing, do not twist or wring the wool or cotton. Such harsh treatment introduces streaks and wrinkles that are difficult to remove.
6. After the final rinse, roll the dyed material in a clean cloth or towel to absorb excess moisture; then shake it well and hang it in the shade to dry. Do not dry wool in a clothes drier. When dyed fabric is dry enough to iron, cover it with a cloth and steam press. Fibers and yarn are ready for use after they are dried.
7. The full amount of yarn or cloth required for each project should be dyed at one time. Vegetable dye materials vary so much that it is impossible to duplicate colors exactly.
8. To lighten or darken colors, decrease or increase the quantity of dyestuffs. Experimentation will result in interesting color effects.
9. These recipes provide basic information on dyeing with natural ingredients and should be regarded as a first step in the exploration of natural dye materials. Many other good dyestuffs are available locally to craftsmen who wish to experiment.

The following plant materials, sometimes suggested for dyeing, do not produce fast colors on wool or cotton, therefore they were not included in the dye recipes: annatto seeds; Japanese barberry root; beets; crab-apple peelings; the fruit of the blackberry, blueberry, cranberry, and pokeweed; purple iris flowers; mosses; peach leaves; red roses; sumach leaves; turmeric and willow leaves.

TESTED DYE RECIPES

ASTER, CHINESE (*Callistemma chinensis*)

The coloring principles callistephin and asterin are found in asters, especially in deep purple-red flowers. The asters used in testing this recipe were rose pink.

Light Greenish-Yellow Wool: chrome mordant
Colorfastness: good

1 pound of wool
½ bushel fresh aster flowers

Use chrome mordant (see pages 67 to 68). Cut the flowers into small pieces, cover with water and boil for 10 minutes. Strain out the flowers, then add water to make a dyebath of 4 to 4½ gallons. Before immersing the mordanted wool in the dyebath, rinse it and squeeze out excess moisture. Immerse wool; heat the dyebath to boiling; boil gently for 20 minutes, rinse and dry.

BARKS

The barks of many trees are good sources of brown dyes. A wide range of tones from the very lightest tan to deepest brown can be extracted from the inner bark of such common trees as oak and maple. Wool can be dyed in the complete range of tones, while only lighter browns can be produced in cotton.

Most barks are best collected in the fall or winter, but resinous ones may be gathered in the spring. The inner bark can be used either fresh or dried: fresh barks are usually most potent. If barks are stored, they should be dried carefully first, then put in a place free from dampness and mold.

The coloring principles of these dyes are combined with a type of tannin; because of the presence of tannin, fabrics dyed with bark extracts often do not retain their original color, becoming darker brown upon exposure to light. This change can be prevented by treating dyed materials with certain chemicals that fix or remove excess tannin such as potassium dichromate, ferrous sulfate, and copper sulfate which are used in dye methods 2, 3, and 4 on the following pages.

Many other barks not included here will produce fast colors in textiles. Experimentation with local materials and application of basic methods of extracting dyes from tree barks can result in attractive and durable colors.

Bark: Dye Method 1

1 pound of wool or cotton
1 peck finely chopped bark

Use alum or chrome mordant on wool, and alum or alum-tannin-alum on cotton (see pages 67 to 69). Soak the bark overnight in 2 to 2½ gallons of soft water. The following morning gradually heat this bath to boiling, boil for 2 hours. Add hot water as necessary to maintain the original water level. Strain the dye liquid twice through cheesecloth, then add cold water to make a dyebath of 4 to 4½ gallons. When the bath is cooled to lukewarm (95° F.), immerse the material after first wetting it thoroughly and squeezing out excess moisture. Heat the dyebath to boiling; boil for 30 minutes, rinse and dry.

Bark: Dye Method 2

1 pound of wool or cotton
1 peck finely chopped bark
⅙ ounce potassium dichromate
⅙ ounce acetic acid, or 6 to 7 tablespoons vinegar

Use alum mordant on wool, and alum or alum-tannin-alum on cotton (see pages 67 to 69). Soak the bark overnight in 2 to 2½ gallons of soft water. The following morning heat this bath to boiling and continue to boil for 2 hours. Add hot water as necessary to maintain the original water level. Strain the dye liquid twice through cheesecloth then add cold water to make a dyebath of 4 to 4½ gallons. When the bath is cooled to lukewarm, immerse the material after first rinsing thoroughly and squeezing out excess moisture. Heat the dyebath to boiling and continue to boil for 30 minutes.

Without rinsing, transfer the yarn or cloth to a boiling bath of potassium dichromate and acetic acid dissolved in 4 gallons of soft water. Stir carefully while boiling for 10 minutes, rinse and dry.

Bark: Dye Method 3

1 pound wool
1 peck finely chopped bark
⅙ ounce copper sulfate (blue vitriol)
⅙ ounce acetic acid or 6 to 7 tablespoons vinegar

Use alum or chrome mordant (see pages 67 to 68). Follow directions for dye method 2, substituting copper sulfate for potassium dichromate.

Bark: Dye Method 4

1 pound wool
1 peck finely chopped bark
⅙ ounce ferrous sulfate (copperas)

72

Use alum mordant (see pages 67 to 68). Follow directions for dye method 2, substituting ferrous sulfate for potassium dichromate and acetic acid or vinegar.

APPLE BARK (*Pyrus malus* or *Malus sylvestris*)

Dark Yellow-Tan Wool: alum mordant
Colorfastness: fair to light, good to washing
Dye Method 1 or 4 (see pages 72 and 73)

Brass Wool: chrome mordant
Colorfastness: fair to light, good to washing
Dye Method 1 (see page 72)

BIRCH BARK, YELLOW (*Betula lutea*)

The yellow birch bark used in these recipes is found in moist forests in Northeastern United States and in some Midwestern States.

Dark Yellow-Tan Wool: alum mordant
Colorfastness: fair to light, good to washing
Dye Method 3 (see page 72)

Yellow-Brown Wool: alum mordant
Colorfastness: good
Dye Method 2 (see page 72)

CHITTAM BARK (*Rhamnus purshiana*)

Chittam bark is collected in Oregon and Washington States for use in manufacturing the drug cascara sagrada.

Dark Yellow-Tan Wool: chrome mordant
Colorfastness: fair
Dye Method 1 (see page 72), using only ¼ peck of bark

Light Brown Wool: alum mordant
Colorfastness: good
Dye Method 2 (see page 72), using only ¼ peck of bark

Tan Cotton: alum-tannin-alum mordant
Colorfastness: good
Dye Method 2 (see page 72), using only ¼ peck of bark

Gray Cotton: alum-tannin-alum mordant
Colorfastness: fair
Dye Method 4 (see pages 72 and 73), using only ¼ peck of bark

Hemlock Bark, Western (*Tsuga heterophylla*)

Hemlock bark is commonly used as a dyeing and tanning material. Western hemlock, which grows in hilly and rocky wooded areas of the western part of the United States, was used in these recipes. The eastern hemlock (*Tsuga canadensis*), sometimes called spruce pine, is also used in dyeing.

Dark Yellow-Tan Wool: chrome mordant
Colorfastness: fair
Dye Method 2 (see page 72)

Dark Rose-Tan Wool: alum mordant
Colorfastness: fair
Dye Method 2 (see page 72)

Rose-Tan Cotton: alum-tannin-alum mordant
Colorfastness: fair to light, good to washing
Dye Method 1 or 2 (see page 72)

Hickory Bark, White (*Carya tomentosa* or *C. alba*)

The hickory used in this recipe grows in Eastern United States.

Dark Yellow-Tan Wool: alum mordant
Colorfastness: fair to light, good to washing
Dye Method 3 (see page 72)

Yellow-Brown Wool: alum mordant
Colorfastness: good
Dye Method 2 (see page 72)

Brass Wool: chrome mordant
Colorfastness: fair to light, good to washing
Dye Method 1 (see page 72)

Gold Cotton: alum-tannin-alum mordant
Colorfastness: good
Dye Method 1 (see page 72)

Brass Cotton: alum-tannin-alum mordant
Colorfastness: good
Dye Method 2 (see page 72)

Maple Bark, Norway (*Acer platanoides*)

The barks of the Norway maple and the silver maple produce similar colors on wool and cotton. These trees are found throughout Eastern North America.

Rose-Tan Wool: alum mordant
Colorfastness: fair to light, good to washing
Use Dye Method 3 (see page 72)

Rose-Tan Wool: chrome mordant
Colorfastness: fair to light, good to washing
Use Dye Method 1 (see page 72)

Light Brown Wool: alum mordant
Colorfastness: fair to light, good to washing
Use Dye Method 2 (see page 72)

Light Gray Cotton: alum-tannin-alum mordant
Colorfastness: fair to light, good to washing
Use Dye Method 1 (see page 72)

Drab Cotton: alum-tannin-alum mordant
Colorfastness: good
Use Dye Method 2 (see page 72)

OAK BARK, BLACK OR QUERCITRON (*Quercus velutina*)

Quercitron, the dyestuff prepared from the inner bark of black- or quercitron-oak trees, is more potent than the dye produced by any other bark mentioned in this publication. It is found in the eastern half of the United States, especially in Pennsylvania, Georgia, and the Carolinas. The bark itself may be used, or a pure dye extract of quercitron may be purchased. The extract has much greater coloring power than the bark.

The dye material in quercitron contains a type of tannin. Since tannin dulls colors, prolonged boiling in a quercitron bath should be avoided.

Gold Wool: chrome mordant
Colorfastness: good
Use Dye Method 1 (see page 72) for quercitron bark

Use the following dye method for quercitron extract:
   1 pound wool
   ½ ounce quercitron extract

Use chrome mordant (see pages 67 to 68). Then dissolve the quercitron extract in 4 to 4½ gallons of soft water. Immerse the material after thoroughly rinsing it and squeezing out excess moisture. Heat to boiling the bath containing the wool; boil for 30 minutes, rinse and dry.

Yellow-Tan Wool: alum mordant
Colorfastness: fair to light, good to washing
Use Dye Method 2 (see page 72) for quercitron bark

Use the following dye method for quercitron extract:
   1 pound wool
   ½ ounce quercitron extract
   ⅙ ounce potassium dichromate
   ⅙ ounce acetic acid, or 6 to 7 tablespoons vinegar

75

Use alum mordant (see page 68). Then dissolve the quercitron extract in 4 to 4½ gallons of soft water. Before immersing mordanted wool in the dyebath, thoroughly rinse it and squeeze out excess moisture. Immerse the wool; heat the bath to boiling; boil for 30 minutes. Then without rinsing, transfer the material into a boiling water solution of potassium dichromate and acetic acid or vinegar. Stir carefully while boiling 10 minutes, rinse and dry.

Gold Cotton: alum-tannin-alum mordant
Colorfastness: good
Use Dye Method 2 (see page 72) for quercitron bark

Use the following dye method for quercitron extract:
 1 pound cotton
 ½ ounce quercitron extract
 ⅙ ounce potassium dichromate
 ⅙ ounce acetic acid, or 6 to 7 tablespoons vinegar

Use alum-tannin-alum mordant (see pages 67 to 69). Then dissolve the quercitron extract in 4 to 4½ gallons of soft water. Before immersing the mordanted material in the dyebath, rinse it and squeeze out excess moisture. Immerse the cotton; heat the dyebath to boiling, boil for 30 minutes. Without rinsing it, transfer the material into a boiling water solution of potassium dichromate and acetic acid. Stir carefully while boiling for 10 minutes, rinse and dry.

Oak Bark, Chestnut (*Quercus prinus*)

The chestnut oak is native to the eastern part of the United States and grows in dry woods from Maine to Alabama.

Dark Yellow-Tan Wool: chrome mordant
Colorfastness: fair to light, good to washing
Dye Method 1 (see page 72)

Light Brown Wool: alum mordant
Colorfastness: good
Dye Method 2 or 3 (see page 72)

Oak Bark, Northern Red (*Quercus rubra* var. *borealis* or *Q. borealis* var. *maxima*)

Northern red-oak trees are found throughout the eastern half of the United States.

Tan Wool: chrome mordant
Colorfastness: good
Dye Method 3 (see page 72)

Rose-Tan Wool: no mordant
Colorfastness: fair
Dye Method 1 (see page 72)

Yellow-Tan Wool: chrome mordant
Colorfastness: good
Dye Method 1 (see page 72)

Light Brown Wool: alum mordant
Colorfastness: good
Dye Method 2 (see page 72)

Rose-Tan Cotton: alum mordant
Colorfastness: fair to light, good to washing
Dye Method 2 (see page 72)

OAK BARK, WHITE (*Quercus alba*)

The white oak grows in the woods of the eastern half of the United States.

Dark Yellow-Tan Wool: alum mordant
Colorfastness: good
Dye Method 1, 3, or 4 (see pages 72 to 73)

Light Brown Wool: alum mordant
Colorfastness: good
Dye Method 2 (see page 72)

Khaki Wool: chrome mordant
Colorfastness: good
Dye Method 1 (see page 72)

TUPELO OR BLACK GUM BARK (*Nyssa sylvatica*)

The tupelo or black-gum tree is common in the eastern half of the United States.

Dark Yellow-Tan Wool: alum mordant
Colorfastness: fair to light, good to washing
Dye Method 1 or 3 (see page 72)

Khaki Wool: alum mordant
Colorfastness: fair to light, good to washing
Dye Method 2 (see page 72)

WALNUT BARK, BLACK (*Juglans nigra*)

Although the hulls of black walnuts are most commonly used for dyeing (see page 105), the bark of the black walnut also yields a satisfactory dye.

Khaki Wool: chrome mordant
Colorfastness: fair to light, good to washing
Dye Method 1 (see page 72)

Yellow-Brown Wool: alum mordant
Colorfastness: good
Dye Method 3 (see page 72)

Dark Brown Wool: alum mordant
Colorfastness: good
Dye Method 2 (see page 72)

WILLOW BARK, BLACK (*Salix nigra*)

The black-willow tree is native to the eastern part of North America, growing in damp soils from eastern Canada to northern Florida.

Rose-Tan Wool: alum mordant
Colorfastness: fair to light, good to washing
Dye Method 1 or 3 (see page 72)

Light Brown Wool: alum mordant
Colorfastness: fair to light, good to washing
Dye Method 2 (see page 72)

BIRCH LEAVES, YELLOW (*Betula lutea*)

Yellow birch is one of the most valuable forest trees of the Northern States. The leaves can be used either fresh or dry; if the leaves are fresh, use twice the quantity stated below.

Yellow-Tan Wool: alum mordant
Colorfastness: fair to light, good to washing

1 pound of wool
¾ peck of dry birch leaves

Use alum mordant (see page 68). Cover the leaves with water and soak overnight. The following morning boil them for 1 hour, strain, then add water to make a dyebath of 4 to 4½ gallons. Before immersing the mordanted wool in the dyebath, rinse it and squeeze out excess moisture. Immerse the wool; heat the dyebath to boiling; boil for 30 minutes, rinse and dry.

BROOMSEDGE (*Andropogon virginicus*)

Broomsedge or "dyer's broom" grows on open waste ground from Massachusetts to Illinois and south to Florida and Texas. The entire stalk and leaves are used for dyeing. Although it can be gathered at any season for use as a dye, the dye is most concentrated in the summer when the plant is green. It can be cut in June and July, dried, then used as needed.

Broomsedge is used in top-dyeing (see pages 107 to 109). Greens are obtained by dipping the material first in a broomsedge dyebath, then in the indigo vat. Henna and brick colors are produced by dipping materials in successive dyebaths of broomsedge and madder.

Light Greenish-Yellow Wool: alum mordant
Colorfastness: good

1 pound wool
¾ peck dry broomsedge
⅙ ounce copper sulfate
⅙ ounce acetic acid, or 6 to 7 tablespoons vinegar

Use alum mordant (see pages 67 to 68). Cut the dry broomsedge stalks cover them with water and boil for 20 minutes. Strain the liquid, then add cold water to make a dyebath of 4 to 4½ gallons. Before immersing mordanted material in the dyebath, thoroughly rinse it and squeeze out excess moisture. Immerse the wool; heat to boiling; boil for 20 minutes. Without rinsing, transfer the dyed wool into a boiling bath containing copper sulfate and acetic acid in 4 gallons of water. Stir gently and boil for 10 minutes, rinse and dry.

Brass Wool: chrome mordant
Colorfastness: good

1 pound wool
¾ peck dry broomsedge

Use chrome mordant (see pages 67 to 68). Cut the dry broomsedge stalks, cover them with water and boil for 20 minutes. Strain the liquid then add cold water to make a dyebath of 4 to 4½ gallons. Before immersing mordanted material in the dyebath, thoroughly rinse it and squeeze out excess moisture. Immerse the wool; heat to boiling; boil for 20 minutes, rinse and dry.

Yellow Cotton: alum-tannin-alum mordant
Colorfastness: fair to light, good to washing

1 pound cotton
¾ peck dry broomsedge

Use alum-tannin-alum mordant (see pages 67 to 69). Follow directions for dyeing "Brass Wool" (above) with broomsedge.

Gold Cotton: alum-tannin-alum mordant
Colorfastness: good

1 pound cotton
¾ peck dry broomsedge
⅙ ounce potassium dichromate
⅙ ounce acetic acid, or 6 to 7 tablespoons vinegar

Use alum-tannin-alum mordant (see pages 67 to 69). Follow directions for dyeing "Light Greenish Yellow Wool" (above) with broomsedge.

79

BUTTERNUT HULLS (*Juglans cinerea*)

The bark, root, leaf, and hull of the butternut tree, found in the woods of the Eastern and Central States, are all used for dyeing. The mature nuts are gathered when still green and allowed to ripen partially. The hulls are then ready for use; they may also be dried and stored for future use.

Butternut produced the warm brown hue found in many overshot coverlets woven in the Northeastern States during the 18th and 19th centuries.

Brown Wool: alum mordant
Colorfastness: good

1 pound wool
1 peck green butternut hulls

Use alum mordant (see pages 67 to 68). Cover the hulls with water, soak for 30 minutes, then boil them for 15 to 30 minutes. After the liquid is strained, add cold water to make a dyebath of 4 to 4½ gallons. Before immersing the mordanted material, thoroughly rinse it and squeeze out excess moisture. Immerse the wool; heat to boiling; boil for 30 minutes, rinse and dry.

To obtain a darker brown, follow the above recipe. Then transfer the dyed, unrinsed material into a boiling bath containing one-sixth of an ounce of ferrous sulfate (copperas) and 4 to 4½ gallons of soft water. Boil for 10 minutes longer, rinse and dry.

Greenish Tan Cotton: alum mordant
Colorfastness: fair

1 pound cotton
1 peck green butternut hulls

Use alum mordant (see pages 67 to 68). Follow directions for dyeing "Brown Wool" (above).

Gray Cotton: alum mordant
Colorfastness: good

1 pound cotton
1 peck green butternut hulls
⅙ ounce ferrous sulfate (copperas)

Use alum mordant (see pages 67 to 69). Follow directions for dyeing "Brown Wool" (above). Without rinsing, transfer the yarn or cloth into a boiling bath of ferrous sulfate. Stir carefully while boiling for 10 to 15 minutes, rinse and dry.

CAMOMILE FLOWERS, YELLOW (*Anthemis tinctoria*)

Yellow camomile flowers or golden marguerites bloom in fields and waste places of this country.

Camomile flowers cannot be used for dyeing cotton.

Buff Wool: alum mordant
Colorfastness: fair

1 pound wool
7 quarts dry, crushed camomile flowers

Use alum mordant (see pages 67 to 68). Cover the dry crushed flowers with water then boil them for 25 minutes or until their color is gone. Strain and add cold water to make a dyebath of 4 to 4½ gallons. Before immersing mordanted wool in the dyebath, thoroughly rinse, and squeeze out excess water. Immerse the wool; heat to boiling; boil for 30 minutes. Wash in soapsuds to brighten the color, then rinse and dry.

Gold Wool: chrome mordant
Colorfastness: good

1 pound wool
7 quarts dry, crushed camomile flowers

Use chrome mordant (see pages 67 to 68). Follow directions for dyeing "Buff Wool" (above).

Khaki Wool: alum mordant
Colorfastness: good

1 pound wool
7 quarts dry, crushed camomile flowers
⅙ ounce potassium dichromate
⅙ ounce acetic acid, or 6 to 7 tablespoons vinegar

Use alum mordant (see pages 67 to 68). Follow directions for dyeing "Buff Wool" (above). Without rinsing, transfer the wool into a boiling bath of potassium dichromate and acetic acid in 4 gallons of water. Stir, then boil for 10 minutes rinse and dry.

CHROME YELLOW

On cotton, without a mordant, lead acetate and potassium dichromate produce a bright yellow. The color is not fast on wool.

Yellow Cotton: no mordant before dyeing
Colorfastness: good

1 pound cotton
3 ounces lead acetate
1 ounce potassium dichromate

Dissolve the lead acetate and potassium dichromate in individual baths, each containing 4 to 4½ gallons of water. Thoroughly wet the cotton, squeeze out excess water, then dip it in each bath, stirring to make certain that the solution reaches all parts of the material. Repeat this process four times. Rinse and dry.

81

COCHINEAL (*Dactylopius coccus*)

Cochineal is prepared from a dried insect, *D. coccus*, found in Mexico and Central America. It can be obtained from drug and dye supply houses. Cochineal is not a satisfactory dye for cotton. Some cochineal-dyed woolens become slightly bluer when washed, though they do not run or bleed.

Rose-Pink Wool: no mordant before dyeing
Colorfastness: good

    1 pound dry wool
    1 ounce powdered cochineal (2 oz. produces a light scarlet)
    4 ounces oxalic acid
    4 ounces stannous chloride
    1 ounce cream of tartar

Soak cochineal overnight in a small amount of water. The following morning add the oxalic acid, stannous chloride, and cream of tartar and boil for 10 minutes. Add cold water to make a dyebath of 4 to 4½ gallons. Before immersing the wool in the dyebath, thoroughly wet it and squeeze out excess moisture. Immerse the wool; heat to boiling; boil for 1 hour, rinse and dry.

Flag-Red Wool: no mordant before dyeing
Colorfastness: good

    1   pound wool
    3⅓ ounces powdered cochineal
    3⅓ ounces cream of tartar
    1⅗ ounces concentrated nitric acid
    ¼ ounce stannous chloride

Soak the cochineal and cream of tartar in water; add this mixture to 4 to 4½ gallons of boiling water. Boil for 10 minutes, strain, then add the nitric acid and stannous chloride which were previously dissolved in 1 cup of water. (CAUTION: *Always pour acid into water; never pour water into acid.*) Immerse the dry wool in the dyebath and allow it to boil for 1½ hours. Stir this dyebath constantly. Rinse wool and dry.

American Beauty Red Wool: alum mordant
Colorfastness: good

    1 pound wool
    1 ounce powdered cochineal

Use alum mordant (see pages 67 to 68). Soak cochineal in water for 1 hour, boil for 15 minutes then strain the liquid. Add cold water until the dyebath contains 4 to 4½ gallons. Before immersing mordanted wool in the dyebath, thoroughly rinse it and squeeze out excess moisture. Immerse the wool; heat to boiling point; boil for 1½ hours, rinse and dry.

Purple Wool: chrome mordant
Colorfastness: good

1 pound wool
2½ ounces powdered cochineal
1 teaspoon vinegar

Use chrome mordant (see pages 67 to 68). Boil the cochineal and vinegar in a small amount of water for 10 minutes. Strain the liquid, then add water to make a dyebath of 4 to 4½ gallons. Before immersing mordanted wool in the dyebath, thoroughly rinse it and squeeze out excess moisture. Immerse the wool; heat to boiling point; boil for 1½ hours, rinse and dry.

COFFEE BEANS (*Coffea arabica*)

Coffee does not produce fast colors on cotton.

Dark Yellow-Tan Wool: chrome mordant
Colorfastness: good

1 pound wool
1¾ pounds ground coffee

Use chrome mordant (see pages 67 to 68). Boil the coffee in water for 20 minutes. Strain out the grounds, then add cold water to make a dyebath of 4 to 4½ gallons. Thoroughly rinse the wool and squeeze out excess moisture. Immerse the wool; heat to the boiling point; boil for 30 minutes, rinse and dry.

Light Brown Wool: alum mordant
Colorfastness: fair

1 pound wool
1¾ pounds ground coffee
⅙ ounce ferrous sulfate (copperas)

Use alum mordant (see pages 67 to 68). Follow directions for dyeing "Dark Yellow Tan Wool" (above). Without rinsing, put the wool into a boiling bath of ferrous sulfate in 4 gallons of water. Stir the bath as it boils for 10 minutes. Rinse and dry the wool.

COREOPSIS FLOWERS (*Coreopsis* sp.)

The coreopsis is commonly called the "yellow dye flower." It does not produce a dye suitable for cotton.

Dark Burnt Orange or Terra Cotta Wool: chrome mordant
Colorfastness: good

1 pound wool
1 to 1½ pecks fresh coreopsis flower heads

83

Use chrome mordant (see pages 67 to 68). Cover the flowers with water and boil for 10 to 15 minutes. Strain out the flowers, then add cold water to make a dyebath of 4 to 4½ gallons. Before immersing mordanted wool in the dyebath, thoroughly rinse it and squeeze out excess moisture. Immerse the wool; heat to boiling; boil for 20 minutes or until the desired color is obtained, rinse and dry.

COTTON FLOWERS (*Gossypium* sp.)

The flowers of the cotton plant, one of our main sources of textile fibers, also furnish a dye.

Brass Wool: chrome mordant
Colorfastness: fair to light, good to washing
1   pound wool
1⅓ quarts dry cotton flowers

Use chrome mordant (see pages 67 to 68). Cover the crushed dried cotton flowers with water and boil them for 20 minutes. Strain out the flowers, then add cold water to make a dyebath of 4 to 4½ gallons. Before immersing mordanted material in the dyebath, thoroughly rinse it and squeeze out excess moisture. Immerse the wool; heat to the boiling point; boil for 30 minutes, rinse and dry.

Yellow-Tan Wool: alum mordant
Colorfastness: good
or
Yellow-Tan Cotton: alum-tannin-alum mordant
Colorfastness: good
1   pound cotton or wool
1⅓ quarts dry crushed cotton flowers
⅙ ounce potassium dichromate
⅙ ounce acetic acid, or 6 to 7 tablespoons vinegar

Use the following directions for dyeing both cotton and wool. Use alum mordant on wool, and alum-tannin-alum on cotton (see pages 67 to 69). Cover the crushed dry cotton flowers with water and allow them to soak for 20 minutes. Strain out the flowers, then add cold water until the dyebath contains 4 to 4½ gallons. Before immersing mordanted material in the dyebath, thoroughly rinse it and squeeze out excess moisture. Immerse the wool; heat to the boiling point; boil for 30 minutes.

Without rinsing, transfer the material into a boiling bath of potassium dichromate and acetic acid in 4 to 4½ gallons of water. Continue to boil for 10 minutes, rinse and dry.

Yellow Cotton: alum-tannin-alum mordant
Colorfastness: fair
1   pound cotton
1⅓ quarts dry cotton flowers

Use alum-tannin-alum mordant (see pages 67 to 69). Follow directions for dyeing "Brass Wool" (above).

CUTCH (*Acacia* sp.)

Cutch or catechu, one of the most important brown vegetable dyes, is the dried extract obtained from the wood of various species of acacia grown in India, Java, and the East Indies. Cutch can be obtained from houses supplying dyes and botanical drugs.

Rich Brown Wool: no mordant before dyeing
Colorfastness: good
or
Rich Brown Cotton: no mordant before dyeing
Colorfastness: fair to light, good to washing

1 pound dry wool or cotton
. 4 ounces cutch
½ ounce copper sulfate
½ ounce potassium dichromate

Use the following directions for both cotton and wool. Place the dry material in water and heat it to the boiling point. In a separate container, dissolve the cutch and copper sulfate by boiling them in water. While the textile material is still hot, transfer it to the cutch solution, stir well and allow it to soak overnight. The following morning squeeze excess moisture out of the material. Place it in a hot bath of potassium dichromate dissolved in 4 to 4½ gallons of water, and stir. Allow the material to steep for 45 minutes just below the boiling point. Rinse and dry.

DAHLIA FLOWERS (*Dahlia* sp.)

The dahlias common in flower gardens furnish a good source of orange dye for wool. Yellow flowers give clearer and brighter colors than pink ones although there is no difference in colorfastness. Dahlia flowers will not dye cotton.

Orange Wool: chrome mordant
Colorfastness: fair to light, good to washing

1 pound wool
1 to 1½ pecks fresh dahlia flowers

Use chrome mordant (see pages 67 to 68). Cover cut-up dahlia flowers with water and boil for 10 to 15 minutes. Strain out the flowers and add cold water to make a dyebath of 4 to 4½ gallons. Before immersing mordanted material in the dyebath, thoroughly rinse it and squeeze out excess moisture. Immerse the wool; heat to boiling; boil for 20 minutes, rinse and dry.

Yellow Wool: alum mordant
Colorfastness: poor to light, good to washing

Follow the directions for dyeing "Orange Wool" (above), but substitute alum for chrome mordant (see pages 67 to 68).

FUSTIC (*Chlorophora tinctoria*)

Fustic is probably one of the best yellow dyes found in nature. It is obtained from the wood of a tree that grows in Mexico, Cuba, and Nicaragua and can be purchased either as wood chips or as an extract.

Gold Wool: chrome mordant
Colorfastness: good

1 pound wool
½ ounce fustic extract

Use chrome mordant (see pages 67 to 68). Dissolve the fustic in 4 to 4½ gallons of water. Before immersing mordanted wool in the dyebath, thoroughly rinse it and squeeze out excess moisture. Immerse the wool; heat it to boiling; boil for 30 minutes, rinse and dry. Prolonged boiling will darken and dull the color.

Dark Yellow-Tan Wool: alum mordant
Colorfastness: good

1 pound wool
½ ounce fustic extract
⅙ ounce potassium dichromate
⅙ ounce acetic acid, or 6 to 7 tablespoons of vinegar

Use alum mordant (see pages 67 to 68). Follow directions for dyeing "Gold Wool" (above). Without rinsing, transfer the material into a boiling bath of potassium dichromate and acetic acid in 4 to 4½ gallons of water. Boil 10 minutes, rinse and dry.

Light Yellow-Tan Cotton: alum-tannin-alum mordant
Colorfastness: good

1 pound cotton
½ ounce fustic extract
⅙ ounce potassium dichromate
⅙ ounce acetic acid, or 6 to 7 tablespoons of vinegar

Use alum-tannin-alum mordant (see pages 67 to 69). Follow directions for dyeing "Gold Wool" (above). Without rinsing, transfer the material into a boiling bath of potassium dichromate and acetic acid in 4 to 4½ gallons of water. Boil 10 minutes, rinse and dry.

GOLDENROD FLOWERS (*Solidago* sp.)

Goldenrod that grows wild in fields and along roadsides is one native American plant recognized early as a source of yellow dye. With indigo, goldenrod can be top-dyed (see pages 107 to 109) to make dark green shades; top-dyeing goldenrod with madder results in terra cotta and rose-brown tones. Goldenrod does not produce lightfast colors on cotton.

Flowers should be picked as they are coming into bloom. They can be used fresh or dried.

Brass Wool: chrome mordant
Colorfastness: good

1 pound wool
1 to 1½ pecks goldenrod flowers

Use chrome mordant (see pages 67 to 68). Cover the flowers with water and boil for 15 minutes. Strain out the flowers, then add cold water to make a dyebath of 4 to 4½ gallons. Before immersing mordanted material in the dyebath, thoroughly wet it and squeeze out excess moisture. Immerse the wool; heat to boiling; boil for 20 minutes, rinse and dry.

Yellow-Brown Wool: alum mordant
Colorfastness: good

1 pound wool
1 to 1½ pecks goldenrod flowers
⅛ ounce potassium dichromate
⅛ ounce acetic acid, or 6 to 7 tablespoons vinegar

Use alum mordant (see pages 67 to 68). Follow directions for dyeing "Brass Wool" (above). Without rinsing, transfer the material into a boiling bath of potassium dichromate and acetic acid in 4 to 4½ gallons of water. Stir and allow to boil for 10 minutes, rinse and dry.

Omitting the potassium dichromate and acetic acid bath will result in a greenish-yellow color with poor lightfastness.

HICKORY NUT HULLS (*Carya laciniosa* or *Hicoria laciniosa*)

This hickory tree, commonly called big shellbark, grows throughout the eastern half of the United States from New York to Iowa and south to Tennessee and Oklahoma. The very large, thick hulls contain the dye material.

Light Brown Wool: alum mordant
Colorfastness: good

1 pound wool
1 peck green hickory nut hulls
⅛ ounce potassium dichromate
⅛ ounce acetic acid, or 6 to 7 tablespoons vinegar

Use alum mordant (see pages 67 to 68). Cut up the green hulls, cover them with water and soak overnight. The following morning, heat the dye material gradually to the boiling point; boil 45 minutes. Strain the liquid, then add water until the dyebath contains 4 to 4½ gallons. Before immersing mordanted wool in the dyebath, thoroughly rinse it and squeeze out excess moisture. Immerse the wool; heat to boiling; boil for 30 minutes. Without rinsing, transfer the material to a boiling bath of potassium dichromate and acetic acid, stir and continue to boil for 10 minutes, rinse and dry.

Hollygrape Root (*Mahonia* sp.)

The coloring matter contained in hollygrape root is berberine, the same as that present in the bark and root of barberry. It is one of the few natural basic dyestuffs. Hollygrape or Oregon grape grows in the Northwestern States. Its colors are not fast on cotton.

Buff Wool: alum mordant
Colorfastness: fair

1 pound wool
1 peck chopped hollygrape root

Use alum mordant (see pages 67 to 68). Cover the chopped root with water and allow it to soak overnight. The following morning, boil it in the soaking liquid for 2 hours. Strain out the particles of dye material and add water to make a dyebath of 4 to 4½ gallons. Before immersing mordanted wool in the dyebath, thoroughly rinse it and squeeze out excess moisture. Immerse the wool; heat to boiling; boil for 30 minutes, rinse and dry.

Light Tan Wool: alum mordant
Colorfastness: fair

1 pound wool
1 peck chopped hollygrape root
⅛ ounce potassium dichromate
⅛ ounce acetic acid, or 6 to 7 tablespoons vinegar

Use alum mordant (see pages 67 to 68) and follow directions for dyeing "Buff Wool" (above). Without rinsing, transfer the material into a boiling bath of potassium dichromate and acetic acid. Stir and boil 10 minutes longer, rinse and dry.

Indigo (*Indigofera* sp.)

Indigo was America's most important dyestuff during the 18th and 19th centuries. Although dyeing with indigo requires both time and patience, the blue shades it produces are very fast to light and washing on both wool and cotton. Indigo does not require a mordant. It belongs to the class of dyestuffs known as vat dyes—so-called because they are applied in a special dyebath called a vat.

The following is a simplified explanation of what takes place in the indigo dye vat:

88

All natural dyestuffs must be dissolved in a liquid before textile materials can absorb them. Since water will not dissolve indigo, it must be dissolved in another liquid. When indigo is combined with a reducing agent, a compound is formed that will dissolve in an alkaline liquid. This process turns the indigo dye liquid yellow. When wool and cotton are dipped into this dyebath (known as the indigo vat) they readily absorb the dye in this yellow, reduced form.

The dye is fixed on the fibers permanently by oxidation when the dyed material is exposed to air. During this final step the blue color returns and the dye reverts to its original insoluble form on the fibers. Repeated dipping and airing of the material results in a gradual build-up of blue color on the yarn or fabric; thus the skillful dyer can obtain almost any depth of the blue desired.

Both methods of indigo dyeing given below can be used by the home dyer.

Method 1: Indigo Fermentation Vat or Blue-Pot

The fermentation vat or blue-pot is the oldest method of dyeing with indigo. Bacteria that develop in the vat act as the reducing agent. Although dyeing by this method is somewhat complicated, repeated dippings result in a good, fast, dark blue on both wool and cotton if the vat is properly prepared.

When top-dyeing (see pages 107 to 109) wool with yellow dyes, mordant (see pages 67 to 69) the material with alum either before or after dyeing. Although treatment before blue-dyeing is not essential, the following methods are sometimes used:

For 1 pound of wool: alum mordanting (see pages 67 to 68) or soaking for 30 minutes in a solution of ½ ounce of washing soda in 4 gallons of luke-warm water. Rinse thoroughly before dyeing.

For 1 pound of cotton: alum mordanting (see pages 67 to 68) or boiling the material for 30 minutes in a solution of ½ ounce of sodium hydroxide in 4 gallons of water. Rinse cotton thoroughly before dyeing.

For each pound of wool or cotton, allow:
  8   ounces finely powdered indigo
  4   ounces wheat bran
  4   ounces madder
  1½ pounds sodium carbonate (washing soda)
  4   gallons water

Mix ingredients in a large vessel and keep it at about 85° F. for 5 to 10 days. This blue-pot should be stirred well each morning. When the mixture

89

develops a disagreeable odor, a bluish-coppery scum on top and green streaks throughout, it is ready to be used.

Wet the wool or cotton thoroughly before dipping it in the dye vat. Throughout the dyeing process the vat should be kept lukewarm (95° F.) and the material turned and stirred occasionally to assure even absorption of dye. The material must also be lifted out and exposed to the air at intervals during the dye process. Though greenish yellow in the dye liquid, the material will turn blue when exposed to the air.

Continue dipping and airing for 30 minutes, then lift the material from the dyebath, squeeze out excess liquid and allow it to air for half an hour. Since depth of color depends on the number of times the material is lifted out and aired, repeat these steps as many times as necessary, increasing each immersion time, until the desired depth of color is achieved. After the last airing the material should be rinsed in lukewarm water and dried.

NOTE: If the sediment in the bottom of the vat is disturbed the material will be streaked and unevenly dyed. If the dyebath is stirred too much it will turn blue, and thus lose its effectiveness. If this should happen, renew the vat by adding more indigo, bran, madder, and sodium carbonate. Allow it to stand undisturbed for one or two days and it will again be ready for use. In this manner the blue-pot can be replenished and reused many times.

Method 2: Indigo Hydrosulfite Vat

The hydrosulfite vat is the most easily regulated of the indigo vats and is used extensively among indigo dyers. Both wool and cotton can be dyed in the hydrosulfite vat without mordants. When top-dyeing, however, the material should be mordanted with alum either before or after dyeing with indigo, depending on the nature of the other dyestuff.

The following quantities are sufficient for dyeing 1 pound of wool or cotton. First make up the following two stock solutions:

(A) *Indigo Hydrosulfite Solution*

4¼ ounces powdered indigo
3 ounces sodium hydroxide
2¾ ounces sodium hydrosulfite

Mix the powdered indigo with sodium hydroxide which has been dissolved in water, add enough water to make 1 gallon of solution; then heat it to 120° F. Stir well while slowly adding the sodium hydrosulfite. Allow the solution to stand for 30 minutes. The liquid should be clear and yellow. A drop running along a glass plate should turn blue in about 25 seconds. Measure out 2 to 2½ quarts of solution for the dye vat. Store extra solution in a stoppered bottle.

Slowly add: ½ ounce sodium hydrosulfite to 1 quart of water

Measure out ½ to ⅔ cup for the dye solution. Keep the extra solution in a stoppered bottle.

The dye vat is made up as follows:

Heat 4 gallons of water to 120° F. Add ½ to ⅔ cup of sodium hydrosulfite solution (B), stir well and set aside for 10 minutes. Add 2 to 2½ quarts of indigo hydrosulfite solution (A). Stir gently and set aside for 20 minutes. When the dye liquor is a clear, yellow liquid it is ready for the textile material.

First wet the cloth thoroughly and dip it in the dye vat. Stir it occasionally during the 30 minutes it is in the vat, making certain that the material is always well covered with dye. Without rinsing or squeezing out excess moisture, hang it outside the dye vat. After exposing the material to the air for 30 minutes, dip it in the vat for another 30 minutes. Repeat dipping and airing until the desired color is obtained. After the last airing the material should be rinsed thoroughly in clear water, washed in soapsuds, and rinsed again.

If the liquid in the vat turns blue, add more sodium hydrosulfite solution (B), stir the liquid in the vat carefully and allow it to stand for 15 minutes before proceeding with the dye process. If repeated dippings and airings fail to produce a noticeably darker blue in the material, the dye vat needs more indigo hydrosulfite solution (A). After renewing the dye vat, proceed as before.

IRON BUFF

Buff Cotton: no mordant before dyeing
Colorfastness: fair

1 pound unmordanted cotton
6 ounces ferrous sulfate (copperas)
6 ounces powdered soap

Dissolve the ferrous sulfate in 4 to 4½ gallons of water. Before immersing the cotton, thoroughly wet it and squeeze out excess moisture. Stir for a few minutes, remove from dyebath and drain. Dip the material into soapsuds, stir and wring out. Repeat these steps three times, rinse and dry.

JUNIPER BERRIES (*Juniperus* sp.)

Juniper, also called red cedar, grows in many sections of the United States. The bark, berries, and twigs are suitable for dyeing purposes. Juniper berries will not dye cotton.

91

Khaki Wool: no mordant before dyeing
Colorfastness: good

1 pound wool
2 quarts ripe juniper berries
2 ounces potash alum
¾ ounce ammonium chloride
1 ounce cream of tartar
1 ounce copper sulfate
1 ounce copper acetate

Dissolve the alum, ammonium chloride, cream of tartar, and copper sulfate in 4 to 4½ gallons of water. Before immersing the wool in the dyebath, thoroughly wet it and squeeze out excess moisture. Heat it to boiling; boil for 1 hour. Allow the material to stand in this mordant liquor until it is cool, then rinse the wool, roll it in a towel and set it aside.

Break up the berries, tie them in a cheesecloth bag, and place the bag in enough water to cover it. Allow the berries to soak overnight. The following morning boil the berries for 1 hour. After removing the cheesecloth bag from the dye extract, add cold water to make a dyebath of 4 to 4½ gallons. Thoroughly wet the previously mordanted wool in water, squeeze out excess moisture and immerse the material in the dyebath. Heat the dyebath to boiling, continue to boil for 1 to 2 hours, then remove the wool. Next dissolve copper acetate in the dye liquor, return the wool material to it and boil it for 15 to 30 minutes longer, rinse and dry.

LICHENS

For many years rural dyers of Sweden, Scotland, and Ireland have used lichens for coloring woolens various shades of brown, yellow, red, and purple. Though lichens were never used as frequently as other dye materials in the United States, many produce interesting colors without mordants. The two recipes which follow merely suggest the possibilities that might be explored with lichen dyeing. A more complete study of this subject is Eileen M. Bolton's book "Lichens for Vegetable Dyeing" which gives details on identification of lichens and directions for using them.

LICHEN 1 (*Peltigera* sp.)

Lichens of the genus *Peltigera* are flat and leaflike. The lobes are large, sometimes overlapping, and are dark greenish brown when wet, but turn ashen when dried (Bolton, 1960). They grow on soil and mosses in damp woods and are abundant in all parts of North America, especially in the mountains of the South.

92

Yellow-Tan Wool: alum mordant
Colorfastness: fair to light, good to washing

1 pound wool
1 peck crushed dry lichens

Use alum mordant (see pages 67 to 68). Cover the lichens with water and soak them overnight. The following morning heat the water to boiling, and boil for 1 hour. Strain out the lichens and add cold water to make a dyebath of 4 to 4½ gallons. Before immersing the wool, thoroughly rinse it and squeeze out excess moisture. Immerse the wool; heat to boiling; boil for 30 minutes, rinse and dry.

Dark Rose-Tan Wool: alum mordant
Colorfastness: fair to light, good to washing

1 pound wool
1 peck crushed dry lichens
⅛ ounce potassium dichromate
⅛ ounce acetic acid, or 6 to 7 tablespoons vinegar

Use alum mordant (see pages 67 to 68), then follow directions for dyeing "Yellow-Tan Wool" (above). Without rinsing, transfer the material to a boiling bath of potassium dichromate and acetic acid or vinegar. Stir and boil for 10 minutes, rinse and dry.

LICHEN 2 (*Usnea* sp.)

These lichens, sometimes called "beard moss," are branched and hairy, forming a shaggy yellowish coating on the barks of old trees. They are distributed throughout the world.

Buff Wool: alum mordant
Colorfastness: good

1 pound wool
1½ to 2 pecks crushed dry lichens

Use alum mordant (see pages 67 to 68). Cover the dry lichens with water and soak overnight. The following morning boil this infusion for 1 hour and strain out all vegetable matter. Add cold water to make a dyebath of 4 to 4½ gallons. Thoroughly rinse, squeeze out excess moisture and immerse the wool in the bath. Heat to boiling; boil for 30 minutes, rinse and dry.

Yellow-Tan Wool: chrome mordant
Colorfastness: good

1 pound wool
1½ to 2 pecks crushed dry lichens

Use chrome mordant (see pages 67 to 68) and follow directions for dyeing "Buff Wool" (above).

Dark Rose-Tan Wool: alum mordant
Colorfastness: good

1 pound wool
1½ to 2 pecks crushed dry lichens
⅙ ounce potassium dichromate
⅙ ounce acetic acid, or 6 to 7 tablespoons vinegar

Use alum mordant (see pages 67 to 68) and follow directions for dyeing "Buff Wool" (above). Without rinsing, transfer the wool to a boiling bath of potassium dichromate and acetic acid or vinegar in 4 gallons of water and boil for 10 minutes, rinse and dry.

LILY-OF-THE-VALLEY LEAVES (*Convallaria majalis*)

Greenish-Yellow Wool: chrome mordant
Colorfastness: fair to light, good to washing

1 pound wool
1½ pecks shredded fresh, young lily-of-the-valley leaves

Use chrome mordant (see pages 67 to 68). Soak the leaves in water overnight. The next morning heat to boiling, boil for 1 hour, strain and add cold water to make a dyebath of 4 to 4½ gallons. Before immersing mordanted wool in the dyebath, thoroughly rinse it and squeeze out excess moisture. Immerse the wool; heat to boiling; boil for 45 minutes, rinse and dry.

Gold Wool: chrome mordant
Colorfastness: fair to light, good to washing

Follow the directions for dyeing "Greenish-Yellow Wool" (above), but use lily-of-the-valley leaves picked in the late summer or fall.

LOGWOOD (*Haematoxylon campechianum*)

Logwood, formerly one of the most extensively used natural dyestuffs, is obtained from a tree that grows in Cuba, Jamaica, and Central America. It can be purchased from dye supply houses either as wood chips or as an extract, in liquid or solid form. With various mordants it gives a wide range of colors, but their fastness to light is generally rather poor.

Black Wool: special sumach mordant
Colorfastness: good

1 pound wool
9 ounces logwood chips
½ ounce fustic extract
1½ pecks chopped sumach leaves and twigs
1 ounce sodium carbonate (washing soda)
¼ ounce ferrous sulfate (copperas)
½ ounce potassium dichromate

94

Soak the fresh sumach leaves and twigs in water overnight. The following morning boil them for 30 minutes, strain the liquid and add water to make a mordant bath of 4 to 4½ gallons. Wet the material thoroughly, squeeze out excess moisture and soak it overnight in the mordant bath.

The next morning squeeze moisture out of material and, without rinsing, work it for 10 minutes in a sodium carbonate solution kept at 120° to 140° F. Remove the wool and set this solution aside. Squeeze excess moisture from the wool and work it in a cool ferrous sulfate solution for 30 minutes. Again remove the wool, squeeze out excess moisture, and return the material to the sodium carbonate solution for 15 minutes. Rinse thoroughly. Tie the logwood chips in a cheesecloth bag, cover with water and heat to boiling; continue to boil for 20 minutes.

Finally, add fustic extract to the dye vessel containing the logwood solution and boiled-out chips. Add enough water to make a dyebath of 4 to 4½ gallons. Immerse the previously treated material and heat to boiling; continue to boil for 30 minutes longer, and pass the material through a warm potassium dichromate solution. Rinse well, work in warm soap suds, rinse again, and dry.

MADDER (*Rubia tinctorum*)

The ground root of the madder plant yields a dye whose attributes have been known for centuries. It can be grown in this country; however, since it takes considerable effort and time to raise it in sufficient quantity for use, a dye house or botanical house would be a better source.

Lacquer-Red Wool: alum mordant
Colorfastness: good

1 pound wool
8 ounces madder

Use alum mordant (see pages 67 to 68). Soak the madder in a small quantity of water overnight. The following morning heat it to boiling and pour the hot liquid into 4 gallons of cool water. Before immersing mordanted wool in the dyebath, thoroughly rinse it and squeeze out excess moisture. Immerse the wool; heat the bath to boiling and continue to boil it for 45 minutes, rinse and dry.

Dark Lacquer-Red Wool: alum mordant
Colorfastness: good

1 pound wool
1 pound madder

Use alum mordant (see pages 67 to 68). Soak the madder in a small quantity of water overnight. The following morning add enough water to make a 4 to 4½ gallon dyebath. Before immersing mordanted wool in the dyebath, thoroughly rinse it and squeeze out excess moisture. Heat the bath gradually until it reaches a temperature of 140° to 160° F. Maintain this temperature while stirring constantly for 2 hours. Allow the bath to cool, then remove the wool, rinse and dry.

Bright Orange Wool: no mordant before dyeing
Colorfastness: fair to light, good to washing

1   pound wool
½   ounce cream of tartar
1   ounce stannous chloride
½   ounce quercitron extract
1½ ounces madder

Dissolve cream of tartar and three-fourths of the stannous chloride in 4 to 4½ gallons of water. Thoroughly wet the wool, squeeze out excess moisture, and immerse it in the stannous chloride solution. Heat to boiling; boil for 45 minutes. Remove the wool. Add the quercitron, madder, and the remainder of stannous chloride to the dyebath, stirring well until dissolved. Return the wool to this dyebath, stir and continue to boil for 30 minutes longer. Rinse and dry.

Garnet-Red Wool: chrome mordant
Colorfastness: good

1 pound wool
8 ounces madder

Use chrome mordant (see pages 67 to 68) then follow directions for dyeing "Lacquer Red Wool" (above).

Dark Red Cotton: alum-tannin-alum mordant
Colorfastness: good to light, fair to washing

1 pound cotton
8 ounces madder

Use alum-tannin-alum mordant (see pages 67 to 69). First dyebath: prepare a 4 to 4½ gallon dyebath using 2 ounces of madder which has been soaked in water overnight. Before immersing cotton in the dyebath, thoroughly rinse it and squeeze out excess moisture. Immerse the cotton; stir until the bath is lukewarm (95° F.); maintain this water temperature for 1 hour. Allow the dyebath containing the material to cool overnight. At the same time prepare a fresh madder infusion, this time soaking 3 ounces of madder in water overnight.

Second dyebath: the following day repeat the entire procedure for the first dyebath, using the 3 ounces of madder soaked the night before. At the same time prepare a final madder infusion, once again soaking 3 ounces of madder in water overnight.

Third dyebath: the following day repeat the entire procedure for the first dyebath once more, using the 3 ounces of madder soaked the night before. Rinse well, wash the material in soapsuds, rinse again, and dry.

MARIGOLD FLOWERS (*Tagetes* sp.)

The coloring matter in the flower of the garden marigold is similar to that in black- or quercitron-oak bark. Either fresh or dry flowers may be used.

Brass Wool: chrome mordant
Colorfastness: good

1 pound wool
1 to 1½ pecks fresh marigold flower heads or ½ to ¾ peck of dried marigold flower heads

Use chrome mordant (see pages 67 to 68). Cover the flower heads with water and boil them for 10 to 15 minutes. Strain out the vegetable material. Add cold water to make a dyebath of 4 to 4½ gallons. Before immersing mordanted wool in the dyebath, thoroughly rinse it and squeeze out excess moisture. Immerse the wool; heat to boiling, boil for 20 minutes, rinse and dry.

Dark Yellow-Tan Wool: alum mordant
Colorfastness: good

1 pound wool
1 to 1½ pecks fresh marigold flower heads or ½ to ¾ peck of dried marigold flower heads
⅛ ounce potassium dichromate
⅛ ounce acetic acid, or 6 to 7 tablespoons vinegar

Use alum mordant (see pages 67 to 68). Follow directions for dyeing "Brass Wool" (above). Without rinsing, transfer the material into a boiling bath of potassium dichromate and acetic acid or vinegar and boil for 10 minutes, rinse and dry.

Yellow-Tan Cotton: alum-tannin-alum mordant
Colorfastness: fair

Follow directions for dyeing "Dark Yellow-Tan Wool" (above) using cotton mordanted with alum-tannin-alum (see pages 67 to 69) instead of wool.

MOUNTAIN-LAUREL LEAVES (*Kalmia latifolia*)

Yellow-Tan Wool: chrome mordant
Colorfastness: fair to light, good to washing

1 pound wool
1½ pecks shredded fresh mountain-laurel leaves

Use chrome mordant (see pages 67 to 68). Cover the shredded leaves with water and soak them overnight. The following morning boil them for 20 minutes, strain the leaves out of the dye liquor and add water to make a dyebath of 4 to 4½ gallons. Before immersing mordanted wool in the cool dyebath, thoroughly rinse it and squeeze out excess moisture. Immerse the wool; heat to boiling; boil for 30 minutes, rinse and dry.

Onion Skins (*Allium cepa*)

The dry outer skins of onion bulbs can be used for coloring textile materials. Easter eggs also take on a bright golden hue when dipped in onion skins boiled in water.

Burnt-Orange Wool: alum mordant
Colorfastness: fair

1 pound wool
10 ounces dry Yellow Globe onion skins

Use alum mordant (see pages 67 to 68). Cover the onion skins with water and boil them for 15 minutes. Strain skins out of the dye liquor and add enough cold water to make a 4 to 4½ gallon dyebath. Before immersing mordanted wool in the dyebath thoroughly rinse it and squeeze out excess moisture. Immerse the wool; heat to boiling; boil for 30 minutes. rinse and dry.

Brass Wool: chrome mordant
Colorfastness: fair to light, good to washing

Use chrome mordant (see pages 67 to 68), then follow directions for dyeing "Burnt-Orange Wool" (above).

Osage Orange or Bois D'Arc (*Maclura pomifera* or *Toxylon pomiferum*)

The Osage-orange trees that grow abundantly in Southwestern U.S. provided the Indians of that area with dyestuffs in the 19th century before their introduction to commercial dyes. This dye material is being used once again by some Navajo weavers for coloring rug materials. The wood can be used in several forms: as wood chips, as a liquid extract, or in solid or powdered form. Directions below are for using powdered extract.

Gold Wool: chrome mordant
Colorfastness: fair to light, good to washing

1 pound wool
½ ounce Osage-orange extract

Use chrome mordant (see pages 67 to 68). Dissolve the Osage-orange extract in 4 to 4½ gallons of water. Before immersing mordanted wool in the dyebath, thoroughly rinse it and squeeze out excess moisture. Immerse the wool; heat the solution to boiling, and boil for 30 minutes, rinse and dry.

Yellow-Tan Wool: alum mordant
Colorfastness: good

1 pound wool
½ ounce Osage-orange extract
⅙ ounce potassium dichromate
⅙ ounce acetic acid, or 6 to 7 tablespoons vinegar

Use alum mordant (see pages 67 to 68). Follow directions for dyeing "Gold Wool" (above). Without rinsing, transfer the material into a boiling bath of potassium dichromate, acetic acid or vinegar, and 4 gallons of water. Stir and boil for 10 minutes, rinse and dry.

Light Yellow-Tan Cotton: alum-tannin-alum mordant
Colorfastness: good

1 pound cotton
½ ounce Osage-orange extract
⅙ ounce potassium dichromate
⅙ ounce acetic acid, or 6 to 7 tablespoons vinegar

Use alum-tannin-alum mordant (see pages 67 to 69). Follow directions for dyeing "Gold Wool" (above). Without rinsing, transfer the material into a boiling bath of potassium dichromate, acetic acid or vinegar, and 4 gallons of water. Stir while boiling for 10 minutes, rinse and dry.

PECAN HULLS (*Carya illinoensis* or *Hicoria pecan*)

Pecan trees grow in Iowa, Indiana, and the Southern States.

Brown Wool: alum mordant
Colorfastness: fair

1 pound wool
¾ peck green pecan hulls

Use alum mordant (see pages 67 to 68). Cut the hulls from nuts and boil them in water for 15 minutes. Strain and add cold water to make a dyebath of 4 to 4½ gallons. Before immersing mordanted wool in the dyebath, thoroughly rinse it and squeeze out excess moisture. Immerse the wool; gradually heat the dyebath to boiling; boil for 30 minutes, rinse and dry.

Dark Gray Cotton: alum mordant
Colorfastness: fair

1 pound cotton
¾ peck green pecan hulls
⅙ ounce ferrous sulfate (copperas)

Use alum mordant (see pages 67 to 69). Follow directions for dyeing "Brown Wool" (above). Without rinsing, transfer the cotton into a boiling bath of ferrous sulfate in 4 gallons of water. Stir, continuing to boil for 10 minutes, rinse and dry.

PERSIAN BERRIES (*Rhamnus infectoria*)

Persian berries, also known as yellow berries or French berries, are grown in France, Spain, Italy, and Persia. Either the dried berries or an extract can be bought from dye- and botanical-drug supply houses.

Gold Wool: chrome mordant
Colorfastness: good

1 pound wool
½ ounce Persian berry extract

Use chrome mordant (see pages 67 to 68). Dissolve the Persian berry extract in 4 to 4½ gallons of water. Before immersing mordanted wool in the dyebath, thoroughly rinse it and squeeze out excess moisture. Immerse the wool; heat to boiling; boil for 30 minutes, rinse and dry.

Dark Yellow-Tan Wool: alum mordant
Colorfastness: good

1 pound wool
½ ounce Persian berry extract
⅙ ounce potassium dichromate
⅙ ounce acetic acid, or 6 to 7 tablespoons vinegar

Use alum mordant (see pages 67 to 68). Follow directions for dyeing "Gold Wool" (above). Without rinsing, transfer the dyed material into a boiling bath of potassium dichromate, acetic acid or vinegar and 4 gallons of water. Stir and boil for 10 minutes, rinse and dry.

Light Yellow-Tan Cotton: alum-tannin-alum mordant
Colorfastness: good

1 pound cotton
½ ounce Persian berry extract
⅙ ounce potassium dichromate
⅙ ounce acetic acid, or 6 to 7 tablespoons vinegar

Use alum-tannin-alum mordant (see pages 67 to 69). Follow directions for dyeing "Gold Wool" (above). Without rinsing, transfer the dyed material into a boiling bath of potassium dichromate, acetic acid or vinegar, and 4 gallons of water. Stir and boil for 10 minutes, rinse and dry.

Poplar Leaves, Lombardy (*Populus nigra* var. *italica*)

The Lombardy poplar tree is widely cultivated in this country as an ornamental. Its leaves can be used for dyeing wool.

Brass Wool: chrome mordant
Colorfastness: good

1 pound wool
1½ pecks shredded fresh Lombardy poplar leaves

Use chrome mordant (see pages 67 to 68). Cut up the fresh leaves, cover with water, and soak them overnight. The following morning heat them gradually to boiling, boil for 15 or 20 minutes, strain out the leaves and add cold water to make a dyebath of 4 to 4½ gallons. Before immersing mordanted wool in the dyebath, thoroughly rinse it and squeeze out excess moisture. Immerse the wool; heat to boiling; boil for 20 minutes, rinse and dry.

Yellow-Brown Wool: alum mordant
Colorfastness: fair to light, good to washing

1   pound wool
1½ pecks shredded fresh Lombardy poplar leaves
⅙ ounce potassium dichromate
⅙ ounce acetic acid, or 6 to 7 tablespoons vinegar

Use alum mordant (see pages 67 to 68). Follow directions for dyeing "Brass Wool" (above). Without rinsing, transfer the dyed material into a boiling bath of potassium dichromate, acetic acid or vinegar, and 4 to 4½ gallons of water. Stir and boil for 10 minutes, rinse and dry.

PRIVET LEAVES (*Ligustrum* sp.)

Gold Wool: chrome mordant
Colorfastness: good

1   pound wool
1½ pecks shredded fresh privet leaves

Use chrome mordant (see pages 67 to 68). Cover the shredded leaves with water and soak overnight. The following morning heat gradually to boiling, boil for 20 to 25 minutes, strain out the leaves, and add cold water to make a 4 to 4½ gallon dyebath. Before immersing mordanted wool in the cooled dyebath, thoroughly rinse it and squeeze out excess moisture. Immerse the wool; heat to boiling; boil for 20 to 30 minutes, rinse and dry.

SASSAFRAS ROOT BARK (*Sassafras albidum* or *S. variifolium*)

Sassafras is a shrub and tree common in the eastern half of the United States. The bark of the sassafras root yields the dyestuff.

Rose-Brown Wool: chrome mordant
Colorfastness: fair to light, good to washing

1   pound wool
12 ounces dry sassafras root bark

Use chrome mordant (see pages 67 to 68). Cover the bark with water and soak it overnight. The following morning boil it for 30 minutes, strain out the bark and add water to make a dyebath of 4 to 4½ gallons. Before immersing mordanted wool in the dyebath, thoroughly rinse it and squeeze out excess moisture. Immerse the wool; heat it to boiling; boil for 30 minutes, rinse and dry.

Brown Wool: alum mordant
Colorfastness: good

1   pound wool
12 ounces.dry sassafras root bark
⅙ ounce potassium dichromate
⅙ ounce acetic acid, or 6 to 7 tablespoons vinegar

101

Use alum mordant (see pages 67 to 68). Cover the bark with water and allow it to soak overnight. The following morning boil it for 30 minutes, strain out the bark and add enough water to make a 4 to 4½ gallon dyebath. Before immersing mordanted wool in the dyebath, thoroughly rinse it and squeeze out excess moisture. Immerse the wool; heat it to boiling; boil 30 minutes. Without rinsing, transfer it to a boiling bath of potassium dichromate, acetic acid and 4 gallons of water.

Rose-Tan Wool: alum mordant
Colorfastness: fair to light, good to washing

1   pound wool
12 ounces dry sassafras root bark
½ ounce ferrous sulfate (copperas)

Mordant the wool with alum. Follow directions for dyeing "Brown Wool" (above), using ferrous sulfate instead of potassium dichromate and acetic acid or vinegar.

Rose-Tan Cotton: alum-tannin-alum mordant
Colorfastness: fair to light, good to washing

1   pound cotton
12 ounces dry sassafras root bark
⅛ ounce potassium dichromate
⅛ ounce acetic acid, or 6 to 7 tablespoons vinegar

Use alum-tannin-alum mordant (see pages 67 to 69). Follow directions for dyeing "Brown Wool" (above).

Dark Gray Cotton: alum-tannin-alum mordant
Colorfastness: fair to light, good to washing

1   pound cotton
12 ounces dry sassafras root bark
⅛ ounce ferrous sulfate (copperas)

Use alum-tannin-alum mordant (see pages 67 to 69). Follow directions for dyeing "Brown Wool" (above), using ferrous sulfate instead of potassium dichromate and acetic acid or vinegar.

SUMACH BERRIES (*Rhus glabra*)

White or smooth sumach is a common shrub growing in dry soil of Eastern United States. The berries, leaves, and roots of this sumach have been used for dyeing textile materials for many years.

Dark Yellow-Tan Wool: alum mordant
Colorfastness: good

1   pound wool
½ peck ripe sumach berries

Use alum mordant (see pages 67 to 68). Cover the berries with water and soak them for an hour. Boil them 30 minutes, strain out the berries

102

and add cold water to make a dyebath of 4 to 4½ gallons. Before immersing mordanted wool in the dyebath, thoroughly rinse it and squeeze out excess moisture. Immerse the wool; heat it to boiling; boil for 30 minutes, rinse and dry.

Gray Wool: no mordant before dyeing
Colorfastness: good to light, fair to washing

1 pound wool
½ peck ripe sumach berries
⅙ ounce ferrous sulfate (copperas)

Follow directions for dyeing "Dark Yellow-Tan Wool" (above), omitting the mordant. Without rinsing, transfer the material into a boiling bath of ferrous sulfate and 4 gallons of water. Stir and boil for 10 minutes, rinse and dry.

Dark Gray Cotton: no mordant before dyeing
Colorfastness: fair

1 pound cotton
½ peck ripe sumach berries
⅙ ounce ferrous sulfate (copperas)

Follow directions for dyeing "Dark Yellow-Tan Wool" (above), omitting the mordant. Without rinsing, transfer the material into a boiling bath of ferrous sulfate and 4 gallons of water. Stir while boiling for 10 minutes, rinse and dry.

Light Tan Cotton: alum mordant
Colorfastness: fair

1 pound cotton
½ peck ripe sumach berries

Follow directions for dyeing "Dark Yellow-Tan Wool" (above). If a deeper color is desired, add more sumach.

SUNFLOWERS (*Helianthus annuus*)

Flowers of the common sunflower plant produce a yellow dye extract that will become more yellow when treated with an alkaline solution.

Gold Wool: alum mordant
Colorfastness: good

1 pound wool
1½ quarts dry sunflower flowers
⅙ ounce potassium dichromate
⅙ ounce acetic acid, or 6 or 7 tablespoons vinegar

Use alum mordant (see pages 67 to 68). Boil the dry crushed flowers in water for 25 minutes, strain out the flowers and add cold water to make a dyebath of 4 to 4½ gallons. Before immersing mordanted wool in the dyebath, thoroughly rinse it and squeeze out excess moisture. Immerse the wool; heat it to boiling, boil for 30 minutes. Without rinsing, transfer the material into a boiling bath of potassium dichromate and acetic acid or vinegar and boil for 10 minutes, rinse and dry.

TEA LEAVES, BLACK (*Camellia sinensis* or *Thea sinensis*)

Tannin in tea leaves imparts brownish hues to woolens and cotton. The colors are not fast on cotton.

Rose-Tan Wool: alum mordant
Colorfastness: good

1 pound wool
8 ounces black tea

Use alum mordant (see pages 67 to 68). Boil the tea in water for 15 minutes, strain out the leaves, and add cold water to make a dyebath of 4 to 4½ gallons. Before immersing mordanted wool in the dyebath, thoroughly rinse it and squeeze out excess moisture. Immerse the wool; heat to boiling; boil for 30 minutes, rinse and dry.

A darker rose tan can be obtained if the dyed material is transferred from the dyebath directly into a boiling bath containing ⅙ ounce of ferrous sulfate (copperas) and 4 gallons of water. Boil for 10 minutes, rinse and dry.

Light Brown Wool: chrome mordant
Colorfastness: good

1 pound wool
8 ounces black tea

Use chrome mordant (see pages 67 to 68). Follow directions for dyeing "Rose-Tan Wool" (above).

TULIP TREE LEAVES (*Liriodendron tulipifera*)

Leaves of the tulip tree or so-called "yellow poplar" found in the eastern half of the United States produce an attractive gold color on wool; however, this dye is unsatisfactory on cotton.

Gold Wool: chrome mordant
Colorfastness: fair to light, good to washing

1   pound wool
1½ pecks shredded fresh tulip tree leaves

Use chrome mordant (see pages 67 to 68). Cover the shredded leaves with water and soak them overnight. The following morning heat them to boiling; boil for 20 to 25 minutes, strain out leaves and add cold water to make a dyebath of 4 to 4½ gallons. Before immersing mordanted wool in the dyebath, thoroughly rinse it and squeeze out excess moisture. Immerse the wool; heat to boiling; boil 20 to 30 minutes, rinse and dry.

WALNUT HULLS, BLACK (*Juglans nigra*)

Both the hulls and shells of the black walnut are used for dyes. The hulls must be collected green, and can be used fresh or dried for future use. Many dyers believe that the dye prepared from dried hulls is more potent than that from fresh ones. The dye can also be prepared from green hulls covered with water and stored away from the light. The color seems to darken when the hulls are stored in this way.

Dark Brown Wool: no mordant
Colorfastness: good

1 pound wool
¾ peck green hulls from black walnuts

Cover the hulls with water and soak them for 30 minutes. Boil them for 15 minutes, strain out hulls and add cold water to make a dyebath of 4 to 4½ gallons. Before immersing wool in the dyebath, thoroughly wet it and squeeze out excess moisture. Immerse the wool; heat to boiling, boil for 20 minutes, rinse and dry.

Using alum-mordanted (see pages 67 to 68) wool in this recipe will brighten color, but reduce its lightfastness. Overboiling wool in a walnut-hull dyebath will make its texture harsh.

Drab Cotton: alum mordant
Colorfastness: good to light, fair to washing

1 pound cotton
¾ peck green hulls from black walnuts

Use alum mordant (see pages 67 to 68). Follow directions for dyeing "Dark Brown Wool" (above). A darker drab is obtained if the dyed material is placed without rinsing into a boiling bath containing ⅛ to ½ ounce of ferrous sulfate (copperas) and 4 gallons of water. Boil this solution for 5 to 10 minutes, rinse and dry.

WALNUT HULLS, PERSIAN OR ENGLISH (*Juglans regia*)

The green hulls can be used immediately after they are collected. They can also be dried and used later as needed or covered with water and stored in a wooden keg, protected from the light.

Light Brown Wool: no mordant
Colorfastness: fair

1 pound wool
1 peck dry Persian walnut hulls

Cover the hulls with water and allow them to soak for 1 hour. Heat to boiling, boil for 1 hour, strain out the hulls, and add enough cold water to make a 4 to 4½ gallon dyebath. Before immersing wool in the dyebath,

105

thoroughly wet it and squeeze out excess moisture. Immerse the wool; heat to boiling; boil for 30 minutes, rinse and dry. Wool previously mordanted with alum will become darker brown than unmordanted wool.

Dark Brown Wool: alum mordant
Colorfastness: good

1 pound wool
1 peck dry Persian walnut hulls
$\frac{1}{6}$ ounce potassium dichromate
$\frac{1}{6}$ ounce acetic acid, or 6 to 7 tablespoons vinegar

Use alum mordant (see pages 67 to 68), then follow direction for dyeing "Light Brown Wool" (above). Without rinsing the material, transfer it to a boiling bath of potassium dichromate and acetic acid in 4 gallons of water. Stir while it boils for 10 minutes, rinse and dry.

A grayer and darker brown will be obtained if the fabric is boiled in a bath of $\frac{1}{6}$ ounce of ferrous sulfate (copperas) instead of potassium dichromate and acetic acid.

Drab Cotton: no mordant
Colorfastness: fair to light, good to washing

1 pound cotton
1 peck dry Persian walnut hulls

Follow directions for dyeing "Light Brown Wool" (above).

ZINNIA FLOWERS (*Zinnia* sp.)

The zinnia flowers used in these tests were of assorted colors.

Light Yellow Wool: alum mordant
Colorfastness: fair

1 pound wool
$\frac{3}{4}$ peck of fresh zinnia petals and flower heads

Use alum mordant (see pages 67 to 68). Cut up the flowers, add enough water to cover them, heat to boiling and boil for 10 to 15 minutes. Strain out the flowers and add cold water to the dye extract to make a bath of 4 to $4\frac{1}{2}$ gallons. Before immersing mordanted wool in the dyebath, thoroughly rinse it and squeeze out excess moisture. Immerse the wool; heat to boiling; boil for 30 minutes, rinse and dry.

Dark Greenish-Yellow Wool: chrome mordant
Colorfastness: good

1 pound wool
$\frac{3}{4}$ peck of fresh zinnia petals and flower heads

Follow the directions for dyeing "Light Yellow Wool" (above).

106

TOP-DYEING

It is often necessary to top-dye or dip material into two differently colored dyebaths in order to obtain a desired hue. See the section on Color (pages 57 to 63) for suggestions on combining colors.

To top-dye successfully one must start with dyebaths that will produce good clear colors. Thus, if a good green is desired, start with a bright clear yellow (not a muddy yellow or yellow tan), then top it with a clear blue. Yellows obtained from broomsedge, fustic extract, privet leaves, or goldenrod flowers are satisfactory, but prolonged boiling of any of these is likely to dull the color. Good greens are also obtained by dyeing first with indigo and top-dyeing with yellow.

The chart below suggests which dyestuffs yielding yellow, red, brown, and blue can be combined to produce fast green, orange, red purple, and black.

Top-Dyeing with Madder
Method 1

1 pound dyed wool
4 ounces madder

Soak madder in water overnight. The following morning add water to the dye extract to make a dyebath of 4 to 4½ gallons. Before immersing wool in the dyebath, thoroughly wet it in water and squeeze out excess moisture. Immerse the wool; heat the bath to between 140° F. and 160° F. and stir while maintaining this temperature for 30 minutes; rinse and dry.

Method 2

1 pound dyed wool
8 ounces madder

Soak madder in water overnight. The following morning add water to the dye extract to make a dyebath of 4 to 4½ gallons. Thoroughly wet the wool and squeeze out excess moisture. Immerse it in the dyebath and heat it to between 140° and 160° F. Stir while maintaining this temperature for 15 minutes; rinse and dry.

Chart for Top-Dyeing

To dye	Mordant with	Dye first with	Following directions for*	Final dye	Following directions for
black wool	alum	indigo	indigo dyeing method 1 or 2*	Persian walnut hulls or black walnut hulls	light brown wool** dark brown wool**

See footnotes at end of chart

To dye	Mordant with	Dye first with	Following directions for*	Final dye	Following directions for
black or dark gray cotton	alum	indigo	indigo dyeing method 1 or 2*	Persian walnut hulls or black walnut hulls	light brown wool** dark brown wool**
green wool	alum	broomsedge	brass wool*	indigo	indigo dyeing method 1 or 2**
dark yellow-green wool	chrome	broomsedge	brass wool*	indigo	indigo dyeing method 1 or 2**
yellow-green cotton	alum-tannin-alum	broomsedge	gold cotton*	indigo	indigo dyeing method 1 or 2**
yellow-green wool	chrome	fustic	gold wool*	indigo	indigo dyeing method 1 or 2**
blue-green cotton	alum-tannin-alum	fustic	light yellow-tan cotton*	indigo	indigo dyeing method 1 or 2**
dark green wool	chrome	goldenrod	brass wool*	indigo	indigo dyeing method 1 or 2**
dark yellow-green wool	alum	goldenrod	brass wool*	indigo	indigo dyeing method 1 or 2**
dark yellow-green wool	chrome	hickory bark	method 1* under "Barks"	indigo	indigo dyeing method 1 or 2**
yellow-green cotton	alum-tannin-alum	hickory bark	method 2* under "Barks"	indigo	indigo dyeing method 1 or 2**
dark yellow-green wool	chrome	Persian berries	gold wool*	indigo	indigo dyeing method 1 or 2**
blue-green cotton	alum-tannin-alum	Persian berries	light yellow-tan cotton*	indigo	indigo dyeing method 1 or 2**

See footnotes at end of chart

To dye	Mordant with	Dye first with	Following directions for*	Final dye	Following directions for
red-purple wool	no mordant	indigo	indigo dyeing method 1 or 2 medium blue*	cochineal	rose pink wool**
light terra cotta wool	alum	broomsedge	brass wool*	madder	top-dyeing with madder, method 1
burnt-orange wool	chrome	broomsedge	brass wool*	madder	top-dyeing with madder, method 1
lacquer red wool	alum	broomsedge	brass wool*	madder	top-dyeing with madder, method 2
dark henna wool	chrome	broomsedge	brass wool*	madder	top-dyeing with madder, method 2
dull orange wool	chrome	fustic	gold wool*	madder	top-dyeing with madder, method 1
rose-brown wool	chrome	fustic	gold wool*	madder	top-dyeing with madder, method 1 boiling the wool in the dye-bath (212°F.)
burnt orange wool	alum	fustic	gold wool*	madder	top-dyeing with madder, method 1
terra cotta wool	alum	goldenrod	brass wool*	madder	top-dyeing with madder, method 1
rose-brown wool	chrome	goldenrod	brass wool*	madder	top-dyeing with madder, method 1
terra cotta wool	chrome	quercitron or black oak	gold wool* method 1 under "Barks"	madder	top-dyeing with madder, method 1
dark coral pink wool	alum	quercitron or black oak	gold wool*	madder	top-dyeing with madder, method 1

* Rinse thoroughly after completing the initial dyeing.
** Final treatment: rinse and dry.

BIBLIOGRAPHY

A. General Bibliography

ADROSKO, RITA J. *A summary of natural dyestuffs most commonly used in the United States.* Report to International Committee on Museum Laboratories (unpubl.), 44 pp., September 1967.

BANCROFT, EDWARD, M. D. *Experimental researches concerning the philosophy of permanent colors.* 2 vols. Philadelphia: 1814.

"Baptisia Tinctoria," *Meehan's monthly.* Philadelphia: Thomas Meehan and Sons, vol. 5, 1895, pp. 80–82.

BEMISS, ELIJAH. *The dyer's companion.* New London: 1806 and New York: Evert Duyckinck, 1815.

BENSON, ADOLF B., ed. *Peter Kalm's travels in North America.* 2 vols. New York: Wilson-Erikson Inc., 1937.

The best system of dying. Bennington, Vt.: 1811.

BIRCH, THOMAS. *History of the Royal Society of London.* 4 vols. London: 1756–1757.

BIRREN, FABER. *Creative color.* New York: Reinhold, 1961.

BISHOP, J. LEANDER. *A history of American manufactures from 1608 to 1860.* 3 vols. Philadelphia: Edw. Young and Co., 1866.

BOLTON, EILEEN M. *Lichens for vegetable dyeing.* Newton Centre, Mass.: Charles T. Branford Co., 1960.

BRONSON, J. and R. *The domestic manufacturer's assistant, and family directory, in the arts of weaving and dyeing.* Utica, N.Y.: 1817.

CATESBY, MARK. *The natural history of Carolina, Florida and the Bahama Islands.* 2 vols. 3rd. ed. London: Benjamin White, 1771.

Ciba Review. *Medieval dyeing* (no. 1, 1937); *India, its dyers* . . . (no. 2, 1937); *Purple* (no. 4, 1937); *Scarlet* (no. 7, 1938); *Dyeing and tanning in classical antiquity* (no. 9, 1938); *Trade routes and dye markets in the Middle Ages* (no. 10, 1938); *Weaving and dyeing in ancient Egypt and Babylon* (no. 12, 1938); *Great masters of dyeing in eighteenth century France* (no. 18, 1939); *Madder and Turkey red* (no. 39, 1941); *Indigo* (no. 85, 1951); *Chromium* (no. 101, 1953); *Sir William Henry Perkin* (no. 115, 1956).

COOPER, THOMAS. *A practical treatise on dyeing, and callicoe printing.* Philadelphia: Thomas Dobson, 1815.

[COXE, TENCH]. *Brief examination of Lord Sheffield's observations on the commerce of the United States.* Philadelphia: M. Carey, 1791.

DAMPIER, CAPT. WILLIAM. *A new voyage round the world.* London: Argonaut Press, 1927.

DAVENPORT, ELSIE G. *Your handspinning.* Big Sur, Calif.: Craft and Hobby Book Service, 1964.

EDELSTEIN, SIDNEY M. *Historical notes on the wet processing industry.* [New York]: American Dyestuff Reporter, 1956.

ELLIS, ASA, JR. *The country dyer's assistant.* Brookfield, Mass.: 1798.

Encyclopédie, ou dictionnaire raisonné des sciences, des arts et des métiers. Paris: 1772, vol. 10.

FIERZ-DAVID, H. E. Chrome Mordants and Chrome Complex Dyes, *Ciba Review.* Basle: no. 101, December 1953, pp. 3633–3638.

FORCE, PETER, ed. *Tracts and other papers relating principally to the origin, settlements, and progress of the colonies in North America, from the discovery of the country to the year 1776.* Washington: vol. 2, no. 8, 1838.

GERARD, JOHN. *The herbal.* London: 1597.

GILROY, CLINTON G. *A practical treatise on dyeing and calico-printing.* 2nd ed., rev. New York: Harper and Bros., 1846.

110

GRAVES, MAITLAND E. *The art of color and design.* 2nd ed. New York: McGraw-Hill, 1951.

GRONOVIUS, JAN. F. *Flora Virginica.* 2nd ed. Leiden: 1762.

HAIGH, JAMES. *The dier's assistant in the art of dyeing wool and woolen goods* . . . Philadelphia: 1810, 1st Amer. ed. and Poughkeepsie, N.Y : Paraclete Potter, 1813, 2nd Amer. ed.

HARRIS, MOSES. *The natural system of colours.* 1766. New York: Privately reprinted, 1963.

HASERICK, E. C. *The secrets of the art of dyeing.* Cambridge [Mass.]: 1869.

HAYNES, WILLIAMS. *American chemical industry.* New York: Van Nostrand Co., vol. 1, 1954.

HAZEN, EDWARD. *The panorama of professions and trades.* Philadelphia: Uriah Hunt, 1836, pp. 48–51.

HOLLAND, J. H. Brazilwood, *Kew bulletin of miscellaneous information.* London: no. 9, 1916, pp. 209–225.

HOLLBERG, ESAIAS. *Norra Americanska Fårge-Örter.* Upsala, Sweden: 1763. (North American dye plants. Transl. Esther Louise Larsen. *Agricultural History,* 1954, vol. 28, no. 1, pp. 30–33.)

HOLMYARD, E. J. Dyestuffs in the nineteenth century, *in* Singer, Charles et al., *A history of Technology.* New York and London: Oxford University Press, 1958, vol. 5, pp. 257–283.

HOWARD, ALEXANDER L. *Timbers of the world.* London: Macmillan Co., 1948.

HURRY, JAMIESON B. *The woad plant and its dye.* London: Oxford University Press, 1930.

ITTEN, JOHANNES. *The art of color.* Transl. Ernst von Haagen. New York: Reinhold, 1961.

JACOBSON, EGBERT. *Basic color.* Chicago: Paul Theobald, 1948.

JEFFERSON, THOMAS. *Thomas Jefferson's garden book.* Edit. Edwin Morris Betts. Philadelphia: Amer. Philos. Soc. Mem., vol. 22, 1944.

KALM, PETER. *Travels into North America.* 2 vols. 2nd ed. Transl. John Reinhold Forster. London: 1772.

KNECHT, RAWSON, ET AL. *A manual of dyeing.* 2 vols. 2nd ed. London: Charles Griffin and Co., 1910.

KOK, ANNETTE. A short history of the orchil dyes, *The Lichenologist.* London: British Lichen Society, vol. 3, part 2, 1966, pp. 248–272.

KREVETSKY, NIK. *Batik art and craft.* New York: Reinhold, 1964.

LAND, EDWIN H. Experiments in color vision, *Scientific American,* vol. 200, no. 5, May 1959, pp. 84–99.

LAWRIE, L. G. *A bibliography of dyeing and textile printing.* London: Chapman and Hall, Ltd., 1949.

LEGGETT, M. D., ed. *Subject matter index of patents for inventions issued by the U.S. Patent Office.* Washington: U.S. Patent Office, vol. 1, 1874.

LYNDE, J. *The domestic dyer.* New York [state]: 1831.

MACKENZIE, COLIN. *Mackenzie's five thousand receipts in all the useful and domestic arts.* Philadelphia: 1831.

MAERZ, A., and PAUL, M. REA. *A dictionary of color.* New York: McGraw-Hill, 1930.

McMAHON, BERNARD. *The American gardener's calendar.* Philadelphia: 1806.

MIJER, RIETER. *Batiks and how to make them.* New York: Dodd, Mead and Co., 1920.

MINNAERT, M. *The nature of light and colour in the open air.* New York: Dover, 1954.

MOLONY, CORNELIUS. *The practical dyer.* Boston: 1833.

MUNSELL, ALBERT HENRY. *A color notation.* 9th ed. Baltimore, Md.: Munsell Color Co., Inc., 1941.

111

O'NEILL, CHARLES. *A dictionary of dyeing and calico printing.* Philadelphia: Henry Carey Baird, 1869.

[PARNELL, EDWARD A.] *A practical treatise on dyeing and calico-printing.* New York: Harper and Bros., 1846.

PARTRIDGE, WILLIAM. *A practical treatise on dying woollen, cotton, and silk.* New York: 1834 and 1847.

PELLEW, CHARLES E. Dyes and dyeing. New York: McBride, Nast and Co., 1913, pp. 192–210.

"Pennsylvania Packet," Philadelphia: January 3, 1798., *in* Prime, Alfred Coxe (ed.). *The arts and crafts in Philadelphia, Maryland and South Carolina 1786–1800.* Series 2. [New York]: The Walpole Society, 1932.

PERSOZ, JEAN FRANCOIS. *Traité théorique et pratique de l'impression des tissus.* 4 vols. Paris: Victor Masson, 1846.

POMET, PIERRE. *Histoire générale des drogues.* Paris: 1694.

RAMSAY, DAVID, M.D. *The history of South-Carolina.* 2 vols. Charleston: David Longworth, 1809.

RAUCH, JOHN. *John Rauch's receipts on dyeing.* New York: Joseph I. Badger & Co., 1815.

RAVENEL, HARRIOTT HORRY. *Eliza Pinckney.* New York: Scribner's, 1909.

RECORD, SAMUEL J., AND HESS, ROBERT W. *Timbers of the new world.* New Haven: Yale University Press 1943.

SARGENT, WALTER. *The enjoyment and use of color.* New York: Dover, 1964.

SCHETKY, ETHEL JANE McD., ed. Dye plants and dyeing—a handbook, *Plants and Gardens,* vol. 20, no. 3. Brooklyn, N.Y.: Brooklyn Botanic Garden, 1964.

SHEFFIELD, LORD JOHN. *Observations on the commerce of the American States.* London: J. Debrett, 1784.

SHELDON, WILLIAM. Application of chestnut wood to the arts of tanning and dyeing. [London, Edinburgh and Dublin] *Philosophical Magazine and Journal.* London, vol. 54, July–December, 1819 [1819], pp. 148–150.

SINGER, CHARLES. *The earliest chemical industry.* London: The Folio Society, 1948.

SPRAT, THOMAS. *History of the Royal Society of London.* London: 1667.

SUDWORTH, GEORGE B., AND MELL, CLAYTON D. Fustic wood: its substitutes and adulterants, *Forest Service Circular 184.* Washington: U.S. Department of Agriculture, 1911. 14 pp.

THORPE, SIR EDWARD. *A dictionary of applied chemistry.* 5 vols. New York: Longmans, Green, and Co., 1912.

TOMLINSON, CHARLES, ed. *Cyclopaedia of useful arts.* 2 vols. London: 1854.

TUCKER, WILLIAM. *The family dyer and scourer.* 4th London ed. Philadelphia: E. L. Carey and A. Hart [ca. 1830].

UPHOF, J. C. TH. *Dictionary of economic plants.* New York: Hafner Publishing Co., 1959.

U.S. Tariff Commission. The dyestuff situation in the textile industries, *Tariff Information Series.* Washington: no. 2, 1918.

U.S. Tariff Commission. Census of dyes and coal-tar chemicals, *Tariff Information Series.* Washington: no. 6, 1918.

WAITE, DANIEL & CO. *The new American dier.* Brookfield, Mass.: 1815.

B. Dye Manuals Printed in America Before 1870*

BANCROFT, EDWARD, M.D. *Experimental researches concerning the philosophy of permanent colours; and the best means of producing them, by dyeing, calico printing, etc.* 2 vols. Philadelphia: 1814.

BEMISS, ELIJAH. *The dyer's companion. In two parts. Part first, containing a general plan of dying wool and woollen, cotton and linen cloths, yarn and thread. Also, directions for milling and finishing, stamping and bleaching cloths. Part second, contains many useful receipts on dying, staining, painting, etc.* New London: 1806 and New York: 1815. 307 pp.

The best system of dying woolen, cotton and silk, of all colors, practised and recommended by the first artists of Europe and America. Bennington, Vt.: 1811. 108 pp.

BORDEN, SPENCER, comp. *Notebook containing over 300 formulas for dyeing and printing cotton, wool and silk, profusely illustrated with sample swatches.* Compiled between 1865 and 1875.

BRONSON, J. AND R. *The domestic manufacturer's assistant, and family directory, in the arts of weaving and dyeing: comprehending a plain system of directions, applying to those arts and other branches nearly connected with them in the manufacture of cotton and woollen goods; including many useful tables and drafts, in calculating and forming various kinds and patterns of goods, designed for the improvement of domestic manufactures.* Utica, N.Y.: 1817. 189 pp.

COOPER, THOMAS. *A practical treatise on dyeing, and callicoe printing: exhibiting the processes in the French, German, English, and American practice of fixing colours on woollen, cotton, silk, and linen.* Philadelphia: Thomas Dobson, 1815. 506 pp.

The domestic dyer, being receipts for dying cotton and linen, hot and cold. New England: 1811. 12 pp.

The dyer and colour maker's companion: containing upwards of two hundred receipts for making colours on the most approved principles, for all the various styles and fabrics now in existence. Together with the scouring process, and plain directions for preparing, washing-off, and finishing the goods. Philadelphia: Henry C. Baird, 1850. 104 pp.

ELLIS, ASA, JR. *The country dyer's assistant.* Brookfield, Mass.: 1798. 139 pp.

GIBSON, RICHARD. *The art of dyeing all colors on raw cotton or cotton waste, for the purpose of working with raw wool: also the methods of dyeing all colors in the piece . . . The system and science of colors, or the principles and practise of woolen dyeing. The properties and composition of the dyestuffs and chymical compounds which enter into the constitution of colors.* Three volumes in one. Willimantic, Conn.: 1861. 409 pp.

GILROY, CLINTON G. *A practical treatise on dyeing and calico-printing; including the latest inventions and improvements; also a description of the origin, manufacture, uses, and chemical properties of the various animal, vegetable, and mineral substances employed in these arts . . .* 2nd ed., rev. New York: Harper & Bros., 1846. 704 pp.

GOTWALT, JACOB. *Vorschriften zum Färben. Um Seiden, Wollen und Canton Cräpe schwarz zur färben.* York, Pa.: December 1831 (Broadside).

GRABILL, EPHRAIM. *The art of dying all sorts of colours, containing 36 secrets. For the use of families.* 2nd. ed. [Hanover, Pa.?]: 1846. 24 pp.

HAIGH, JAMES. *The dier's assistant in the art of dying wool and woollen goods. Extracted from the philosophical and chymical works of those most eminent authors, Ferguson, Dufay, Hellot, Geoffery, Colbert; and that reputable French dier Mons. De Julienne. Translated from the French with additions and practical experiments.* Philadelphia: 1810, 1st Amer. ed.; Poughkeepsie, N.Y.: Paraclete Potter, 1813, 2nd Amer. ed. 278 pp.

HARDT, PETER. *The family dyer.* (English and German). York [Pa.]: 1819. 70 pp.

---

*Only books devoted entirely to textile dyeing are listed here. Several general works printed before 1870 which contained sections on dyeing are listed in section C.

HARTMANN, HEINRICH. *Besondere Kunst, auf eine leichte und wohlfeile Art zu färben; allerley Farbe, so wohl auf Wolle, Halbwolle, Leinen und Seide.* Für den Land und Stadtman (A special art of dyeing by an easy and cheap method; all kinds of dyes on wool as well as on half-wool, linen and silk. For the country and city man). York, [Pa.]: 1797. 30 pp.

HASERICK, E. C. *The secrets of the art of dyeing wool, cotton, and linen, including bleaching and coloring wool and cotton hosiery and random-yarns. A treatise based on economy and practice.* Cambridge [Mass.]: 1869. 131 pp.

HOMAN, JOHANN GEORGE. *Die Land-und Haus-Apotheke, oder getreuer und gründlicher Unterricht für den Bauer und Stadtmann, Enthaltend die allerbesten Mittel, sowohl für die Menschen als für das Vieh besonders für die Pferde. Nebst einem grossen Anhang von der ächten Färberey, um Türkisch-Roth, Blau, Satin-Roth, Patent-Grün und viele andere Farben mehr zu färben* (The country and home apothecary, or faithful and thorough instruction for the farmer and townsman, containing the very best remedies, both for men and beast especially for horses. Furthermore a large appendix of the true dyeing, to dye further Turkey-red, blue, satin-red, patent-green and many other colors). Elsass Taunschip, Berks County, Pa.: 1818.

HOWE AND STEVENS. *Treatise upon dyeing and scouring, as adapted to their family dye colors. With many other valuable receipts.* Boston: 1864. 48 pp.

IMSCHWILLER, P. *The family dyer containing: a number of excellent dyes. Carefully selected for the use of private families; in the English and German language.* York, Pa.: 1826. 70 pp.

Instructions for washing wool and woollen yarns, and for dyeing wool and cotton, adapted to the use of farmers and planters of the Confederate States. Richmond: 1864. 10 pp.

KOEHLER, FRED. AUG. *Dye book comprising the receipts . . . to weavers, manufacturers and others . . . for dyeing . . . cotton, wool and silk . . .* n.p.n.d. [ca. 1870] 8 pp.

KRAMB, CHRISTIAN. *Auf Erfahrung gegründete Vorschriften, um Wolle, Leinen und Baumwolle zu färben* (Rules based on experience for dyeing wool, linen and cotton). Libanon, Pa.: 1809. 52 pp.

KUDER, SOLOMON. *The practical family-dyer containing all practical processes of dyeing for wool, cotton, linen, silk, cloth, garments, etc.* (Dr. Edwin M. Fogel, transl., *in* The Pennsylvania German Folklore Society [Yearbook] n.p., vol. 13, 1948). Trexlertown, Pa.: 1858 and Allentown, Pa.: 1866.

LOCHMAN, CHRISTIAN L. *Grundrisse der Färbekunst. Nach Chemischen Grundsätzen bearbeitet, enthaltend Recepten für allerley Farben, für Wollenes, Baumwollenes und Leinenes Zeug* (Basic principles of the art of dyeing worked out according to chemical principles, containing recipes for various dyes, for wool, cotton and linen cloth). Hamburg, Pa.: 1843.

LOVE, THOMAS. *The art of dyeing, cleaning, scouring, and finishing, on the most approved methods; being practical instructions in dyeing silks, woollens, and cottons, feathers, chips, straw, etc., scouring and cleaning bed and window curtains, carpets, rugs, etc. French and English cleaning for any color or fabric of silk, satin, or damask.* 2nd Amer. ed., with added general instructions for the use of aniline colors. Philadelphia: Henry C. Baird, 1869. 343 pp.

LYNDE, J. *The domestic dyer, or philosophy of fast colours: being a compilation from the most approved American and European authors.* New York [State]: 1831. 44 pp.

MOLONY, CORNELIUS. *The modern wool dyer containing the most approved methods as practised in the first clothing establishments in Great Britain.* Lowell, Mass.: 1834. 114 pp.

———. *Molony's masterpiece on wool, silk, and cotton dyeing: containing his best receipts, without the least reserve; according to his practice in Great Britain and America.* Lowell, Mass.: 1837. 122 pp.

114

————. *The practical dyer.* Boston: Monroe and Francis, 1833. 107 pp.

NAPIER, JAMES. *Chemistry applied to dyeing.* Philadelphia: Henry C. Baird, 1853. 405 pp.

————. *A system of chemistry applied to dyeing. A new and thoroughly revised edition, completely brought up to the present state of the science, including the chemistry of coal tar colors.* Edit. A. A. Fesquet. Philadelphia: H. C. Baird, 1869. 422 pp.

O'NEILL, CHARLES. *A dictionary of dyeing and calico printing: containing a brief account of all the substances and processes in use in the arts of dyeing and printing textile fabrics; with practical receipts and scientific information.* Philadelphia: Henry Carey Baird, 1869. 491 pp.

O'RORK, JAMES T. *The family dyer and weaver: being a treatise on dyeing and weaving, including recipes for scouring, discharging colors, and re-dyeing, to which is added a description of various waters, with their component parts and effects on different colors.* Winchester, Va.: 1844. 34 pp.

[PARNELL, EDWARD A.]. *A practical treatise on dyeing and calico-printing; including the latest inventions and improvements; also a description of the origin, manufacture, uses, and chemical properties of the various . . . substances employed in these arts.* New York: Harper & Bros., 1846. 704 pp.

PARTRIDGE, WILLIAM. *A practical treatise on dying woollen, cotton, and silk, including recipes for lac reds and scarlets—chrome yellows and oranges—and Prussian blues—on silks, cottons and woollens, with every improvement in the art, made since the year 1823. Also, a correct description of sulphuring woollens.* New York: Wm. Partridge's Son and Co., 1834 and 1847. 180 pp. First published in 1823 as *A practical treatise on dying of woollen, cotton, and skein silk, the manufacturing of broadcloth and cassimere, including the most improved methods pursued in the west of England, in which the various manipulations are accurately delineated. Also, a correct description of sulphuring woollens, and chemical bleaching of cottons.* New York: William Partridge. 288 pp.

Practical treatise on dyeing and calico printing. New York: 1860.

RAUCH, JOHN. *John Rauch's receipts on dyeing, in a series of letters to a friend. Containing correct and exact copies of all his best receipts on dyeing cotton and woollen goods, obtained and improved by him, during twelve years practice at different manufactories, in Switzerland, France, Germany and America; also a true description of his invented substitute for woad, being a cheap and preferable material, and the produce of this country.* New York: Joseph I. Badger and Co., 1815. 97 pp.

SELLERS, JOHN. *The color mixer containing nearly four hundred receipts for colors, pastes, acids, pulps, blue vats, liquors, etc. For cotton and woollen goods including the celebrated Barrow delaine colors.* Philadelphia: 1865. 155 pp.

SMITH, D. *The dyers' instructor.* Philadelphia: 1853, 1857, 1866. 338 pp.

SWARTZ, JOSEPH. *The family dyer and scourer. Also, fullers' guide and assistant.* Liberty-town, Md.: 1841 (*in* The farmers book, vol. 1, June 1840–June 1841). 38 pp.

TAMONEY, PATRICK. *The art of dyeing simplified. Dyeing cotton, woolen, linen, and silk goods; bleaching cotton; extracting mildew, and all kinds of vegetable stains from cotton and linen; sulphuring silk and woolen goods; whiting straw and leghorn bonnets; dyeing straw and leghorn bonnets. Finishing silk dresses and leghorn bonnets after being dyed; scouring woolen yarn; preparing goods for dyeing after being fulled.* Mountain Valley, Pa.: 1852. 32 pp.

TUCKER, WILLIAM. *The family dyer and scourer; being a complete treatise on the arts of dyeing and cleaning every article of dress, bed and window furniture, silks, bonnets, feathers etc.* From the 4th London ed. Philadelphia: E. L. Carey and A. Hart [ca. 1830]. 180 pp.

ULRICH, LOUIS. *A complete treatise on the art of dyeing cotton and wool, as practised in Paris, Rouen, Mulhausen, and Germany . . . To which are added the most important receipts for dyeing wool, as practiced in the Manufacture Imperiale des Gobelins, Paris by Prof. H. Dussance.* Philadelphia: H. C. Baird, 1863. 274 pp.

WAITE, DANIEL & CO., *The new American dier or, an entirely new and superior method of dying woolen cloths.* Brookfield, Mass.: 1815. 80 pp.

WARFIELD, HAZAEL. *The clothiers guide, a correct plan of colouring wool and woolen, cotton, and linen cloths, for milling, finishing, etc. of woolen cloths.* Mountpleasant, [Pa.]: 1832. 52 pp.

C. Books Printed in America Before 1870 Which Include a Section of Dye Recipes

AIKEN, JESSE. *The citizen's tutor, containing a variety of valuable receipts for the cure of the different diseases of man and beast; also for colouring wool, cotton and hat.* Mountpleasant [Pa.?]: 1831, pp. 98–100.

BIGELOW, JACOB, M. D. *The useful arts considered in connexion with the applications of science . . .* Boston: Marsh, Capen, Lyon, and Webb, 1840, pp. 183–193.

CUTBUSH, JAMES. *The American artist's manual, or dictionary of practical knowledge in the application of philosophy to the arts and manufactures. Selected from the most complete European systems, with original improvements and appropriate engravings adapted to the use of the manufactures of the United States.* 2 vols. Philadelphia: Johnson and Warner, and R. Fisher: 1814. (Dyeing, vol. 1.) 31 pp.

Ein vortrefliches Kräuter-Buch für Haus-Väter und Mütter, nebst etlichen auserlesenen Recepten. Wie auch eine Anweisung zur Färbe-Kunst, Blau, Roth, Gelb, etc. zu färben. (An excellent herbal for fathers and mothers of families, including selected recipes. As also instructions for dyeing cloth blue, red, yellow, etc.) Hannover, Pa.: 1809. pp. 29–32.

Encyclopaedia: or, a dictionary of arts, sciences, and miscellaneous literature . . . 18 vols. 1st Amer. ed. Philadelphia: 1798. (Dyeing: pp. 185–225; other entries under names of individual dyestuffs.)

FULHAME, MRS. *An essay on combustion, with a view to a new art of dying and painting wherein the phylogistic and antiphlogist hypotheses are proved erroneous.* Philadelphia: 1810. 248 pp.

The golden cabinet being the laboratory or handmaid to the arts. Containing such branches of useful knowledge, as nearly concerns all kinds of people from the squire to the peasant: and will afford both profit and delight. Philadelphia: 1793. (Dyeing: part 2, pp. 113–122.)

KRAUSS, JOHANN. *Oeconomisches Haus- und Kunst-Buch, oder Sammlung ausgesuchter Vorschriften, zum Nutzen und Gebrauch für Land- und Hauswirthe, Handwerker, Künstler und Kunst-Liebhaber. Zusammengetragen aus den besten Englischen und Deutschen Schriften.* (Home economics and art book or a collection of select recipes for the profit and use of farmers and householders, artisans, artists and art lovers. Collected from the best English and German sources.) Allentown, Pa.: 1819. 452 pp.

Kurzgefasstes Weiber-Büchlein, Welches sehr nützlichen Unterricht für schwangere Weiber und Hebammen enthält; wie auch, die auserlesendsten Artzney-Mittel für aller Arten Krankheiten Beyderley Geschlechts. Ferner: Eine Anweisung zur Färbe-Kunst, Blau, Roth, etc. zu Färben. (Short book for women which contains useful instructions for pregnant women and midwives; also it gives the most select medicines for all kinds of diseases for either sex; Further: Instructions for the art of dyeing blue, red, etc.) n.p. 1818. 64 pp.

LESLIE, MISS ELIZA. *The house book: or, a manual of economy for town and country.* 8th ed. Philadelphia: Carey & Hart, 1845. pp. 93–104.

MACKENZIE, COLIN. *Mackenzie's five thousand receipts in all the useful and domestic arts . . .*

A new American, from the latest London edition. Philadelphia: 1831, pp. 81–92.

A new collection of genuine receipts, for the preparation . . . *and execution of curious arts and interesting experiments.* Concord, N.H.: Fisk and Chase, 1831, pp. 51–84. (Copies many passages from Tucker [ca. 1830].)

PARKER, M. *The arcana of arts and sciences, or, farmers' and mechanics' manual; containing a great variety of valuable receipts and useful discoveries, in the various departments of human knowledge; many of which were never before published.* Washington, Pa.: 1824. (Dyeing pp. 88–118.)

PLATTES, GABRIEL. *A discovery of subterranean treasure, viz all manner of mines and minerals . . . also a sure way to try what colour any berry, leaf, flower, stalk, root, seed, bark, or wood will give together with directions for making colours that shall not stain or fade.* Philadelphia: 1792. pp. 21–24.

PORTER, ARTHUR L. *The chemistry of the arts* . . . *with treatises on calico printing, bleaching* . . . 2 vols. Philadelphia: 1830. (Calico printing.)

URE, ANDREW. *A dictionary of arts, manufactures and mines.* 2 vols. New York: Appleton, 1856. (Dyeing, vol. 1, pp. 601–611; other dye articles under names of individual dyestuffs.)

Valuable secrets in arts and trades, etc., selected from the best authors and adapted to the situation of the United States. New York: 1809. (Dyeing: pp. 219–235.)

WEBSTER, THOMAS. *An encyclopaedia of domestic economy.* New York: Harper & Brothers, 1845, pp. 984–991.

WILLICH, A. F. M. *The domestic encyclopaedia; or, a dictionary of facts, and useful knowledge. Comprehending a concise view of the latest discoveries, inventions, and improvements, chiefly applicable to rural and domestic economy together with* . . . *practical hints respecting the arts and manufactures, both familiar and commercial.* 5 vols. Philadelphia: Birch and Small: 1804. (Dyeing, vol. 2, pp. 406–432.)

WRIGHT, A. S. *Three thousand receipts. The American receipt book, or, complete book of reference, containing valuable and important receipts for cookery, pastry, preserving, pickling, confectionary, distilling, perfumery, varnishing, chemicals, dyeing, and agriculture.* Philadelphia: Lindsay & Blakiston, 1844 (scattered short recipes on dyeing).

Common Names of Chemicals Used in Dyeing**

Alum	Potassium aluminum sulfate	$KAl(SO_4)_2 \cdot 12 H_2O$
Aqua ammonia	Ammonium hydroxide solution	NH_4OH
Aqua fortis	Nitric acid	HNO_3
Aqua regia	Mixture of HCl and HNO_3	$HCl + HNO_3$
Argol (Argal or Argil)	Crude potassium bitartrate, red or white, depending on whether it is deposited from red or white grapes	—
Bleaching powder	Calcium hypochlorite	$CaOCl_2$
Blue stone	Blue vitriol (below)	—
Blue vitriol	Hydrated copper sulfate	$CuSO_4 \cdot 5 H_2O$
Borax	Hydrated sodium tetraborate	$Na_2B_4O_7 \cdot 10 H_2O$
Brimstone	Sulfur	S
Caustic potash	Potassium hydroxide	KOH
Caustic soda	Sodium hydroxide	NaOH
Chalk	Calcium carbonate	$CaCO_3$
Chrome mordant	Potassium dichromate	$K_2Cr_2O_7$
Chrome yellow	Lead chromate	$PbCrO_4$
Cinnabar	Mercuric sulfide	HgS
Copperas	Hydrated ferrous sulfate	$FeSO_4 \cdot 7 H_2O$
Cream of tartar	Potassium acid tartrate	$KHC_4H_4O_6$
Fuller's earth	Hydrated magnesium and aluminum silicates	—
Glycerine	Glycerol	$C_3H_5(OH)_3$
Green vitriol	Copperas (above)	—
Javelle water	Sodium hypochlorite solution	NaOCl
Lime water	Water solution of calcium hydroxide	$Ca(OH)_2 \cdot H_2O$
Lye	Caustic soda (above)	—
Marine acid	Muriatic acid (below)	—
Milk of lime	Calcium hydroxide suspended in water	$Ca(OH)_2$
Muriatic acid	Hydrochloric acid	HCl
Nitre	Potassium nitrate	KNO_3
Oil of vitriol	Concentrated sulfuric acid	H_2SO_4
Orpiment	Arsenic trisulfide	As_2S_3
Pearl ash	Purified potash (below)	K_2CO_3

**Chief reference: Francis M. Turner, ed., *The condensed chemical dictionary*, 2nd ed., rev. New York: The Chemical Catalog Co., Inc., 1930.

Peroxide	Hydrogen peroxide	H_2O_2
Potash	Potassium carbonate	K_2CO_3
Prussian blue	Ferric ferrocyanide	$Fe_4(Fe(CN)_6)_3$
Prussic acid	Hydrocyanic acid	HCN
Realgar	Arsenic monosulfide	AsS
Red orpiment	Arsenic bisulfide	As_2S_2
Sal ammoniac	Ammonium chloride	NH_4Cl
Sal soda	Hydrated sodium carbonate	$Na_2CO_3 \cdot 10\ H_2O$
Saleratus	Pearl ash overcharged with carbonic acid gas	—
Saltpetre	Nitre (above)	—
Sig	Urine, whose principal constituent is urea, a weakly basic nitrogenous compound	$CO(NH_2)_2$ (urea)
Slaked lime	Hydrated calcium hydroxide	$Ca(OH)_2$
Soda ash	Sodium carbonate	Na_2CO_3
Sour water	Dilute sulfuric acid	H_2SO_4
Spirit of salt	Muriatic acid (above)	—
Spirits of nitre	Dilute nitric acid	$HNO_3 \cdot H_2O$
Sugar of lead	Lead acetate	$Pb(C_2H_3O_2)_2 \cdot 3\ H_2O$
Tannic acid (tannin)	Gallotannic acid	$C_{14}H_{10}O_9$
Tartar	Argol (above)	—
Verdigris	Basic copper acetate	$CuO \cdot 2Cu(C_2H_3O_2)_2$
Vermillion	Cinnabar (above)	—
Vinegar	Dilute impure acetic acid	CH_3COOH
Vitriol	A sulfate, usually of iron or copper	—
Vitriolic acid	Oil of vitriol (above)	—
Washing soda	Sal soda (above)	—

Dyes Occasionally Mentioned in Dyers' Manuals Printed in America

Agaric		Black
Almond leaves		Yellow
Aloes		Purple
Artichokes		Green
Bear-berry	*Arctostaphylos uva-ursi*	Brown
Bindweed		Yellow-orange
Blackwood bark		Grey
Bloodroot	*Sanguinaria canadensis*	Red
Buckwheat		Blue
Chrysanthemum		Yellow
Convolvulus		Yellow-orange
Corn-marigold		Yellow
Dyers' savory	*Serratula tinctoria*	Yellow
Dyers' woodroof	*Asperula tinctoria*	Red
Ebony wood		Yellow-green
Fenugrec	*Trigonella foenum-graecum*	Yellow
Fenugreek	*Trigonella foenum-graecum*	Yellow
Hairy mistletoe		Yellow
Lady's bedstraw	*Galium tinctorium*	Red
Lombardy poplar	*Populus dilata* (= *P. nigra* var. *italica*)	Yellow
Magnolia	*Magnolia virginiana*	Yellow
Malacca bean	*Semecarpus anacardium*	Black
Mangrove bark	*Sweitenia mahogani*	Brown
Nephritic wood	Lignum peregrinum***	Yellow
Privet berries	*Ligustrum vulgare*	Green
Saffron	*Crocus sativus*	Yellow
Saw-wort	*Serratula tinctoria*	Yellow
Savory	*Serratula tinctoria*	Yellow
Sorrel	*Rumex acetosella*	Black
Sweet gale	*Myrica gale*	Yellow
Zant		Yellow
	Andromeda arborea (*A. Ferruginea* var. *arborescens*)	Black
	Cistus ledon	Yellow
	Coccus polonicus	Red
	*Mespilus canadensis*****	Red
	*Virga aura canadensis****	Green

*** Not a botanical name.
****Contemporary botanical name, *Crataegus canadensis*.

Excerpt from David Ramsay, *The history of South-Carolina.* Charleston: David Longworth, 1809, 2 vol. (vol. 2, pp. 249–252).

The art of dying ought to make a conspicuous figure among the arts of the carolinians; for nature has blessed them with a profusion of materials for that purpose. To encourage their attention to this subject, the following facts are mentioned: captain Felder, near Orangeburgh, procured a paste from the leaves of the sweet leaf, hopea tinctoria, and those of the yellow indigo, a species of cassia, for which he obtained one guinea per pound during the american revolutionary war. Unfortunately his process died with him.

Doctor Bancroft, the ingenious author of experimental researches concerning the philosophy of permanent colors, informed the writer of this history that his patent for introducing into England several dye-stuffs gained for him 5000£. per annum for some of the last years of his patent. In the course of his experiments, doctor Bancroft found that some materials for dying could be procured in the greatest abundance from the woods of America, which were of equal efficacy with others which commanded a high price in England. This was particularly the case with the bark of the quercus tinctoria or black oak, which is very common in Carolina. Of this he annually imported and sold as much as gained him the above sum.

It may be of service to some persons residing in the country to be informed that Carolina affords, among many other dye-stuffs, the following materials for dying the colors to which they are respectively annexed:

BLACK.

Rhus toxicodendron, *poison oak*—the acrid juice of this small shrub imparts a durable black without any addition.

Gall-berry bush grows in profusion on the margin of our bays, creeks, and ponds; the leaves and berries of it are employed by hatters for giving a black to hats, as also by weavers for staining yarn.

Lycopus europaeus, *water hoarhound*, or *gypsywort*—the juice of this plant also gives a fixed black dye.

Actea spicuta, *herb christopher, or baneberries*—the juice of the berries boiled with alum affords a fine black dye, or ink.

Quercus Rubra, *red oak*, the capsules and bark of the oak afford a good fixture for brown or black dyes. Copperas or alum is commonly used for the *mordant*, or setting ingredients as they are vulgarly called.

BLUES.

Indigofera tinctoria, *common indigo*.

Amorpha fruticosa, *false indigo*—these are well known dyes.

Fraxinus excelsior, *common ash tree*—the inner bark is said to give a good blue color to cloth.

Note.—Preparations of the *cuprum, vitriolatum*, or blue stone, are used in dying blues.

YELLOW.

Urtica dioica, *common nettle*—the roots of this give a faint yellow to cotton.

Rhamnus frangula, *black berry*, bearing alder—the bark tinges a dull yellow.

121

Berberis vulgaris, *barberry bush*—the root gives wool a beautiful yellow.

Prunus chicasa, *common plumb tree.*

Pyrus malus, *apple tree*—the barks of both these are used in dying yellow.

Betula, *birch tree*—the leaves give a faint yellow.

Seratula tinctoria, *saw wort*, and contaurea jacea, *common knapweed*, give to wool a good yellow.

Polygonum persicaria—*spotted arsemart.*

Lysimachia vulgaris, *yellow willow herb*, or *loose strife.*

Scabiosa succisa, or *devil's bit*—the leaves impart a yellow color.

Hypericum perforatum, *St. John's wort*, the flowers.

Calnendula officinalis, *garden marygold*, the petals or flower leaves dried.

Cuscuta americana, *american dodder*, or *love vine*, produces a bright though not permanent yellow; it is however in great esteem.

Hopea tinctoria, *horse laurel, horse honey, sweet or yellow leaf*, this shrub abounds in the country, and on James island—is greedily eaten by cows and horses. The leaves are used for dying yellow.

Helianthus Tuberosa, *tuberose sun-flower, Jerusalem or ground artichoke*—the petals of this plant are used for imparting a yellow color to wool.

Zanthoriza apüfolia, *parsley leaved root, yellow root.*

Hydrastis canadensis, *yellow root*, both impart a beautiful yellow.

RED.

But few articles of this kind are known in South-Carolina. Carthamus tinctoria, *bastard saffron*, is used for cotton; it is said to impart a fine red color to silks—the blossoms only are used.

Rumex allosa, *common sorrel*—the roots impart a faint red, but is not lasting.

Gallium soreale, *crosswort madder*, and indeed the roots of several species of gallium impart a red color to wool.

Sanginaria canadensis, *puccoon*, or *bastard turmeric* the roots impart a yellowish red color to wool.

Cactus opuntia, *prickly pear*, imparts a beautiful red color.

CRIMSON.

Phytolacea discaudea, *american night shade*, or *poke*—the juice of poke berries boiled in rain water and set with alum, imparts to wool a beautiful crimson, and when fixed with limewater, produces a yellow color.

GREEN.

Arundo phragmatis, *common reed* or *cane*, the leaves of which impart to wool a fine green color.

This color is principally obtained by first dying the stuffs yellow, and then dipping them in indigo dye.

BROWN, GOLD, AND OLIVE SHADES.

Acer campestris, *common maple*, the bark imparts to cotton or wool, a brownish purple, as does also the tops of the origanum vulgare, or *wild majoram.*

Quercus rubra, *red oak*, the inner bark of the tree produces an orange or reddish brown color with alum—set with copperas, a good black.

Juglans nigra, *black walnut*, the bark of the tree and fruit imparts to wool or cotton an excellent dark olive color.

Humulus lupuli, *common hops*, the plant dyes a good brown.

Agrimonia eupatorium, *common agrimony*, affords a tolerable gold color.

122

Excerpt from Thomas Cooper, *A practical treatise on dyeing and callicoe printing*. Philadelphia: Thomas Dobson, 1815, pp. 483–506.

APPENDIX.

On the Colours produced on Woollen, by means of various plants. From D'Ambourney, of Rouen.

THIS gentleman instituted a set of experiments to ascertain what permanent colours could be produced by means of plants, chiefly those in common use, and easily procured. They appear to be made with considerable care, and were deemed of such importance as to be published by order of the French government, under the administrationship of M. Calonne, in 1786.

I have already intimated my opinion, that a few drugs in common use and well known, whether of foreign or domestic growth, would better answer the purpose of a dyer, than a multiplicity of dye stuffs whose virtues were not ascertained with equal precision, and which produced no better effect at the same price than the drugs in use. The more chemical knowledge extends, the more will the Materia Tinctoria, like the Materia Medica, be reduced in number and in price.

But these observations ought not to extend to the experiments of the laboratory, the true source of future improvement in the art of dyeing. The experiments and perseverance of Dr. Bancroft has sent into every dye house, and every printing shop in Europe, without any exception, an article so common in the American woods, that it was never noticed here, though a chemist could hardly pass by a tanner's establishment without being struck with the colour of the skins. I mean the quercitron, or bark of the common American black oak. This drug has nearly superseded weld and fustic, both in the woollen and the cotton dye; in so much, that I may venture to say, not one-fiftieth part of those drugs are now used in England, France, and Germany, that were used thirty years ago.

The experiments of D'Ambourney on the birch, the Lombardy poplar, and the black alder in particular; the use of walnut peel, and of soot on the continent of Europe, so little employed in England and this country, promise improvements in dyeing by means of common and cheap articles, by no means to be slighted or overlooked.

Homassel, or Bouillon Le Grange for him, have republished the kind of abridgment of D'Ambourney's experiments, which D'Ambourney himself inserted at the end of his book: this presents a general idea only of what vegetables may be employed in dyeing, but does not afford information sufficiently accurate for a dyer to follow at once. I shall republish this abridgment with the English names of the plants, not so much for the use of the dyer as of the experimentalist; and to open a door to a kind of knowledge, which

123

our own country is better calculated to afford than any other, and to an employment for leisure hours, in a very high degree amusing, interesting, and instructive.

The mordants employed by D'Ambourney were not well calculated for the dyer's work shop: they were the following:

1. Bismuth dissolved in single aqua fortis: of this solution one part, with brine of common salt, two parts, and tartar in powder, one part, was used to woollen sixteen parts by weight. Water, as much as necessary.

2. A solution of tin made by dissolving four ounces of sal ammoniac and nine ounces of grain tin in four pounds of single aqua fortis. Five pounds and one ounce of this solution, with an equal quantity of tartar, and twice the quantity of brine, formed the mordant for sixty pounds weight of cloth.

3. A solution of tin in aqua fortis and common salt.

4 and 5. Another solution of tin with less tin: both hot and cold.

6. A solution of tin with a small quantity of gold, in aqua regia.

7. Tin dissolved in strong muriatic acid only.

8. Tin dissolved in nitro-muriatic acid; nitrous acid, one part; muriatic acid, one part; tin, one-eighth of a part.

9. Tin dissolved in various proportions in nitro-muriatic acid, wherein the muriatic was one-third of the nitrous.

10. Solution of nitrat of copper.

11. Muriatic solution of iron.

12. Solution of three pounds of red argol or tartar in boiling water, and nine pounds of alum, for sixty pounds of cloth.

It is evident that the experiments are less valuable, in proportion as you employ new, unusual, and expensive mordants: so that M. D'Ambourney's experiments do not bear upon practice so much as they might do.

I have had a good deal of experience in this kind of experiment myself, and I feel myself therefore entitled to offer to others who would pursue the same very entertaining employment of leisure hours, the following advice.

The object is, not so much to procure brilliant colours, as permanent colours: by permanent colours meaning always such as will stand the three tests of air, soap, and acids.

The substances to be dyed may be confined to woollen and cotton. The mordants ought to be the mordants in common use. I have a very high opinion of nitrat, and nitro-muriat of bismuth; and also of nitrat of iron; but I fear, the necessary attention to economy will confine their utility to brilliant colours, and very high priced goods. They ought to be the subjects of a separate set of comparative experiments.

For experiments on WOOLLEN, take well scoured, clean, white flannel as the subject to be dyed. Boil it in clean snow or rain water for half an hour. Take it out, wring it, dry it. Water of calcareous soils will modify the effect of the colouring substances employed; not so the water of mountainous and siliceous soils. Of such flannel, take any quantity of a given weight, as one, two, three, or four pounds.

1. Let it soak in the common boiling hot mordant of alum three ounces and a half, to finely-powdered tartar one ounce and a half, for each pound of cloth. It may remain covered up for twelve hours. Then take it out, wring it moderately, rince it in cold water moderately, and dry it not perfectly, but so as to be slightly damp, and keep it in an under-ground room. Tartar in proportion of *one-third* of the alum I consider as too small, in the proportion of *one-half*, rather too much; that is, as a general rule. Alum without the tartar, crystallizes too readily, gives the cloth a harshness to the touch, and though the colours are equally full in most cases, they are not equally bright.

I do not believe that any decided decomposition of the alum takes place without the intervention of the cloth; and perhaps too, not without the further intervention of colouring matter. But these facts have not yet been chemically ascertained; and every chemist knows the obscurity that yet hangs about the operation of common tartar in the silvering of brass and copper, and the tinning of brass wire for pins.

2. Mordant for woollens. To a pound of aqua fortis, add a pound of pure clean rain water, and two ounces of sal ammoniac. In this mixture, slowly dissolve two ounces of grain tin, then add one ounce of powdered white tartar. When you dye with the woods or plants, first let the cloth stay for fifteen minutes in this solution diluted, using it in the proportion of one-fifth or one-sixth part the weight of the cloth. Then having soaked it in this solution and dried it moderately, enter it into a hot decoction of the plant, and when it has taken up as full a colour as it will, take it out of the decoction, rinse it well in cold water, soak it again in the mordant and dye it again. Then wash it well and dry it, as a specimen of the colour with the tin mordant.

3. From some experiments I have made, I believe the tin mordant may be as usefully prepared in the following as in any other way, but it is not the actual dyer's practice; which the preceding method approaches as far as may be: except that I have directed the usual dose of tartar to be put to the mordant instead of putting it to the dye stuff, as in the scarlet dye.

Make an aqua regia thus. Muriatic acid, from iron, three parts; nitric acid, one part. Dissolve slowly as much tin as it will take up, pour it off clear, and then add muriatic acid in like proportion to the amount of one-sixth in quantity of the solution, so that there shall be an excess of acid. Of this, when diluted with an equal quantity of water, employ one part by weight to six or eight parts of cloth.

But the second process being the process of practice, I should upon the whole prefer it. We sadly want a judicious set of experiments on mordants. Indeed no man but a dyer by practice and a good chemist into the bargain, can even guess at the multitude of desiderata in the art of dyeing; and how little we know about it as yet.

These, with iron and copper, will be mordants enough for woollen. The pieces of flannel used for these experiments should be not more than six inches square, cut off *after* the cloth has been mordanted with alum and tartar, but divided *before* the tin mordant is used. The weight of each piece may be ascertained by weighing the whole piece first.

4. Dissolve four ounces of green copperas in a pint of water, and add two ounces of finely powdered tartar. Stir them till dissolved; this will be the utmost proportion for one pound of cloth.

Mordant the cloth with this in all proportions, (noting them) and mix it also occasionally with the alum and tartar mordant, wherever you want saddened colours, as is done in practice for olives and drabs.

5. Make a similar mordant, using blue instead of green copperas.

Secondly. Mordants for Cotton.

1. Take a given weight of callicoe well bleached. Immerse it for six hours in water acidulated with sulphuric acid; to wit, one part oil of vitriol to fifty parts water. Take it out, wash it perfectly and scrupulously. This is necessary to dissolve any alkaline or earthy mordant which the cloth in bleaching is apt to imbibe. The callicoe printer never dispenses with this.

2. Make a mordant merely of alum: using four ounces of alum to one pound of callicoe, and soak your callicoe in this mordant boiling hot, for six hours. Keep it in a damp place.

3. Make a mordant of acetat of alum, as in common practice, though it be not perfect: but for these experiments common practice is the best foundation to build upon: thus,

125

Take one part by weight of alum finely powdered; dissolve it in as much hot water as is necessary, and no more; that is five pints of water and half a pint of vinegar to one pound of alum. Then add to it three-fourths of a part of sugar of lead: stir them well, let them settle, pour off the clear liquor after the sediment has settled for a day: add to each pint of the clear liquor four ounces of gum arabic, bruised into a coarse powder; keep stirring it occasionally until dissolved.

Divide your callicoe so cleared by an acid, into pieces of four or six inches square. In the middle of each piece print a figure or make a spot with your thickened acetat of alumine. Let it dry. Then let it soak for half an hour in a liquor composed of one part by measure of fresh cow dung to four parts boiling water. Then take out the piece: rince it: dry it: lay it by for use, to be dyed in the decoction of the proposed vegetable. Boil it, or rather keep it in a full scalding heat of the decoction for an hour. Then boil it in bran and water, and bleach it in the air for a day.

4. Make a mordant of iron in the acetous acid thus: dissolve in four parts by weight of hot water one part of green copperas; add more water if necessary when cold, to keep it in solution. To this solution add an equal weight of sugar of lead. Let the sediment subside, thicken the clear liquor with gum arabic, and use it on the callicoe in the same manner as you use the acetate of alumine. This will be the same with the common iron liquor.

You may mix these two mordants at your pleasure, so as to produce browns, purples, and chocolates, with reds; and olives, drabs, &c. with yellows. So, you may use for mordanting the whole piece of callicoe, sulphat of iron (green copperas) either mixed or unmixed with common alum-solution: for the colours are thus greatly varied with the same drug, or colouring material.

These mordants might be increased in number, and varied; but then the experiments would become too complicated, and would vary too much from the usual and approved practice.

I have stated in the beginning of this work, that the quantity and brilliancy of the colouring matter of a dye-drug might be ascertained by a solution of acetat of alumine or of muriat of tin generally speaking. I prefer the former, particularly for cotton: but the muriat or nitro-muriat of tin is very useful for colours to be applied to woollen.

Make a filtered decoction of the vegetable to be tried: drop into it a solution of acetat of alumine not thickened with gum, and a little diluted. Or, a saturated solution of nitro-muriat of tin, wherein the muriatic is in the proportion of three parts, and the nitric acid of one.

The quantity and colour of the colouring matter may be thus ascertained.

Such a course of experiments with the woods, herbs, fruits and flowers of our own country, would be a very valuable and interesting work: that ought indeed to be a national work, but that is not to be expected.

I have already mentioned that the birch tree, and the Lombardy poplar, promise useful and permanent colours, and deserve to be the subject of many experiments not yet made, particularly in the back country, for which these experiments seem peculiarly calculated.

Table and Classification of Colours procured from Indigenous Plants.

According to the experiments of D'Ambourney.

Homassel, or Bouillon Le Grange, have omitted the Linnaean names of the vegetables, which I have supplied from D'Ambourney's original work. I cannot always answer for the English names, though I believe there are very few mistakes; but as I have added the Linnaean ones, there can be no difficulty to a botanist.

126

Aurora.

Golden-yellow aurora, from the stalks and fresh leaves of *Bidens tripartita*, the trifid water hemp agrimony: not so bright from the dry plant.

Tarnished, from the yew tree. *Taxus baccata.*

Brilliant, with nitro-muriat of tin and alum in the decoction of the same.

From the dry flowers of furze, *Ulex Europaea*, with a little madder.

Cinnamon-aurora, from the young shoots of the Lombardy poplar, *Populus Pyramidalis*, with one forty-eighth of madder.

From the roots of a wild apple-tree.

Aurora-capuchine, from the Virginia sumach, *Rhus Virginiana*, Stags-horns. Quere, if this be also the *Rhus typhinum*? This required two baths.

The capuchin tinge increased by a small quantity of madder.

From the dry straw of buckwheat, *Polygonum fagopyrum*, with a nitro-muriat of tin.

Rich and brilliant with nitro-muriat of tin and gold from the dried straw of buckwheat, the fruit of the berries of the black berry-bearing alder, *Rhamnus frangula*, and a little madder.

Blue.

The blue vat, Saxon blue, and logwood blue as usual.

Logwood blue, made more solid by the bark of the birch tree, *Betula alba*, with the nitro-muriat of tin.

Bluish gray, from the common black elder berries, *Sambucus nigra*.

Handsome blue, but fugitive, from the same berries and sulphat of copper.

Browns.

Rappie snuff brown: fresh alder, *Betula alnus*.

Olive brown, from the shoots of *Agnus castus*.

Deep brown, from the stalks and leaves of *Leonurus cardiaca*, mother wort.

The most beautiful and solid colour from fresh walnut peel.

Puce-brown, from the fresh bark of the black walnut, *Juglans nigra*.

Same from the shoots of the marsh elder, or Guelder rose while in sap, *Viburnum opulus*.

Gray-olive, deep brown, from the stalks and leaves of *Parietaria*, Pellitory of the wall.

Caca-Dauphin, or Bright Fawn Colour.

Bright greenish, from common heath, *Erica vulgaris*, and buckwheat straw, both dry, with nitro-muriat of tin.

Light fawn, from buckwheat straw dried: beautiful with solution of tin and gold.

Olive fawn, from dry buckwheat straw and dried berries of the *Rhamnus frangula*.

Avanturin-fawn, from the same, with bismuth mordant.

Cinnamon.

From the shoots of the rose-acacia, *Robinia hispida*, with bismuth.

From the shoots of the apricot tree.

From the stem and roots of the bilberry or whortle-berry, *Vaccinium myrtillus*.

From the branches of the broad-leaved trumpet flowers, *Bignonia Catalpa*.

Rich, from a half spent bath of logwood and sumach with tin and gold solution.

Light nankin, from the fresh wood of the common horn beam, *Carpinus Betulus*, barked.

Yellowish, (very good) from the Cyprus, *Cupressus foliis acaciae deciduis: Virginia:* mixed with the dry shoots of the horn beam.

From the roots of the *Fragaria vesca*, or strawberry.

127

Reddish, brilliant, in a fresh bath or decoction of madder with bismuth.

Deep, from the common broom, *Spartium scoparium.*

Reddish, from the shoots of the *Grevia occidentalis,* elm-leaved, with purple flowers.

Mordorè, cinnamon, from the bark of the common beech, *Fagus sylvatica,* with nitro-muriat of tin.

Nankin, from the green stalks of the hop, *Lupulus.*

Mordorè, from the roots of yew, *Taxus baccata,* and birch bark.

Rich colour, from the dried flowers of furze and a little madder.

Mordorè, from the shoots of the Portugal laurel.

From the fresh roots of *Convolvulus sepium,* great bindweed.

Light rose-coloured cinnamon from the branches of *Prunus Mahaleb,* perfumed cherry.

Same, from the branches of the sallow or black willow, *Salix Capraea,* with bismuth.

Yellowish, from the shoots without leaves of the larch, *Pinus Larix,* with bismuth mordant. Same, from the wood of the wild cherry tree.

Delicate, from the bark of the Dutch medlar, *Mespilus Germanica,* with bismuth.

From the shoots of the five-leaved bladder nut, *Staphylea Pinnata.*

Reddish, from the barks of the elm and birch.

Light, from the shoots of the peach tree.

Golden, from the ripe fruit of the wake robin, *Arum maculatum.*

From the branches of a three year old pear tree.

Rose coloured, from the shoots of *Syringa, Philadelphus Coronarius.*

Carmelite.

From a mixture of shoots of alder, a little madder, dry berries of the black alder, and shoots of Lombardy poplar.

From a half spent bath or decoction of balsamine, *Impatiens Balsamina,* then in the decoction of black alder berries.

From wine of the black alder berry with a little madder.

Light from dry hay, which is improved greatly by a little madder.

From the stalks of lavender.

Rich from the shoots of scarlet flowering chestnut, *Esculus octandra Pavia,* with dried black berries.

From shoots of buckthorn, *Rhamnus catharticus,* and then in madder.

From dried wheat straw, a little sumach, and solution of iron.

From the Italian or Lombardy poplar, dried berries of black alder, madder, and solution of iron.

Light and brilliant from buck-wheat straw, dried black alder berries, Lombardy poplar, and madder, with bismuth mordant.

At once from buck-wheat bran, dried black alder berries and Lombardy poplar.

From chimney soot (which in France is generally wood soot) madder, dried black alder berries, and poplar.

From red clover and a little madder.

The ivy leaved speedwell, *Veronica hederifolia,* furnishes a very good ground for carmelites.

Citron or Lemon Yellow.

From the young branches of the acacia. *Robinia Caragagna seu Sibirica.*

Greenish, from the *Aristolochia clematitis,* Birthwort.

From the shoots of the *Daphne mezereum,* red mezereon.

From the branches and leaves of *Guilandina Dioica,* Canada Bonduc.

128

Brilliant, from the common heath, *Erica vulgaris*, with tin mordant.
Brimstone, from the green leaves of myrrh, *Scandix odorata*.
Light citron, from the meadow saffron, *Colchicum autumnale*.
From the *Coronilla glauca*, seven-leaved Colutea.
From the shoots of Cyprus.
Brilliant, from the counter poison, *Asclepias Vincetoxicum*.
From the shoots of the hairy broom, *Genista pilosa*.
From the dyers' broom, *Genista tinctoria*.
From the musk Geranium, *Geranium moschatum*.
From the common knapweed, *Centaurea nigra*.
From the swamp golden rod, *Senecio paludosus*.
From the common yellow jessamin of the woods, *Jasminum fruticans*.
From the *Tagetes patula*, (Oillet d'Inde) African marigold?
From the shoots of the olive, *Olea Europaea*.
From the larger nettle, *Urtica dioica;* common nettle.
From the *Scandix pecten veneris*, a species of cicely.

From the black, Virginia poplar,
    Populus Balsami fera, Tacamahac,
    white poplar, *populus alba*,
    aspen tree, *populus tremula*,

{ Solid colours on wool mordanted with bismuth, and after being dyed run through tin solution. The older wood gives sadder colours but solid. }

From the larkspur, *Delphinium Ajacis multiplex*.
From the green leaves of pitch pine, *pinus maritima*.
From the common red pepper, Guinea pepper, *Capsicum annuum:* (while green.)
From the leaves of the potatoe.
From the double white meadow sweet, *Spiraea ulmaria*.
From the China aster, *Aster Sinensis*.
From the green stalks of rue, *Ruta graveolens*.
From the buckwheat, *Polygonum fagopyrum*, twining bindweed, *polygonum convolvulus*, on wool with tin mordant.
From African ragwort, *Othonna Cheirifolia*.
From the fresh stalks of Canada (common) golden rod, *Solidago Canadensis*.
From the leaves of the same.

Crimson.

Venetian scarlet, from brazil wood on woollen, grounded with birch bark, after being mordanted with tin solution.
More intense, from the same, using only a stronger dose of brazil wood of Fernambouca, called amaranthine brazil wood.
Less brilliant, when the colour was fixed by the shoots of the birch tree instead of the bark.
Light crimson, by birch bark and wood of St. Martha (Nicaragua.)
Same in a half spent bath of the same.
Same with varied proportions.
Rose red, nearly crimson from a decoction of birch bark, brazilletto, and alum.
Less brilliant from brazilletto and alum without birch bark.
More lively and solid by brazilletto, birch bark, alum and cream of tartar, in two successive baths.
Same in the same bath half spent.

129

From Angola wood (Cam wood, the most lively of the woods, *T.C.*) birch bark and alum in the same bath or decoction.

Yellow.

Two dippings in a decoction of the shoots of large leaved privet, *Rhamnus alaternus.*
Jonquil yellow from the straight leaved privet, *Alaternus folio minore.*
From the shoots in leaf of the American arbor vitae, *Thuya occidentalis.*
Jonquil yellow, from the shoots of *Calycanthus floridus,* Carolina alspice foliis internis longioribus.
From two baths of the old wood of acacia.
July-flower yellow, from the bark of the alder: and from the leaves of artichoke.
Bright yellow, from the shoots of *Ceanothus Americanus,* New Jersey tea tree.
Olive yellow, from two baths of Canada bonduc, *Guilandina Dioica.*
July-flower yellow, from the flowers of balsamine.
Dull yellow, from the green shoots of birch.
Bright yellow, from the unripe berry of black alder.
July-flower yellow, from the common heath with tin mordant.
Same with the addition of black alder berries ripe, and dried.
Dull capuchin yellow, from the ripe berries of bryony.
Chamoy yellow, from beech-mast.
Apricot yellow, from alpine chervil, or honeysuckle, *Lonicera.*
Golden yellow, from the male dogwood, *Cornus mas.*
From turmeric, altered by soap.
From the trefoil cytisus.
From fumitory, fresh and dry.
From fustic made solid by birch bark with tin mordant.
From dry weld; better from green weld.
From hairy broom, *Genista pilosa.*
From *Genista tinctoria,* dyers' broom.
Intense olive yellow, from herb Robert, *Geranium Robertianum.*
Jonquil yellow, from furze fresh: and dry.
From the bark of horse chesnut.
Apricot yellow from the bark of black willow, *Salix Caprae*
Olive yellow, from the fresh stalks of buckthorn.
Good yellow, from the Italian aster, starwort, *Aster Amellus.*
Delicate, from the bark of elm, dried black alder berries and buckwheat straw with tin mordant.
From the shoots of yellow osier, *Salix Vitellina.*
Greenish yellow, from fermented pansy, hearts' ease, *Viola tricolor.*
From the larger pusicaria, *Polygonum orientale.*
From the bark and also from the shoots of the Italian poplar, particularly from the fresh shoots with tin mordant.
Another shade with the same and dried berries of black alder. This ingredient is economical and renders other colours solid.
Jonquil yellow, with the black Virginia poplar, tin mordant.
From the fresh plants of common field basil, *Clinopodium vulgare.*
From the bark of pitch pine.
From the shoots of the Indian date plum, Placqueminier, *Diospyros Lotus.*
From the bark of the plane tree.
From the roots of wild apple.

130

From the fresh China aster.

From the Virginia sumach or stagshorn (*Rhus Virginiana.*)

From the fresh flowers of African marygold, *Tagetes erecta.*

From the plants nearly dry of common saw-wort, *Serratula.*

From wild sage.

From the white willow, *Salix alba.*

From thyme.

From the roots of tormentil.

From the fresh plants of yellow trefoil.

From the common golden rod, *Solidago, Virga aurea.*

Wine Lees.

Wool mordanted with a precipitate of alum and tin becomes a deep brown-red in a decoction of bran of sorgho.

Maron. Chesnut.

From the Carolina alspice, *Calycanthus floridus.*

From the bark of common maple.

Deep, from brazil, archil and madder.

From dry hay with madder.

From madder with bismuth mordant.

From beech bark.

From horse chesnut bark, scarlet flowering chesnut, *Esculus octandra.*

Reddish from Italian or Lombardy poplar and madder.

From the dry wood of the apple tree.

From the bran of sorgho, son de sorgho. Millet?

Merd'orè. Goose dung.

From the shoots of the snow drop tree, *Chiananthus Virginiana.*

From the bark of alder.

From the *Aristolochia clematitis*, birthwort.

From the restharrow, *Ononis arvensis.*

From the common southernwood, *Artemisia.*

From the *Cucubalus Behen*, bottle campion.

From the cow wheat, *Melampyrum nemorosum.*

Brilliant, from the black alder berry, with mordant of blue copperas.

Yellowish from terragon, *Artemisia Dracunculus.*

From the *Euphorbia Cyparissas*, a species of spurge.

From the leaves of the fig tree.

From the narrow leaved all-heal, *Galeopsis Ladanum.*

From the cotton weed, *Filago Impia.* Quere cudweed?

From the *Gnafolium silvaticum*, wood everlasting.

From the common red rosebay, *Nerion Oleander.*

From the *Leonurus marubiastrum.* Quere, whether horehound or motherwort?

From ground ivy, *Glecoma Hederacea.*

From black horehound, *Manubium nigrum.*

After long boiling from common field basil, *Clinopodium vulgare.*

From marsh horehound, with small leaves, *Lycopus palustris glaber.*

From the Siberian plum, *Prunus Sibirica.*

From wild sage.

From stalks and leaves of rue.

131

From the shoots of *Rhus coriaria,* true sumach.
Rich colour from the shoots of the *Sambucus racemosa,* or scarlet berried alder.

Mordorè.

From the straight leaved privet, *Rhamnus alaternus;* three dippings.
Light, from the shoots of alder with a little madder.
From the bark and shoots of *Crataegus oxiacantha,* haw-thorn or white thorn.
From the shoots of Christ's thorn, *Algalon, Paliurus aculeatus rhamnus.*
From cinquefoil, *Potentilla anscrina,* the leaves.
Mordorè chesnut, from the whole plant.
Almost purple, from the shoots and bark of the birch tree with archil, which is fixed thereby.
From dried black alder berries and a little madder.
Beautiful from the shoots of the flowering Virginia hornbeam, *Carpinus Virginiana florescens.*
From dried hay with madder; the decoction somewhat acidulated.
Rich, from the common broom, *Spartium scoparium,* with bismuth.
Better still, with a mordant of tin.
From the shoots of the common or cherry laurel, *Prunus lauro-cerasus.*
Light colour from Luzerne (*medica*) and madder.
From the bark of horse chesnut, *Aesculus hypocastanum.*
From a half spent bath of *Salix capraea,* black willow.
From the dried shoots of buck thorn, *Rhamnus catharticus.*
From the bark of elm.
From the shoots of yellow osier, *Salix Vitellina.*
From the Italian poplar, with a little madder in the bath when nearly spent; the cloth mordanted with blue copperas.
From Italian poplar, brazil of Fernambouca, and dried black alder berries.
From the bark of pitch pine.
From the fresh bark of Geneva pine, Scotch pine, *Pinus sylvestris.*
From the coloured heart of the wood of the cultivated plum, *Prunus domestica,* hedge plum or white bullace?
From the fresh shoots of *Pyracantha.*
From the ripe berries of the bramble, *Rubus fruticosus.* (Common blackberry.)

Musk.

From the half spent decoction of the large leaved privet.
From the *Thuya Canadensis,* American arbor vitae.
From the *Thuya Sinensis,* Chinese arbor vitae.
From a third dipping in decotion of Carolina alspice, *Calycanthus floridus.*
From the shoots of the poison tree *Rhus toxicodendron.*
From the wood of the *Acacia,* in a strong dose.
From the flowers of *althaea frutex, Hybiscus Syriacus.*
From the branches of *Crataegus torminalis,* wild service.
From the ripe stalks of agrimony.
From the shells of the apricot kernel.
Musk-cinnamon, from the shoots of bilberry, *Vaccinium myrtillus.*
From the common bladder sena, *Colutea arborescens.*
Chesnut musk, from the flowers of *Balsamine,* with blue copperas.
Golden, from roots of common avens, *Geum urbanum.*

132

From betony.

From roots of bistort.

From wood of red mezereon, *Daphne mezereon.*

From the shoots of black birch, *Betula nigra.*

From the fine-leaved heath, *Erica cinerea.*

From the roots of asarabacca, *Azuram Europaeum.*

From the lesser Indian cress, *Tropaeolum minus.*

From black currants.

From chesnut bark.

From comfrey, *Symphytum officinale.*

From the dogwood of New Holland, and of Virginia.

From common cyprus.

From the *Dierilla acadiensis.*

From the fruit of the sloe or black thorn, *Prunus sylvestris.*

From Dutch or hemp agrimony, *Eupatorium cannabinum.*

Rich, from the green shoots of Venice sumach, *Rhus cotinus.*

Light, from the nettle hemp, *Galeopsis tetrahit.*

From a weak bath of *Genista pilosa.*

From the large flowering geranium, bloody crane's bill, *Geranium sanguineum.* Also from *Geranium Robertianum.*

Beautiful, from the dwarf cistus, *Cistus helyanthemum.*

From hawk weed, *Hieracium majus.*

From the shoots of the beech.

From rag wort, *Senecio jacobaea,* and from *Senecio palustris,* or marsh golden rod.

From elecampane, *Inula dysenterica.*

From wild lettuce.

From the broad-leaved sweet bay tree, *Laurus nobilis.*

From the young leafy branches of *Liriodendron tulipfera,* tulip tree.

From yellow toad's flax, *Antirrhinum linaria.*

From the leafy shoots of liquid amber.

From the shoots of the smaller bind weed, *Convolvulus arvensis.*

From the roots of *Lysimachia vulgaris,* loose strife.

From the young leafy branches of horse chesnut, *Aesculus hypocastanum.*

Richer colour, from the scarlet flowering chesnut, *Aesculus octandra pavia.*

From the wood and bark of *Salix capraea,* black willow.

From the leafy shoots of the larch tree, *Pinus larix.*

From the stalks and leaves of water mint, *Mentha aquatica.*

From *Mercurialis annua.*

From the fresh plants of the greater snap dragon, *Antirrhinum majus.*

From the shoots of sweet gale, *Myrica gale.*

From the dry roots of the common nut, (walnut) *Juglans regia.*

From the thick bark of the walnut tree.

From black walnut bark, and from the shoots and leaves, fresh and dry.

From the red fruits of the Guelder rose, *Viburnum opulus.*

From the stalks of common marjoram, *Origanum.*

From the roots of sorrel, *Rumex acetosella.*

From the roots of garden patience, *Rumex patientia.*

———————————bloody dock, *Rumex sanguineus.*

From the Virginian silk, *Periploca graeca.*

From spignel, pasil de montagne, *Athamanta libanotis.*

133

From the barked wood of the Italian poplar.

Beautiful, from fresh pimpernel.

From the shoots of the Indian date plum, *Diospiros lotus.*

From the bark of the plane tree, and from the wood and bark.

From the flowers of piony.

From the mark or pressed fruit of the pear.

From the *Campanula* or bell flower, *Pyramidalis.*

From the double white meadow sweet, *Spiraea ulmaria.*

From the yellow *Ranunculus.*

From the stalks of rosemary.

From a weak decoction of *Tagetus erecta,* African marigold.

From the shoots of the yellow Austrian rose, *Rosa lutea.*

From Spanish sain foin, *Hedasyrum coronarium.*

From the leafy shoots of purple spiked willow herb, *Lythrum salicarlia.*

From the tops of the *Pinus abies,* or fir tree.

From the fresh stalks of buckwheat.

From the stalks of climbing bindweed, *Polygonum scandens.*

From the twining bindweed, *Polygonum convolvulus.*

From the fresh plant of knotty fig wort, *Scrophularia nodosa.*

From the sun flower.

From the dry flowers of the common black elder, and from its berries, fermented and unfermented.

From the dried uncured leaves of tobacco: and from the green leaves.

From the stalks of tansy.

Light musk, from the *Thlaspi aranse,* penny-cross, a kind of shepherd's purse.

From the bark of the roots of tormentil.

From the common native golden rod.

From vervain, *Verbena.*

From vine cuttings.

From the ripe berries of *Sambucus ebulus:* and from the same dried.

Nankin.

From the shoots of the Judas tree, *Circis siliquastrum.*

————————————————rose acacia.

————————————————Italia azedarach, *Melia azedarach.*

————————————————Dutch medlar, *Mespilus inermis.*

From the leafy stalks of agrimony.

From the New Jersey tea tree, apalachine, *Ceanothus Americanus.*

From birch bark.

From ripe cherries.

From the cherries of Zara.

From Dutch or hemp agrimony, *Eupatorium Cannabinum.*

From red gooseberries.

From the flowers of the queen's bean, haricot a la reine, (kidney bean with red flower?) *Phaseolus coccineus.*

From the hairy trefoil, *Lotus hirsutus, or hemorrhoidalis.*

From the European nettle tree, *Celtis australis.*

From the wood of an orange tree.

From the kernel of peaches.

From the bark of all the poplars.

134

From the barked wood of the Scotch pine, *Pinus sylvestris.*
From the shoots of the double cinnamon rose, *Rosa Cinnamomea.*
From the barked wood of the willow.
From the shoots of the mountain ash, *Sorbus occuparia.*
From the Guelder rose, *Spircea opulifolia.*

Hazle-nut Colour (*Noisette.*)

From the shoots of button wood, *Cephalanthus occidentalis.*
From the bilberry or whortle-berry, *Vaccinium myrthyllus.*
From common avens, *Geum urbanum.*
From the catalpa.
From the dry white birch, *Betula alba.*
From fresh common heath, *Erica vulgaris.*
From the evergreen box tree, *Buxus sempervirens.*
From the cones of the pitch pine, *Pinus maritima.*
From the red bark of the roots of the male dogwood or cornelian cherry.
Cornus mas, reddish hazle colour.
From the barked wood of the same.
From the mixture of laburnum and ptaelea.
From the roots of the black thorn or sloe, *Prunus sylvestis.*
Hazle-nankin, from the wood of the common maple, *Acer campestre.*
From dry hay, and madder acidulated.
From the bark of the spindle tree, *Eronymus Europaeus.*
From the wood of the juniper.
From the shoots of the red currant tree, *Ribes rubrum.*
From the dry wood of the yew.
From the fresh barked wood of the sallow or black willow, *Salix Capraea.*
From the wood of the laurustinus, *Viburnumtinus.*
From the wood of the buckthorn, *Rhamnus catharticus.*
From the shoots of the Persian or narrow-leaved wild olive, *Eleagnus angustifolia.*
From the barked wood of the elm.
From the flowers of the common purple orpine, *Sedum telephium.*
From the black poppy, *Papaver nigrum.*
From the wood of all the poplars.
From the leaves of pitch pine, *Pinus sylvestris.*
From dried plums, and from the black grape.
From the shoots of sea buck-thorn, *Hippophae Rhamnoides.*
From the African rag wort, *Othonna cheirifolia.*
From the green barked lime tree, *Tilia Europaea.*
From the roots of tormentil.

Olive.

From the stalks of wormwood, *Artemisia absynthium.*
From the fresh stalks of the silk plant, swallow-wort, *Asclepias Syriaca*, or *Apocynum*, Syrian dog's bane.
From cow wheat, *Milampyrum nemorosum.*
From the green shoots of the black alder, *Rhamnus franguld*, with green vitriol: and from the roots of the same plant.
Green olive, from the ripe plants of *Bromus tectorum*, broom grass.
From common self heal, *Prunella vulgaris.*

135

From the poplar with logwood.

From the scabious leaved centaury, or common knap weed, *Centaurea scabiosa*.

From the toadstool, *Boletus viscidus*.

From the Germander, *Teucrium chamaedris*.

From the flowers of meadow saffron, *Colchicum autumnale*.

From the branches of common hazel, *Corglus avellana*.

From the hairy evergreen laburnum or trefoil tree, *Cytisus hirsutus*.

From the dried husks of the common bean, *Vicia faba*.

From a weak bath of green weld, *Reseda luteola*.

————— *Geranium moschatum*.

From winter cresses, or rocket, *Erisimum barbarea*.

From common knap weed, *Centaurea nigra*.

From the ripe stalks of drop wort, *Aenanthe pimpinelloides*.

From the ripe berries of ground ivy.

From mercurialis, French mercury, fermented.

From the bark of the branches of the walnut, *Juglans regia*.

From the roots of water patience, *Rumex aquatica*, particularly with solution of iron.

From the leaves of black poppy, *Papaver nigrum*.

From pansy, or heart's ease, *Viola tricolor*, fermented and unfermented.

From fresh shoots of the poplar, with nine grains of logwood.

More intense by doubling the logwood.

From the poplar, redyed in wine of the berries of *Rhamnus frangula*, and in the dried berries of the same.

Ombre, or Brownish Yellow: ground for Carmelite.

From two dippings in the straight-leaved privet, *Alaternus*.

From the shoots of the southernwood, *Artemisia absynthium*.

From the shoots of the common alder, *Betula alnus*.

From the twigs of *Celastrus scandens*, climbing staff tree.

From the lesser centaury.

From the scabious leaved centaury.

From the roots of celandine, *Chelidonium majus*.

From virgin's bower, *Clematis vitalba*.

From the three leaved cytisus.

From the dog rose, *Rosa canina*.

From the shoots of scorpion sena, *Coronilla emerus*.

From fennel, *Anethum faeniculum*.

From Spanish broom, *Spartium junceum*.

From the bear's-foot hellebore, *Helleborus faetidus*.

From the cotton weed, *Filago arvensis*.

From the *Erysimum officinale*, sauce alone? Hedge mustard?

From the wood of the ivy, *Hedera helix*.

From the dry wood of the laylock or lilac, *Syringa vulgaris*.

From the leafy stalks of common loose-strife, *Lysimachia vulgaris*.

From the melilot, *Melilotus officinalis; trifolium*. (The seeds of this plant ground and mixed with curd, give the colour and the flavour to the shap-zugar, or sapsago cheese, as I know. *T. C.*)

From the half spent decoction of the olive tree.

From the wood of the black mulberry, *Morus nigra*.

From the shoots of the orange tree, and the skin (ecorce) of ripe oranges.

136

From the stalks and leaves of the *Palma Christi.*
From *Scandix pecten veneris.*
From the pansy: and the pansy of Rouen, *Viola Rothomagensis.*
From the white meadow sweet, *Spiraea ulmaria.*
From the bramble roots, *Rubus fruticosus,* black-berry.
From savory, *Satureia hortensis.*
From the evergreen golden rod, *Solidago semper virens.*
From the shoots of the common black elder, *Sambucus nigra.*
From soot.
From the shoots of the red bark tamarisk, *Tamarix gallica.*
From the feathered columbine, *Thalictrum Aquilegi folium.*
From the small yellow trefoil, *Trifolium luteum flore lupuli.*
From fresh red clover, *Trifolium rubens pratense.*
From the Canada golden rod, *Solidago.*
From the ivy-leaved speedwell, *Veronica hederifolia.*
Better from the same with bismuth.

Purple.

From brazil wood fixed by birch bark, with tin mordant.

Plum.

From the fresh and dry berries of the black alder, *Rhamnus frangula.*
From birch bark and logwood.
From bran of millet, sorgho.

Ronce d'Artois, Artois Bramble.

From the stalks and leaves of stinking orach, *Chenopodium vulvaria.*
From the plant balsamine.
From a weak bath of fermented berries of black alder: also from the dried berries.
From the plant of stinking chamomile, *Anthemis cotula.*
From myrrh, (sweet scented myrrh) *Scandix odorata.*
From the leaves of the large oblong citron, *Citrus medica.*
From the lesser hemlock or fool's parsley, *Othusa cynapium.*
From spinach, *Spinacea oleracea.*
From spurge, *Euphorbia palustris.*
From the leafy stalks of tythy malle, *Euphorbia cyperisasis,* Euphorbia tythy malliodes, Curassao-myrtle spurge.
From the weak decoction of green weld.
From the yellow everlasting pea, *Lathyrus aphaca.*
From the bark of the European nettle tree, *Celtis australis.*
From shoots of poplar, with dried berries of black alder.
From wild germander, *Veronica chamaedris.*

Rose.

From the purple kidney bean. Haricots d'espagne. *Phaseolus purpureus.*
———— spotted kidney bean, *Phaseolus rufus variegatus.*
From wild germander, *Veronica chamaedris.*
From the roots of the greater bindweed, *Convolvulus sepium.*
From the archil of the Canaries reddened by acids.

Red.

From the roots of the red ladies bed straw, *Gallium verum*.

From the Portugal cross, *Cruciata, Lusitanica, latifolia, glabra, flore, albo*.

The two preceding equal to madder.

Chesnut red, from madder and sumach.

Purple red with madder, after mordanting with bismuth and galling.

Scarlet red from fine madder: rose red from the same, with mordant containing one-eighth of tin.

More fiery from Cyprus, Smyrna, or Lizari madder.

From the flowers of *Glaucium*.

Several other varieties of red from madder with different mordants.

Ventre de crapaud (toad's belly). Ground for Carmelite.

From the branches of the varnish tree, *Rhus vernix*.

From the goat's rue-leaved vetch, *Astragalus galegi formis*. Milk vetch?

From bastard or wild indigo, *Amorpha fruticosa*.

From shepherd's purse, *Thlaspi, Bursa pastoris*.

From flea bean, *Conyza squanosa*.

From the shoots and leaves of holly, *Ilex aquifolium*.

From the wood of furze, (jonc marin) *Ulex Europaea*.

From white horehound, *Manubium vulgare*.

From the basil called *Thymus acinos*.

From savory, *Satureia hortensis*.

Ventre de Biche (literally Doe's belly) Tan Colour.

From the wood of *Althaea*.

From the bark of young oak.

From Alpine ebony, *Cytisus laburnum*.

From the bark of common broom, *Spartium scoparium*.

From the shoots of the three-thorned acacia, *Gleditsia triacanthos*.

From common lettuce, *Lactuca sativa*.

From the shoots of sophora.

Green.

From the ripe, and from the fermented berries of black alder.

From the bark of the common ash, *Fraxinus excelsior*.

From Italian poplar on a blue ground, mordanted with bismuth.

From the flowers of the violet.

Vigogna, (colour of Vigogna wool.)

From the shoots of the Siberian acacia.

From the dry shoots of the elder.

From the leaves of artichoke.

From rest harrow, *Ononis arvensis*.

From wild angelica, *Angelica sylvestris*.

From tuberose crowfoot, *Ranunculus bulbosus*.

From common bladder sena, *Colutea arborescens*.

From flowers of balsamine.

From the water parsnip, *Sium latifolium*.

From *Gallium verum*, lady's bedstraw.

From the round leaved bell flower, *Campanula rotundifolia*.

From the sea holly with pinnated cut leaves, *Eryngium campestre*.

138

From the blue berried upright honeysuckle, *Lonicera caerulea.*
From the common hedge honeysuckle, *Lonicera periclimenum.*
From the pasque flower, *Anemone pulsatilla.*
From the seven leaved colutea, *Coronilla glauca.*
From the branches of the fig tree, *Ficus carica.*
From the rose flowering raspberry, *Rubus odoratus.*
From the barked wood of the common ash, *Fraxinus excelsior.*
From the heart of the common broom, *Spartium scoparium.*
From the yellow everlasting pea, *Lathyrus aphaca.*
From the *Valantia aparine.*
From the thorny hedge gooseberry, *Uva crispa.*
From the dwarf cistus, *Cistus helianthemum.*
From catmint, *Nepeta cataria.*
From the stalks of knee-holly or butcher's broom, *Ruscus aculeatus.*
From the shoots of white jessamin, *Jasminum officinale.*
From sow-thistle, *Sonchus oleraceus.*
From *Sonchus maximus plumerii,* Japonese thistle.
From wild lettuce, *Lactuca scariola.*
From common lettuce, *Lactuca sativa,* with tin mordant.
From the young branches of the laylock or lilac.
From the hay of Luzerne, *Medica.*
From the *Lychen prunasti.*
From the lesser snap dragon, *Antirrhinum Orontium.*
From sweet myrtle, *Myrica gale.*
From Dutch medlar, *Mespilus Germanica.*
From the shoots of buckthorn, *Rhamnus catharticus.*
From the dried shells of walnuts, *Juglans regia.*
From elm bark with tin.
From the French willow, narrow leaves, red flowers, *Epilobium angustifolium.*
From the dry straw of wheat.
From the stalks of parsnip, *Pastinacea sativa.*
From the vines of the *Vinca major,* Periwinkle.
From all the poplars.
From bark of the plane tree.
From China aster, Aster Sinensis.
From knot grass, *Polygonum aviculare.*
From green sain foin, *Hedasyrum onobrychis.*
From scorzonera.
From the flowers, &c. of common elder, *Sambucus nigra.*
From the bark of sycamore.
From the stalks of *Thalictrum.*
From the shoots of common lime tree, *Tilia Europaea.*
From the roots of upright tormentil, *Tormentilla erecta.*
From common privet, *Ligustrum vulgare.*
From the shoots of the wayfaring tree, *Viburnum lantana.*
From viper's bugloss, *Echium vulgare.*

Violet.

From logwood fixed by birch bark, with bismuth mordant, of various shades: and also with tin mordant.
From the skins of the fruit of *Uva crispa.*

Appendix E

Excerpt from Cornelius Molony, *The practical dyer*. Boston: 1833, pp. 41–59. The following recipes produced the colors seen on the frontispiece. Although color photography and printing processes cannot reproduce the exact colors of Molony's wool swatches, the frontispiece gives a good idea of the wide range of lively, rich colors achieved by this 19th-century craftsman.

The recipes reveal a great deal about the craftsman's methods of working, as well as the actual ingredients he combined.

RECEIPTS FOR WOOLLEN GOODS

Woollen goods, of all descriptions, ought to be well cleansed from oil or grease, and thoroughly wet, going into the dyeing kettle.

Pattern No. 1. *Stone Drab.*

50 lbs. weight.
Use the strength of 1 lb. of fustick, 1 lb. of red tartar (argil); bring the liquor to 150 degrees of heat; enter the goods, turn briskly on poles for 7 turns; then, if you see it necessary, bring the kettle to a greater heat; then turn the worsted or woollen yarn one turn every five minutes, until you come almost to a conclusion; lift up or take out the yarn; use a few drops of chemic (sulphate of indigo . . .) very cautiously, observing to cool the liquor with water every time the chemic is used. Done.

When I mention the proportions of dye drugs for any given quantity of goods, it signifies that these Patterns can be produced and done on the same principle, or method; but I do not pretend to say that the same quantity of drugs, &c. will always produce the shade according to the numbered pattern, as the strength of dye drugs varies so materially, and the different coarse and fine goods will have so different an affinity for the dye drugs, as to alter the shade materially. The difference of wove goods from carpet yarn, with regard to the quantity of dye drugs necessary for producing the colours, will also vary materially, so that the practical workman must use his own skill in order to come exactly to his pattern. These patterns of goods were dyed on the exact principle and quantity of drugs as stated; they are true methods of producing these colours. The methods are so simple, that, acting with caution, every shade of these colours can be easily obtained by any dyer of common abilities.

Pattern No. 2. *Light Drab.*

Of 50 lb. wt.

Bring the kettle to 120 degrees for this shade. First put in 1 lb. of red tartar, ground; then enter the yarn; observing that 1 lb. of fustick and 6 oz. of camwood will produce the colour, by using one half of the quantity in the kettle before you enter the goods. Turn all colours briskly for 7 turns; then allow 5 minutes' interval between the turns. This is a regular system, practised on carpet yarn.

Lift out the carpet yarn. There ought to be bearers over every kettle on which to hang the yarn, when you take it out, so as to be high enough to keep the yarn from reaching into the kettles. When you think the dye stuff is well nigh spent, take out. Put in the remainder of the dye stuff; bring the kettle to 170 degrees of heat, put in the yarn, handle until deep enough; add or diminish the drugs as you see necessary, the quality of drugs, as I have already observed, being very different.

Pattern No. 3.

50 pounds weight.

This colour is dyed on the same method as No. 2, by using 1 lb. of red tartar, 24 ozs. of camwood, 1 lb. of ground fustick. Enter the goods in the kettle 140 degrees of heat; handle 7 turns, then a turn every 5 minutes.

In dyeing either drab worsted yarn or wove cloth, do not use or put in all the drugs at once, for fear of your shade being uneven. When the drugs already used are almost on the goods, use the other half; keep in until deep enough. I do not wish to allow the kettle to boil with the yarn in it for any light drab.

Pattern No. 4. *Red Drab.*

50 lbs. weight.

Put in the dye drugs at 140 degrees, which is a regular standard heat to enter drabs, or 150 at most. 1 lb. of red tartar, 44 ozs. of camwood, 24 ozs. of fustick.

Enter but half the drugs for the first 30 minutes. Lift up on the bearers; then put in the other half, and heat up the kettle according as the colour requires.

Pattern No. 5. *Mazarine Blue.*

Of 50 lbs. weight.

Bring the kettle to 120 degrees of heat, use about a pint of sulphate of indigo and 8 ozs. of sulphuric acid, both together; handle at that heat 7 turns. Heat up to 150 degrees; take out; run off the liquor; fill the kettle with clean water; bring up to a boil; then put in 1 lb. of ground logwood; wash or rinse the yarn in cold water; put it on the poles over the kettle; cool the liquor, and use about half a pint of No. 2 tin liquor, as is used for logwood purple cotton spirit. Stir up the liquor, go 7 turns; if deep enough, take out.

Pattern No. 6. *Light Drab.*

50 lbs. of this light drab. Enter the dye stuff at 100 degrees of heat. Use 1 lb. of red tartar; 4 ozs. of fustick, and 4 ozs. of good madder. Enter the goods, go 7 turns; lift out;

141

put in 4 ozs. more of madder, and 4 ozs. more of fustick; handle until deep enough, and heat the kettle up much hotter, if the colour goes on slowly.

Pattern No. 7. *Drab.*

50 lbs. weight.

Bring the kettle to a boil; put in 40 ozs. of fustick, 8 ozs. of sumach; boil 20 minutes; cool down; enter the yarn; handle briskly for 7 turns, then turn every five minutes; bring the liquor to 170 degrees of heat; take a thread of the yarn out, and dissolve a very little copperas, and dip the thread into it, and if the shade does not appear almost deep enough, add a little more fustick, and handle until you have body enough of colour; take out, and sadden with about 6 ozs. of copperas.

Pattern No. 8. *Crimson.*

50 lbs. weight.

Bring the kettle to a boil, and put in 2¾ lbs. of cochineal of good quality, boil it 20 minutes, then cool down the liquor, put in 3 lbs. of cream of tartar, 3 lbs. of alum, also 2 quarts of No. 4 cochineal tin liquor. Enter the goods, bring the kettle to a boil as speedy as possible, and continue the boil 90 minutes; take out, empty the kettle, get up a kettle of water 140 degrees of heat, use some pearlash or urine to blue the colour to the pattern; handle very briskly; rinse in cold water, and done.

Pattern No. 9. *Brown Olive.*

50 lbs. of yarn.

Boil up 16 lbs. of fustick, 1 lb. of logwood, 4 lbs. of common madder, 2 lbs. of camwood; cool the liquor, enter the yarn, bring the liquor to a boil, then turn the yarn 6 or 8 turns, then a turn every 5 minutes; continue boiling 1 hour, take out, cool the liquor; dissolve come copperas, and put in about 1 lb. Put in the yarn handle until deep enough. I advise all dyers to try how a thread of the yarn will sadden, before they put in the copperas.

Pattern No. 10. *Yellow.*

50 lbs. weight.

Bring the kettle to 180 degrees of heat, put in 4 lb. of quer-citron, or yellow oak bark, do not allow it to boil, as the tanning matter will come out if it does boil, which would dull the colour very much. Put in 2 lbs. of alum, 1 lb. of cream of tartar, 1 quart of No. 2 tin liquor . . . ; rake up the liquor well, allow it to settle 15 minutes, enter the yarn, keep it in until deep enough.

Pattern No. 11. *Yellow.*

50 lbs. weight.

The ingredients for this yellow are the same as those of Pattern No. 10, except by using 1 lb. more (that is, 5 lb.) of quer-citron bark, 2 lb. of alum, 1 quart of tin liquor; use no tartar, as tartar serves to green the colour which is very necessary for light shades of yellow.

142

Pattern No. 12. *Orange.*

50 lbs. weight.

First dye this pattern a full yellow up to pattern No. 11, then run off the liquor out of the kettle, fill it with clear water, put a fire to the kettle; when it gets a little warm, put in 4 lbs. of mungeete, keep heating the kettle, and continue turning until deep enough.

Pattern No. 13. *Orange.*

Of 50 lbs. weight.

Is dyed the same as the No. 12 orange. Orange, dyed this way, is a fast colour to a certainty.

Pattern No. 14. *Fast Red.*

50 lbs. weight. Boil up 20 lbs. camwood 15 minutes, cool the liquor a little, put in 1 lb. of sulphuric acid, enter the goods, turn briskly for 7 turns, then one turn for every five minutes. Continue boiling one hour, take out, cool the liquor a little, put in two pints of No. 2 tin liquor cotton spirit . . . ; go 7 ends; done.

Pattern No. 15. *Green.*

50 lbs. weight. Boil up 25 lbs. of fustick, 5 lbs. of alum, cool the kettle a little with a few pails of water, then put in a pint and a half of sulphate of indigo, rake up well, enter the yarn or worsted, bring up to a boil, turn the goods carefully, continue boiling 1 hour, take out, and, if not blue enough, use a little more sulphate of indigo; handle until deep enough. Rinse in cold water.

Pattern No. 16. *Lilach.*

50 lbs. weight. Boil up the kettle and put in 12 lbs. of archil; cool the liquor a little, enter the yarn or cloth, handle carefully until deep enough; you need not boil the goods in the liquor.

Pattern No. 17. *Lilach.*

This is done the same way by using less archil; rinse in cold water when dyed.

Pattern No. 18. *Clothier's Drab.*

50 lbs. weight.

Bring the kettle to a boil, then put in 2 lbs. of red tartar, 2 lbs. of madder, 2 lbs. of fustick, boil the goods until you have colour enough on, take out, put in 8 ozs. of copperas, enter the goods, handle until deep enough, done.

Pattern No. 19. *Claret.*

50 lbs. weight.

Boil up twenty pounds of camwood for fifteen minutes, cool a little, put in 24 oz. of sulphuric acid, enter the goods, turn briskly 7 turns, then a turn every five minutes; bring

143

the kettle to a boil, continue boiling the cloth 1 hour, take it out, rinse well at the river, or in a great supply of cold water. Rinse the kettle with cold water, observing to rinse with a little wood ashes or urine, to master the acid; then fill up the kettle with clear water, dissolve 9 lbs. of sulphate of iron in hot water, put it into the kettle; when the kettle is nearly warm, enter the goods, make up a good fire, turn the goods, and continue the fire; keep turning until deep enough. There is no colour faster on woollen goods than this claret.

Pattern No. 20. *Lavender.*

50 lbs. weight. Bring the kettle to a boil, put in 12 ozs. of cudbear, 24 ozs. of logwood, enter the goods, handle them well, boil 30 minutes; observe to use 3 lbs. of archil with the logwood and cudbear. Take the goods out, and put in 8 ozs. of copperas, 8 ozs. of sulphate of copper; rake up well, handle until deep enough.

Pattern No. 21. *Brown.*

50 lbs. weight. Boil 20 lbs. of camwood, 7 lbs. of fustick, cool the liquor a little, enter the goods, turn briskly 7 turns, then a turn every five minutes; bring up to a boil, continue boiling two hours, then take out the goods, and dissolve 4 or 5 lbs. of copperas and 3 lbs. of red tartar, cool the liquor to 120 degrees of heat, enter the goods, handle until deep enough. This is a good clothier's brown, as no colour can be more permanent.

Pattern No. 22. *Green Olive.*

50 lbs. weight. Boil up 12 lbs. of fustick, 3 lbs. of logwood, cool the liquor a little, enter the goods, handle briskly 7 turns, then a turn every five minutes, as usual; bring the kettle to a boil, and continue boiling 1 hour, take out, and put in 2 lbs. of copperas and 8 oz. of sulphate of copper, cool the liquor a little, handle until dark enough.

Pattern No. 23. *Deep Lilach, or Light Purple.*

50 lbs. weight. Bring the kettle to boil, put in 4 lbs. of logwood, 2 lbs. of alum, boil 10 minutes, cool the liquor, enter the goods, handle well, bring to a boil, continue the boil one hour, take out the goods, cool the kettle, put in half a pint of No. 3 tin liquor for cotton purple . . . , enter the goods, go 7 turns, do not boil.

Pattern No. 24. *Dark Prune.*

50 lbs. weight. Boil 7 lbs. of logwood and 2 lbs. of camwood in the kettle, cool down a little, enter the yarn or cloth, handle briskly, boil it one hour, turning it occasionally as usual, take it out, dissolve 5 lbs. of copperas in hot water, put it in the kettle, enter the yarn, handle until deep enough, rinse well in cold water.

Pattern No. 25. *Peachwood Red.*

50 lbs. weight. Boil the goods 2 hours in 8 lbs. of alum, 2 lbs. of red tartar, do not rinse from that preparation; boil up 18 lbs. of peachwood in clean water, boil 10 minutes, cool to 190 degrees of heat on the thermometer, use 8 ozs. of No. 2 tin liquor cotton spirit . . . ; enter the yarn, handle until deep enough.

144

Pattern No. 26. *Dark Slate.*

50 lbs. weight of carpet yarn.

Boil up forty ounces of logwood, four ounces of cudbear, four ounces of alum, boil it in the dye kettle 15 minutes, cool the liquor with 5 or 6 pails of water, enter the goods, handle briskly, bring the kettle to a boil, and continue boiling and turning 1 hour, take out the goods, dissolve 1 lb. of copperas in boiling water, put it in the kettle, cool the liquor, enter the goods, handle until deep enough of colour. Rinse all wool colours in cold water.

———

Pattern No. 27. *Mazarine Blue.*

50 lbs. weight. Use chemick or sulphate of indigo to a light blue, in the water in the dye kettle, at 150 degrees of heat, run off the liquor, fill up the dye kettle with clean water, bring it up to a boil, put in 20 ozs. of logwood, 8 ozs. of No 2 tin liquor for cotton; observe to boil the logwood 15 minutes before the tin liquor is put in; cool the liquor with water, enter the yarn, turn until deep enough.

———

Pattern No. 28. *Milk Chocolate.*

50 lbs. weight. Boil up 2 lbs. of fustick, 1 lb. of cudbear, 4 ozs. of logwood, cool the liquor in the kettle, enter the goods, turn briskly 1 hour, observing to bring the kettle to a boil, and keep in until deep enough; then darken to shade with 1 lb. of copperas. Observe to take out the yarn before you put in the copperas.

———

Pattern No. 29. *Pink.*

50 pounds weight.

Bring the kettle to a boil; put in 9 ozs. of cochineal, 18 oz. of cream of tartar, 4 ozs. of alum, 2 pints of No. 4 tin liquor for cochineal scarlet, boil all together 20 minutes, take the yarn and put it on large round poles, cool the kettle, turn in the yarn, handle it as usual. Bring the kettle to a boil; boil the yarn 90 minutes, take out, get up a kettle of hot water, and put about a pound of dissolved pearl-ash into it. Rinse the yarn in cold water, and put it in the kettle of warm water, that the pearl-ash is in; turn briskly; if it is not blue enough to the pattern, use a little more pearl-ash in the water to blue it.

———

Pattern No. 30. *Pink.*

This pattern is done exactly the same as Pattern No. 29, with the small difference of not blueing it in hot water and pearl-ash.

———

Pattern No. 31. *Pink.*

Is done exactly the same as the other pink patterns, with the difference to use 2 ozs. less cochineal, and the difference in not blueing it in hot water and pearlash.

———

Pattern No. 32. *Brown Olive.*

50 lbs. weight.

Boil sixteen pounds of fustick, three pounds of crust madder, 2 lbs. of barwood, 1 lb. of logwood, 2 lbs. of sumach; boil the dye stuff in the kettle 20 minutes, cool down,

145

enter the yarn, turn briskly 7 turns, then a turn every 5 minutes; bring the liquor to a boil, and continue turning 90 minutes; cool the liquor, take out, and put 3 lbs. of dissolved copperas in the liquor; enter again, turn seven or eight turns; if not deep enough, use more copperas.

Pattern No. 33. *Crimson.*

50 lbs. weight. Boil up 8 lbs. of alum, 2 lbs. of red tartar, 1 lb. of sulphate of copper, all in the kettle together; boil the yarn in that liquor 3 hours, take it out, and, if you can allow it to remain 4 or 5 days without colouring, it will be a better colour. Put the yarn into a barrel and cover it with coarse cloths to keep every part of it from drying; do not rinse it from the preparation. Then boil up 20 lbs. of good peachwood; cool to 190 degrees of heat, enter, turn for 40 minutes. If not deep enough, use more peachwood, and blue to pattern with urine in a warm kettle.

Pattern No. 34. *Yellow.*

50 lbs. weight of carpet yarn.

Bring the dyeing kettle to one hundred and ninety degrees of heat; put in 3 lbs. of quercitron bark (yellow oak bark), also 2 lbs. of alum, and 1 lb. of cream of tartar, two pints of No. 2 tin liquor; stir up all together with a large rake or stick; allow the bark to settle 15 minutes, then cool the liquor; enter the yarn, handle until deep enough. If the colour is not deep enough, use more bark, but do not allow the bark to boil. When bark boils, the colour assumes a brown appearance, owing to the tanning matter naturally boiling out.

Pattern No. 35. *Light Blue.*

50 lbs. weight. Bring a kettle of water to 110 degrees of heat, and put in 8 oz. of sulphuric acid, and use a little sulphate of indigo by degrees, until the colour is full enough. Do not allow the kettle to exceed 120 degrees of heat; if you make your liquor any hotter, the colour will assume a greenish appearance.

Refined sulphate of indigo will dye the brightest light blues. If you dye light blue with sulphate of indigo refined, observed to use alum instead of sulphuric acid. By dyeing with sulphate of refined indigo, you may heat your liquor to 170 degrees without any green appearance.

Pattern No. 36. *Common Pink.*

50 lbs. weight. Boil the yarn 2 hours in 5 lbs. of alum, and 1 lb. of orgil, (some dyers term it red tartar,) then boil up about 10 lbs. of peachwood; continue boiling 20 minutes, cool the liquor to 160 degrees of heat, enter the yarn in the kettle, handle until deep enough; observe to put in about 6 oz. of No. 3 tin liquor.

Pattern No. 37. *Beet Root.*

50 lbs. weight. Bring the kettle to a boil, put in 3 lbs. of good cochineal, ground fine in a mill like a coffee mill, and 3 lbs. of cream of tartar, and two quarts of Tin Liquor No. 4, and three lbs. of alum; boil all together 20 minutes, cool the liquor; enter the yarn; turn

briskly 7 turns, then a turn every 5 minutes; commence boiling and continue boiling 90 minutes, take out, rinse the yarn in cold water; bring up a kettle of hot water to 110 degrees of heat, and put in 5 or 6 pails of urine; handle until blue enough. Pearlash will also blue the colour.

———

Pattern No. 38. *Lac Scarlet.*

50 pounds weight.
Boil up 6¼ lbs. of the best lac dye, 3 lbs. of cream of tartar, and 3 lbs. of red tartar; boil 20 minutes; cool the liquor; boil up 8 oz. of quer-citron bark with the other drugs; then put in 6 pints of No. 1 Lac Spirit; enter the yarn; turn as usual; bring the kettle to a boil, and continue boiling one hour. Rinse very well in cold water.

———

Pattern No. 39. *Light Blue.*

50 pounds weight.
Bring the kettle to 110 degrees of heat, and put in 8 ozs. of sulphuric acid; use about a pint of sulphate of indigo; rake up the kettle; enter the yarn; do not allow the heat to exceed 120 degrees. If not deep enough, use a little more sulphate of indigo.

———

Pattern No. 40. *Dark Brown, or Damson Colour.*

50 pounds weight.
Boil 20 lbs. of camwood for 20 minutes; cool the kettle, and put in 1 lb. of oil of vitriol; enter the goods; turn in the usual way; bring the kettle to a boil, and continue boiling and turning the yarn one hour; take it out, and rinse well in cold water. Bring in another kettle of hot water; put in 9 lbs. of copperas; enter the goods; bring on the kettle to a strong heat; handle until deep enough.

———

Pattern 41. *Scarlet.*

50 pounds weight of yarn.
Boil up 3 lbs. of cochineal, well ground and sifted; 6 lbs. of cream of tartar; and 1 lb. of citron bark. Cool down the liquor; then put in 5 pints of No. 4 Tin Liquor. Enter the goods; turn briskly 7 turns, then a turn every 5 minutes. Bring the kettle to a boil, and continue boiling and turning two hours. Rinse well in cold water.

———

It would add very much to the beauty of lac or cochineal colours to cleanse the yarn or cloth with fullers' earth, when dyed.

———

Pattern No. 42. *Sage Drab.*

50 pounds weight of yarn.
Boil up 3 lbs. of fustick, 2 lbs. of sumach, 8 ozs. of nutgalls. Allow these drugs to boil half an hour. Cool the liquor; enter the yarn; go 7 turns; bring the kettle to 180 degrees

147

of heat; handle until you obtain body enough of colour. If not green enough, use a little more powdered or ground nutgalls; take out; put in about 1 lb. of copperas, observing to cool the liquor.

Pattern No. 43. *Claret.*

50 lbs. weight of yarn.

Boil the yarn 2 hours in 9 lbs. of alum, 2 lbs. of red tartar; do not rinse in water: boil up a kettle with 20 lbs. of peachwood and 3 lbs. of logwood; cool the liquor to 180 degrees of heat; handle or turn until deep enough; take out; use 3 or 4 pails of urine; go 5 turns.

INDEX

149

151

A CATALOGUE OF
SELECTED DOVER BOOKS
IN ALL FIELDS OF INTEREST

A CATALOGUE OF SELECTED DOVER BOOKS IN ALL FIELDS OF INTEREST

CELESTIAL OBJECTS FOR COMMON TELESCOPES, T. W. Webb. The most used book in amateur astronomy: inestimable aid for locating and identifying nearly 4,000 celestial objects. Edited, updated by Margaret W. Mayall. 77 illustrations. Total of 645pp. 5⅜ x 8½.
20917-2, 20918-0 Pa., Two-vol. set **$10.00**

HISTORICAL STUDIES IN THE LANGUAGE OF CHEMISTRY, M. P. Crosland. The important part language has played in the development of chemistry from the symbolism of alchemy to the adoption of systematic nomenclature in 1892. ". . . wholeheartedly recommended,"—Science. 15 illustrations. 416pp. of text. 5⅝ x 8¼. **63702-6 Pa. $7.50**

BURNHAM'S CELESTIAL HANDBOOK, Robert Burnham, Jr. Thorough, readable guide to the stars beyond our solar system. Exhaustive treatment, fully illustrated. Breakdown is alphabetical by constellation: Andromeda to Cetus in Vol. 1; Chamaeleon to Orion in Vol. 2; and Pavo to Vulpecula in Vol. 3. Hundreds of illustrations. Total of about 2000pp. 6⅛ x 9¼.
23567-X, 23568-8, 23673-0 Pa., Three-vol. set $32.85

THEORY OF WING SECTIONS: INCLUDING A SUMMARY OF AIRFOIL DATA, Ira H. Abbott and A. E. von Doenhoff. Concise compilation of subatomic aerodynamic characteristics of modern NASA wing sections, plus description of theory. 350pp. of tables. 693pp. 5⅜ x 8½.
60586-8 Pa. $9.95

DE RE METALLICA, Georgius Agricola. Translated by Herbert C. Hoover and Lou H. Hoover. The famous Hoover translation of greatest treatise on technological chemistry, engineering, geology, mining of early modern times (1556). All 289 original woodcuts. 638pp. 6¾ x 11.
60006-8 Clothbd. $19.95

THE ORIGIN OF CONTINENTS AND OCEANS, Alfred Wegener. One of the most influential, most controversial books in science, the classic statement for continental drift. Full 1966 translation of Wegener's final (1929) version. 64 illustrations. 246pp. 5⅜ x 8½.(EBE)61708-4 Pa. $5.00

THE PRINCIPLES OF PSYCHOLOGY, William James. Famous long course complete, unabridged. Stream of thought, time perception, memory, experimental methods; great work decades ahead of its time. Still valid, useful; read in many classes. 94 figures. Total of 1391pp. 5⅜ x 8½.
20381-6, 20382-4 Pa., Two-vol. set $17.90

YUCATAN BEFORE AND AFTER THE CONQUEST, Diego de Landa. First English translation of basic book in Maya studies, the only significant account of Yucatan written in the early post-Conquest era. Translated by distinguished Maya scholar William Gates. Appendices, introduction, 4 maps and over 120 illustrations added by translator. 162pp. 5⅜ x 8½.
23622-6 Pa. $3.00

THE MALAY ARCHIPELAGO, Alfred R. Wallace. Spirited travel account by one of founders of modern biology. Touches on zoology, botany, ethnography, geography, and geology. 62 illustrations, maps. 515pp. 5⅜ x 8½.
20187-2 Pa. $6.95

THE DISCOVERY OF THE TOMB OF TUTANKHAMEN, Howard Carter, A. C. Mace. Accompany Carter in the thrill of discovery, as ruined passage suddenly reveals unique, untouched, fabulously rich tomb. Fascinating account, with 106 illustrations. New introduction by J. M. White. Total of 382pp. 5⅜ x 8½. (Available in U.S. only)   23500-9 Pa. $5.50

THE WORLD'S GREATEST SPEECHES, edited by Lewis Copeland and Lawrence W. Lamm. Vast collection of 278 speeches from Greeks up to present. Powerful and effective models; unique look at history. Revised to 1970. Indices. 842pp. 5⅜ x 8½.   20468-5 Pa. $9.95

THE 100 GREATEST ADVERTISEMENTS, Julian Watkins. The priceless ingredient; His master's voice; 99 44/100% pure; over 100 others. How they were written, their impact, etc. Remarkable record. 130 illustrations. 233pp. 7⅞ x 10 3/5.   20540-1 Pa. $6.95

CRUICKSHANK PRINTS FOR HAND COLORING, George Cruickshank. 18 illustrations, one side of a page, on fine-quality paper suitable for watercolors. Caricatures of people in society (c. 1820) full of trenchant wit. Very large format. 32pp. 11 x 16.   23684-6 Pa. $6.00

THIRTY-TWO COLOR POSTCARDS OF TWENTIETH-CENTURY AMERICAN ART, Whitney Museum of American Art. Reproduced in full color in postcard form are 31 art works and one shot of the museum. Calder, Hopper, Rauschenberg, others. Detachable. 16pp. 8¼ x 11.
23629-3 Pa. $3.50

MUSIC OF THE SPHERES: THE MATERIAL UNIVERSE FROM ATOM TO QUASAR SIMPLY EXPLAINED, Guy Murchie. Planets, stars, geology, atoms, radiation, relativity, quantum theory, light, antimatter, similar topics. 319 figures. 664pp. 5⅜ x 8½.
21809-0, 21810-4 Pa., Two-vol. set $11.00

EINSTEIN'S THEORY OF RELATIVITY, Max Born. Finest semi-technical account; covers Einstein, Lorentz, Minkowski, and others, with much detail, much explanation of ideas and math not readily available elsewhere on this level. For student, non-specialist. 376pp. 5⅜ x 8½.
60769-0 Pa. $5.00

THE SENSE OF BEAUTY, George Santayana. Masterfully written discussion of nature of beauty, materials of beauty, form, expression; art, literature, social sciences all involved. 168pp. 5⅜ x 8½.   20238-0 Pa. $3.50

ON THE IMPROVEMENT OF THE UNDERSTANDING, Benedict Spinoza. Also contains *Ethics, Correspondence,* all in excellent R. Elwes translation. Basic works on entry to philosophy, pantheism, exchange of ideas with great contemporaries. 402pp. 5⅜ x 8½.   20250-X Pa. $5.95

THE TRAGIC SENSE OF LIFE, Miguel de Unamuno. Acknowledged masterpiece of existential literature, one of most important books of 20th century. Introduction by Madariaga. 367pp. 5⅜ x 8½.
20257-7 Pa. $6.00

THE GUIDE FOR THE PERPLEXED, Moses Maimonides. Great classic of medieval Judaism attempts to reconcile revealed religion (Pentateuch, commentaries) with Aristotelian philosophy. Important historically, still relevant in problems. Unabridged Friedlander translation. Total of 473pp. 5⅜ x 8½.   20351-4 Pa. $6.95

THE I CHING (THE BOOK OF CHANGES), translated by James Legge. Complete translation of basic text plus appendices by Confucius, and Chinese commentary of most penetrating divination manual ever prepared. Indispensable to study of early Oriental civilizations, to modern inquiring reader. 448pp. 5⅜ x 8½.   21062-6 Pa. $6.00

THE EGYPTIAN BOOK OF THE DEAD, E. A. Wallis Budge. Complete reproduction of Ani's papyrus, finest ever found. Full hieroglyphic text, interlinear transliteration, word for word translation, smooth translation. Basic work, for Egyptology, for modern study of psychic matters. Total of 533pp. 6½ x 9¼. (USCO)   21866-X Pa. $8.50

THE GODS OF THE EGYPTIANS, E. A. Wallis Budge. Never excelled for richness, fullness: all gods, goddesses, demons, mythical figures of Ancient Egypt; their legends, rites, incarnations, variations, powers, etc. Many hieroglyphic texts cited. Over 225 illustrations, plus 6 color plates. Total of 988pp. 6⅛ x 9¼. (EBE)
22055-9, 22056-7 Pa., Two-vol. set $20.00

THE STANDARD BOOK OF QUILT MAKING AND COLLECTING, Marguerite Ickis. Full information, full-sized patterns for making 46 traditional quilts, also 150 other patterns. Quilted cloths, lame, satin quilts, etc. 483 illustrations. 273pp. 6⅞ x 9⅝.   20582-7 Pa. $5.95

CORAL GARDENS AND THEIR MAGIC, Bronsilaw Malinowski. Classic study of the methods of tilling the soil and of agricultural rites in the Trobriand Islands of Melanesia. Author is one of the most important figures in the field of modern social anthropology. 143 illustrations. Indexes. Total of 911pp. of text. 5⅝ x 8¼. (Available in U.S. only)
23597-1 Pa. $12.95

THE PHILOSOPHY OF HISTORY, Georg W. Hegel. Great classic of Western thought develops concept that history is not chance but a rational process, the evolution of freedom. 457pp. 5⅜ x 8½.   20112-0 Pa. $6.00

LANGUAGE, TRUTH AND LOGIC, Alfred J. Ayer. Famous, clear introduction to Vienna, Cambridge schools of Logical Positivism. Role of philosophy, elimination of metaphysics, nature of analysis, etc. 160pp. 5⅜ x 8½. (USCO)   20010-8 Pa. $2.50

A PREFACE TO LOGIC, Morris R. Cohen. Great City College teacher in renowned, easily followed exposition of formal logic, probability, values, logic and world order and similar topics; no previous background needed. 209pp. 5⅜ x 8½.   23517-3 Pa. $4.95

REASON AND NATURE, Morris R. Cohen. Brilliant analysis of reason and its multitudinous ramifications by charismatic teacher. Interdisciplinary, synthesizing work widely praised when it first appeared in 1931. Second (1953) edition. Indexes. 496pp. 5⅜ x 8½.   23633-1 Pa. $7.50

AN ESSAY CONCERNING HUMAN UNDERSTANDING, John Locke. The only complete edition of enormously important classic, with authoritative editorial material by A. C. Fraser. Total of 1176pp. 5⅜ x 8½.
20530-4, 20531-2 Pa., Two-vol. set $16.00

HANDBOOK OF MATHEMATICAL FUNCTIONS WITH FORMULAS, GRAPHS, AND MATHEMATICAL TABLES, edited by Milton Abramowitz and Irene A. Stegun. Vast compendium: 29 sets of tables, some to as high as 20 places. 1,046pp. 8 x 10½.   61272-4 Pa. $17.95

MATHEMATICS FOR THE PHYSICAL SCIENCES, Herbert S. Wilf. Highly acclaimed work offers clear presentations of vector spaces and matrices, orthogonal functions, roots of polynomial equations, conformal mapping, calculus of variations, etc. Knowledge of theory of. functions of real and complex variables is assumed. Exercises and solutions. Index. 284pp. 5⅝ x 8¼.   63635-6 Pa. $5.00

THE PRINCIPLE OF RELATIVITY, Albert Einstein et al. Eleven most important original papers on special and general theories. Seven by Einstein, two by Lorentz, one each by Minkowski and Weyl. All translated, unabridged. 216pp. 5⅜ x 8½.   60081-5 Pa. $3.50

THERMODYNAMICS, Enrico Fermi. A classic of modern science. Clear, organized treatment of systems, first and second laws, entropy, thermodynamic potentials, gaseous reactions, dilute solutions, entropy constant. No math beyond calculus required. Problems. 160pp. 5⅜ x 8½.
60361-X Pa. $4.00

ELEMENTARY MECHANICS OF FLUIDS, Hunter Rouse. Classic undergraduate text widely considered to be far better than many later books. Ranges from fluid velocity and acceleration to role of compressibility in fluid motion. Numerous examples, questions, problems. 224 illustrations. 376pp. 5⅝ x 8¼.   63699-2 Pa. $7.00

CATALOGUE OF DOVER BOOKS

THE AMERICAN SENATOR, Anthony Trollope. Little known, long unavailable Trollope novel on a grand scale. Here are humorous comment on American vs. English culture, and stunning portrayal of a heroine/villainess. Superb evocation of Victorian village life. 561pp. 5⅜ x 8½.
23801-6 Pa. $7.95

WAS IT MURDER? James Hilton. The author of *Lost Horizon* and *Goodbye, Mr. Chips* wrote one detective novel (under a pen-name) which was quickly forgotten and virtually lost, even at the height of Hilton's fame. This edition brings it back—a finely crafted public school puzzle resplendent with Hilton's stylish atmosphere. A thoroughly English thriller by the creator of Shangri-la. 252pp. 5⅜ x 8. (Available in U.S. only)
23774-5 Pa. $3.00

CENTRAL PARK: A PHOTOGRAPHIC GUIDE, Victor Laredo and Henry Hope Reed. 121 superb photographs show dramatic views of Central Park: Bethesda Fountain, Cleopatra's Needle, Sheep Meadow, the Blockhouse, plus people engaged in many park activities: ice skating, bike riding, etc. Captions by former Curator of Central Park, Henry Hope Reed, provide historical view, changes, etc. Also photos of N.Y. landmarks on park's periphery. 96pp. 8½ x 11.
23750-8 Pa. $4.50

NANTUCKET IN THE NINETEENTH CENTURY, Clay Lancaster. 180 rare photographs, stereographs, maps, drawings and floor plans recreate unique American island society. Authentic scenes of shipwreck, lighthouses, streets, homes are arranged in geographic sequence to provide walking-tour guide to old Nantucket existing today. Introduction, captions. 160pp. 8⅞ x 11¾.
23747-8 Pa. $7.95

STONE AND MAN: A PHOTOGRAPHIC EXPLORATION, Andreas Feininger. 106 photographs by *Life* photographer Feininger portray man's deep passion for stone through the ages. Stonehenge-like megaliths, fortified towns, sculpted marble and crumbling tenements show textures, beauties, fascination. 128pp. 9¼ x 10¾.
23756-7 Pa. $5.95

CIRCLES, A MATHEMATICAL VIEW, D. Pedoe. Fundamental aspects of college geometry, non-Euclidean geometry, and other branches of mathematics: representing circle by point. Poincare model, isoperimetric property, etc. Stimulating recreational reading. 66 figures. 96pp. 5⅝ x 8¼.
63698-4 Pa. $3.50

THE DISCOVERY OF NEPTUNE, Morton Grosser. Dramatic scientific history of the investigations leading up to the actual discovery of the eighth planet of our solar system. Lucid, well-researched book by well-known historian of science. 172pp. 5⅜ x 8½.
23726-5 Pa. $3.50

THE DEVIL'S DICTIONARY. Ambrose Bierce. Barbed, bitter, brilliant witticisms in the form of a dictionary. Best, most ferocious satire America has produced. 145pp. 5⅜ x 8½.
20487-1 Pa. $2.50

HISTORY OF BACTERIOLOGY, William Bulloch. The only comprehensive history of bacteriology from the beginnings through the 19th century. Special emphasis is given to biography-Leeuwenhoek, etc. Brief
accounts of 350 bacteriologists form a separate section. No clearer, fuller
study, suitable to scientists and general readers, has yet been written. 52
illustrations. 448pp. 5⅝ x 8¼.   23761-3 Pa. $6.50

THE COMPLETE NONSENSE OF EDWARD LEAR, Edward Lear. All
nonsense limericks, zany alphabets, Owl and Pussycat, songs, nonsense
botany, etc., illustrated by Lear. Total of 321pp. 5⅜ x 8½. (Available
in U.S. only)   20167-8 Pa. $4.50

INGENIOUS MATHEMATICAL PROBLEMS AND METHODS, Louis
A. Graham. Sophisticated material from Graham *Dial*, applied and pure;
stresses solution methods. Logic, number theory, networks, inversions, etc.
237pp. 5⅜ x 8½.   20545-2 Pa. $4.50

BEST MATHEMATICAL PUZZLES OF SAM LOYD, edited by Martin
Gardner. Bizarre, original, whimsical puzzles by America's greatest puzzler.
From fabulously rare *Cyclopedia*, including famous 14-15 puzzles, the
Horse of a Different Color, 115 more. Elementary math. 150 illustrations.
167pp. 5⅜ x 8½.   20498-7 Pa. $3.50

THE BASIS OF COMBINATION IN CHESS, J. du Mont. Easy-to-follow,
instructive book on elements of combination play, with chapters on each
piece and every powerful combination team—two knights, bishop and
knight, rook and bishop, etc. 250 diagrams. 218pp. 5⅜ x 8½. (Available
in U.S. only)   23644-7 Pa. $4.50

MODERN CHESS STRATEGY, Ludek Pachman. The use of the queen,
the active king, exchanges, pawn play, the center, weak squares, etc.
Section on rook alone worth price of the book. Stress on the moderns.
Often considered the most important book on strategy. 314pp. 5⅜ x 8½.
                                                            20290-9 Pa. $5.00

LASKER'S MANUAL OF CHESS, Dr. Emanuel Lasker. Great world
champion offers very thorough coverage of all aspects of chess. Combinations, position play, openings, end game, aesthetics of chess, philosophy of
struggle, much more. Filled with analyzed games. 390pp. 5⅜ x 8½.
                                                            20640-8 Pa. $5.95

500 MASTER GAMES OF CHESS, S. Tartakower, J. du Mont. Vast
collection of great chess games from 1798-1938, with much material no-
where else readily available. Fully annotated, arranged by opening for
easier study. 664pp. 5⅜ x 8½.   23208-5 Pa. $8.50

A GUIDE TO CHESS ENDINGS, Dr. Max Euwe, David Hooper. One
of the finest modern works on chess endings. Thorough analysis of the
most frequently encountered endings by former world champion. 331
examples, each with diagram. 248pp. 5⅜ x 8½.   23332-4 Pa. $3.95

THE COMPLETE BOOK OF DOLL MAKING AND COLLECTING, Catherine Christopher. Instructions, patterns for dozens of dolls, from rag doll on up to elaborate, historically accurate figures. Mould faces, sew clothing, make doll houses, etc. Also collecting information. Many illustrations. 288pp. 6 x 9. 22066-4 Pa. $4.95

THE DAGUERREOTYPE IN AMERICA, Beaumont Newhall. Wonderful portraits, 1850's townscapes, landscapes; full text plus 104 photographs. The basic book. Enlarged 1976 edition. 272pp. 8¼ x 11¼.
23322-7 Pa. $7.95

CRAFTSMAN HOMES, Gustav Stickley. 296 architectural drawings, floor plans, and photographs illustrate 40 different kinds of "Mission-style" homes from The Craftsman (1901-16), voice of American style of simplicity and organic harmony. Thorough coverage of Craftsman idea in text and picture, now collector's item. 224pp. 8⅛ x 11. 23791-5 Pa. $6.50

PEWTER-WORKING: INSTRUCTIONS AND PROJECTS, Burl N. Osborn. & Gordon O. Wilber. Introduction to pewter-working for amateur craftsman. History and characteristics of pewter; tools, materials, step-by-step instructions. Photos, line drawings, diagrams. Total of 160pp. 7⅞ x 10¾. 23786-9 Pa. $3.50

THE GREAT CHICAGO FIRE, edited by David Lowe. 10 dramatic, eyewitness accounts of the 1871 disaster, including one of the aftermath and rebuilding, plus 70 contemporary photographs and illustrations of the ruins—courthouse, Palmer House, Great Central Depot, etc. Introduction by David Lowe. 87pp. 8¼ x 11. 23771-0 Pa. $4.00

SILHOUETTES: A PICTORIAL ARCHIVE OF VARIED ILLUSTRATIONS, edited by Carol Belanger Grafton. Over 600 silhouettes from the 18th to 20th centuries include profiles and full figures of men and women, children, birds and animals, groups and scenes, nature, ships, an alphabet. Dozens of uses for commercial artists and craftspeople. 144pp. 8⅜ x 11¼.
23781-8 Pa. $4.50

ANIMALS: 1,419 COPYRIGHT-FREE ILLUSTRATIONS OF MAMMALS, BIRDS, FISH, INSECTS, ETC., edited by Jim Harter. Clear wood engravings present, in extremely lifelike poses, over 1,000 species of animals. One of the most extensive copyright-free pictorial sourcebooks of its kind. Captions. Index. 284pp. 9 x 12. 23766-4 Pa. $8.95

INDIAN DESIGNS FROM ANCIENT ECUADOR, Frederick W. Shaffer. 282 original designs by pre-Columbian Indians of Ecuador (500-1500 A.D.). Designs include people, mammals, birds, reptiles, fish, plants, heads, geometric designs. Use as is or alter for advertising, textiles, leathercraft, etc. Introduction. 95pp. 8¾ x 11¼. 23764-8 Pa. $4.50

SZIGETI ON THE VIOLIN, Joseph Szigeti. Genial, loosely structured tour by premier violinist, featuring a pleasant mixture of reminiscenes, insights into great music and musicians, innumerable tips for practicing violinists. 385 musical passages. 256pp. 5⅝ x 8¼. 23763-X Pa. $4.00

TONE POEMS, SERIES II: TILL EULENSPIEGELS LUSTIGE STREICHE, ALSO SPRACH ZARATHUSTRA, AND EIN HELDEN-LEBEN, Richard Strauss. Three important orchestral works, including very popular *Till Eulenspiegel's Marry Pranks*, reproduced in full score from original editions. Study score. 315pp. 9⅜ x 12¼. (Available in U.S. only)
23755-9 Pa. $8.95

TONE POEMS, SERIES I: DON JUAN, TOD UND VERKLARUNG AND DON QUIXOTE, Richard Strauss. Three of the most often performed and recorded works in entire orchestral repertoire, reproduced in full score from original editions. Study score. 286pp. 9⅜ x 12¼. (Available in U.S. only)
23754-0 Pa. $8.95

11 LATE STRING QUARTETS, Franz Joseph Haydn. The form which Haydn defined and "brought to perfection." (*Grove's*). 11 string quartets in complete score, his last and his best. The first in a projected series of the complete Haydn string quartets. Reliable modern Eulenberg edition, otherwise difficult to obtain. 320pp. 8⅜ x 11¼. (Available in U.S. only)
23753-2 Pa. $8.95

FOURTH, FIFTH AND SIXTH SYMPHONIES IN FULL SCORE, Peter Ilyitch Tchaikovsky. Complete orchestral scores of Symphony No. 4 in F Minor, Op. 36; Symphony No. 5 in E Minor, Op. 64; Symphony No. 6 in B Minor, "Pathetique," Op. 74. Bretikopf & Hartel eds. Study score. 480pp. 9⅜ x 12¼. 23861-X Pa. $10.95

THE MARRIAGE OF FIGARO: COMPLETE SCORE, Wolfgang A. Mozart. Finest comic opera ever written. Full score, not to be confused with piano renderings. Peters edition. Study score. 448pp. 9⅜ x 12¼. (Available in U.S. only)
23751-6 Pa. $12.95

"IMAGE" ON THE ART AND EVOLUTION OF THE FILM, edited by Marshall Deutelbaum. Pioneering book brings together for first time 38 groundbreaking articles on early silent films from *Image* and 263 illustrations newly shot from rare prints in the collection of the International Museum of Photography. A landmark work. Index. 256pp. 8¼ x 11.
23777-X Pa. $8.95

AROUND-THE-WORLD COOKY BOOK, Lois Lintner Sumption and Marguerite Lintner Ashbrook. 373 cooky and frosting recipes from 28 countries (America, Austria, China, Russia, Italy, etc.) include Viennese kisses, rice wafers, London strips, lady fingers, hony, sugar spice, maple cookies, etc. Clear instructions. All tested. 38 drawings. 182pp. 5⅜ x 8.
23802-4 Pa. $2.75

THE ART NOUVEAU STYLE, edited by Roberta Waddell. 579 rare photographs, not available elsewhere, of works in jewelry, metalwork, glass, ceramics, textiles, architecture and furniture by 175 artists—Mucha, Seguy, Lalique, Tiffany, Gaudin, Hohlwein, Saarinen, and many others. 288pp. 8⅜ x 11¼. 23515-7 Pa. $8.95

THE CURVES OF LIFE, Theodore A. Cook. Examination of shells, leaves, horns, human body, art, etc., in *"the* classic reference on how the golden ratio applies to spirals and helices in nature . . . . "—Martin Gardner. 426 illustrations. Total of 512pp. 5⅜ x 8½.   23701-X Pa. **$6.95**

AN ILLUSTRATED FLORA OF THE NORTHERN UNITED STATES AND CANADA, Nathaniel L. Britton, Addison Brown. Encyclopedic work covers 4666 species, ferns on up. Everything. Full botanical information, illustration for each. This earlier edition is preferred by many to more recent revisions. 1913 edition. Over 4000 illustrations, total of 2087pp. 6⅛ x 9¼.   22642-5, 22643-3, 22644-1 Pa., Three-vol. set **$28.50**

MANUAL OF THE GRASSES OF THE UNITED STATES, A. S. Hitchcock, U.S. Dept. of Agriculture. The basic study of American grasses, both indigenous and escapes, cultivated and wild. Over 1400 species. Full descriptions, information. Over 1100 maps, illustrations. Total of 1051pp. 5⅜ x 8½.   22717-0, 22718-9 Pa., Two-vol. set **$17.00**

THE CACTACEAE,, Nathaniel L. Britton, John N. Rose. Exhaustive, definitive. Every cactus in the world. Full botanical descriptions. Thorough statement of nomenclatures, habitat, detailed finding keys. The one book needed by every cactus enthusiast. Over 1275 illustrations. Total of 1080pp. 8 x 10¼.   21191-6, 21192-4 Clothbd., Two-vol. set **$50.00**

AMERICAN MEDICINAL PLANTS, Charles F. Millspaugh. Full descriptions, 180 plants covered: history; physical description; methods of preparation with all chemical constituents extracted; all claimed curative or adverse effects. 180 full-page plates. Classification table. 804pp. 6½ x 9¼.
23034-1 Pa. **$13.95**

A MODERN HERBAL, Margaret Grieve. Much the fullest, most exact, most useful compilation of herbal material. Gigantic alphabetical encyclopedia, from aconite to zedoary, gives botanical information, medical properties, folklore, economic uses, and much else. Indispensable to serious reader. 161 illustrations. 888pp. 6½ x 9¼. (Available in U.S. only)
22798-7, 22799-5 Pa., Two-vol. set **$15.00**

THE HERBAL or GENERAL HISTORY OF PLANTS, John Gerard. The 1633 edition revised and enlarged by Thomas Johnson. Containing almost 2850 plant descriptions and 2705 superb illustrations, Gerard's *Herbal* is a monumental work, the book all modern English herbals are derived from, the one herbal every serious enthusiast should have in its entirety. Original editions are worth perhaps $750. 1678pp. 8½ x 12¼.
23147-X Clothbd. **$75.00**

MANUAL OF THE TREES OF NORTH AMERICA, Charles S. Sargent. The basic survey of every native tree and tree-like shrub, 717 species in all. Extremely full descriptions, information on habitat, growth, locales, economics, etc. Necessary to every serious tree lover. Over 100 finding keys. 783 illustrations. Total of 986pp. 5⅜ x 8½.
20277-1, 20278-X Pa., Two-vol. set **$12.00**

GREAT NEWS PHOTOS AND THE STORIES BEHIND THEM, John Faber. Dramatic volume of 140 great news photos, 1855 through 1976, and revealing stories behind them, with both historical and technical information. Hindenburg disaster, shooting of Oswald, nomination of Jimmy Carter, etc. 160pp. 8¼ x 11. 23667-6 Pa. $6.00

CRUICKSHANK'S PHOTOGRAPHS OF BIRDS OF AMERICA, Allan D. Cruickshank. Great ornithologist, photographer presents 177 closeups, groupings, panoramas, flightings, etc., of about 150 different birds. Expanded *Wings in the Wilderness*. Introduction by Helen G. Cruickshank. 191pp. 8¼ x 11. 23497-5 Pa. $7.95

AMERICAN WILDLIFE AND PLANTS, A. C. Martin, et al. Describes food habits of more than 1000 species of mammals, birds, fish. Special treatment of important food plants. Over 300 illustrations. 500pp. 5⅜ x 8½. 20793-5 Pa. $6.50

THE PEOPLE CALLED SHAKERS, Edward D. Andrews. Lifetime of research, definitive study of Shakers: origins, beliefs, practices, dances, social organization, furniture and crafts, impact on 19th-century USA, present heritage. Indispensable to student of American history, collector. 33 illustrations. 351pp. 5⅜ x 8½. 21081-2 Pa. $4.50

OLD NEW YORK IN EARLY PHOTOGRAPHS, Mary Black. New York City as it was in 1853-1901, through 196 wonderful photographs from N.-Y. Historical Society. Great Blizzard, Lincoln's funeral procession, great buildings. 228pp. 9 x 12. 22907-6 Pa. $8.95

MR. LINCOLN'S CAMERA MAN: MATHEW BRADY, Roy Meredith. Over 300 Brady photos reproduced directly from original negatives, photos. Jackson, Webster, Grant, Lee, Carnegie, Barnum; Lincoln; Battle Smoke, Death of Rebel Sniper, Atlanta Just After Capture. Lively commentary. 368pp. 8⅜ x 11¼. 23021-X Pa. $11.95

TRAVELS OF WILLIAM BARTRAM, William Bartram. From 1773-8, Bartram explored Northern Florida, Georgia, Carolinas, and reported on wild life, plants, Indians, early settlers. Basic account for period, entertaining reading. Edited by Mark Van Doren. 13 illustrations. 141pp. 5⅜ x 8½. 20013-2 Pa. $6.00

THE GENTLEMAN AND CABINET MAKER'S DIRECTOR, Thomas Chippendale. Full reprint, 1762 style book, most influential of all time; chairs, tables, sofas, mirrors, cabinets, etc. 200 plates, plus 24 photographs of surviving pieces. 249pp. 9⅞ x 12¾. 21601-2 Pa. $8.95

AMERICAN CARRIAGES, SLEIGHS, SULKIES AND CARTS, edited by Don H. Berkebile. 168 Victorian illustrations from catalogues, trade journals, fully captioned. Useful for artists. Author is Assoc. Curator, Div. of Transportation of Smithsonian Institution. 168pp. 8½ x 9½. 23328-6 Pa. $5.00

SECOND PIATIGORSKY CUP, edited by Isaac Kashdan. One of the greatest tournament books ever produced in the English language. All 90 games of the 1966 tournament, annotated by players, most annotated by both players. Features Petrosian, Spassky, Fischer, Larsen, six others. 228pp. 5⅜ x 8½.   23572-6 Pa. $3.50

ENCYCLOPEDIA OF CARD TRICKS, revised and edited by Jean Hugard. How to perform over 600 card tricks, devised by the world's greatest magicians: impromptus, spelling tricks, key cards, using special packs, much, much more. Additional chapter on card technique. 66 illustrations. 402pp. 5⅜ x 8½. (Available in U.S. only)   21252-1 Pa. **$5.95**

MAGIC: STAGE ILLUSIONS, SPECIAL EFFECTS AND TRICK PHO-TOGRAPHY, Albert A. Hopkins, Henry R. Evans. One of the great classics; fullest, most authorative explanation of vanishing lady, levitations, scores of other great stage effects. Also small magic, automata, stunts. 446 illus-trations. 556pp. 5⅜ x 8½.   23344-8 Pa. $6.95

THE SECRETS OF HOUDINI, J. C. Cannell. Classic study of Houdini's incredible magic, exposing closely-kept professional secrets and revealing, in general terms, the whole art of stage magic. 67 illustrations. 279pp. 5⅜ x 8½.   22913-0 Pa. $4.00

HOFFMANN'S MODERN MAGIC, Professor Hoffmann. One of the best, and best-known, magicians' manuals of the past century. Hundreds of tricks from card tricks and simple sleight of hand to elaborate illusions involving construction of complicated machinery. 332 illustrations. 563pp. 5⅜ x 8½.   23623-4 Pa. $6.95

THOMAS NAST'S CHRISTMAS DRAWINGS, Thomas Nast. Almost all Christmas drawings by creator of image of Santa Claus as we know it, and one of America's foremost illustrators and political cartoonists. 66 illustrations. 3 illustrations in color on covers. 96pp. 8⅜ x 11¼.
                                                                  23660-9 Pa. $3.50

FRENCH COUNTRY COOKING FOR AMERICANS, Louis Diat. 500 easy-to-make, authentic provincial recipes compiled by former head chef at New York's Fitz-Carlton Hotel: onion soup, lamb stew, potato pie, more. 309pp. 5⅜ x 8½.   23665-X Pa. $3.95

SAUCES, FRENCH AND FAMOUS, Louis Diat. Complete book gives over 200 specific recipes: bechamel, Bordelaise, hollandaise, Cumberland, apri-cot, etc. Author was one of this century's finest chefs, originator of vichyssoise and many other dishes. Index. 156pp. 5⅜ x 8.
                                                                  23663-3 Pa. $2.75

TOLL HOUSE TRIED AND TRUE RECIPES, Ruth Graves Wakefield. Authentic recipes from the famous Mass. restaurant: popovers, veal and ham loaf, Toll House baked beans, chocolate cake crumb pudding, much more. Many helpful hints. Nearly 700 recipes. Index. 376pp. 5⅜ x 8½.
                                                                  23560-2 Pa. $4.95

ILLUSTRATED GUIDE TO SHAKER FURNITURE, Robert Meader. Director, Shaker Museum, Old Chatham, presents up-to-date coverage of all furniture and appurtenances, with much on local styles not available elsewhere. 235 photos. 146pp. 9 x 12. 22819-3 Pa. $6.95

COOKING WITH BEER, Carole Fahy. Beer has as superb an effect on food as wine, and at fraction of cost. Over 250 recipes for appetizers, soups, main dishes, desserts, breads, etc. Index. 144pp. 5⅜ x 8½. (Available in U.S. only) 23661-7 Pa. $3.00

STEWS AND RAGOUTS, Kay Shaw Nelson. This international cookbook offers wide range of 108 recipes perfect for everyday, special occasions, meals-in-themselves, main dishes. Economical, nutritious, easy-to-prepare: goulash, Irish stew, boeuf bourguignon, etc. Index. 134pp. 5⅜ x 8½. 23662-5 Pa. $3.95

DELICIOUS MAIN COURSE DISHES, Marian Tracy. Main courses are the most important part of any meal. These 200 nutritious, economical recipes from around the world make every meal a delight. "I . . . have found it so useful in my own household,"—N.Y. Times. Index. 219pp. 5⅜ x 8½. 23664-1 Pa. $3.95

FIVE ACRES AND INDEPENDENCE, Maurice G. Kains. Great back-to-the-land classic explains basics of self-sufficient farming: economics, plants, crops, animals, orchards, soils, land selection, host of other necessary things. Do not confuse with skimpy faddist literature; Kains was one of America's greatest agriculturalists. 95 illustrations. 397pp. 5⅜ x 8½. 20974-1 Pa. $4.95

A PRACTICAL GUIDE FOR THE BEGINNING FARMER, Herbert Jacobs. Basic, extremely useful first book for anyone thinking about moving to the country and starting a farm. Simpler than Kains, with greater emphasis on country living in general. 246pp. 5⅜ x 8½. 23675-7 Pa. $3.95

PAPERMAKING, Dard Hunter. Definitive book on the subject by the foremost authority in the field. Chapters dealing with every aspect of history of craft in every part of the world. Over 320 illustrations. 2nd, revised and enlarged (1947) edition. 672pp. 5⅜ x 8½. 23619-6 Pa. $8.95

THE ART DECO STYLE, edited by Theodore Menten. Furniture, jewelry, metalwork, ceramics, fabrics, lighting fixtures, interior decors, exteriors, graphics from pure French sources. Best sampling around. Over 400 photographs. 183pp. 8⅜ x 11¼. 22824-X Pa. $6.95

ACKERMANN'S COSTUME PLATES, Rudolph Ackermann. Selection of 96 plates from the Repository of Arts, best published source of costume for English fashion during the early 19th century. 12 plates also in color. Captions, glossary and introduction by editor Stella Blum. Total of 120pp. 8⅜ x 11¼. 23690-0 Pa. $5.00

THE ANATOMY OF THE HORSE, George Stubbs. Often considered the great masterpiece of animal anatomy. Full reproduction of 1766 edition, plus prospectus; original text and modernized text. 36 plates. Introduction by Eleanor Garvey. 121pp. 11 x 14¾.   23402-9 Pa. **$8.95**

BRIDGMAN'S LIFE DRAWING, George B. Bridgman. More than 500 illustrative drawings and text teach you to abstract the body into its major masses, use light and shade, proportion; as well as specific areas of anatomy, of which Bridgman is master. 192pp. 6½ x 9¼. (Available in U.S. only)
22710-3 Pa. **$4.50**

ART NOUVEAU DESIGNS IN COLOR, Alphonse Mucha, Maurice Verneuil, Georges Auriol. Full-color reproduction of *Combinaisons ornementales* (c. 1900) by Art Nouveau masters. Floral, animal, geometric, interlacings, swashes—borders, frames, spots—all incredibly beautiful. 60 plates, hundreds of designs. 9⅜ x 8-1/16.   22885-1 Pa. **$4.50**

FULL-COLOR FLORAL DESIGNS IN THE ART NOUVEAU STYLE, E. A. Seguy. 166 motifs, on 40 plates, from *Les fleurs et leurs applications decoratives* (1902): borders, circular designs, repeats, allovers, "spots." All in authentic Art Nouveau colors. 48pp. 9⅜ x 12¼.
23439-8 Pa. **$6.00**

A DIDEROT PICTORIAL ENCYCLOPEDIA OF TRADES AND IN-DUSTRY, edited by Charles C. Gillispie. 485 most interesting plates from the great French Encyclopedia of the 18th century show hundreds of working figures, artifacts, process, land and cityscapes; glassmaking, paper-making, metal extraction, construction, weaving, making furniture, clothing, wigs, dozens. of other activities. Plates fully explained. 920pp. 9 x 12.
22284-5, 22285-3 Clothbd., Two-vol. set **$50.00**

HANDBOOK OF EARLY ADVERTISING ART, Clarence P. Hornung. Largest collection of copyright-free early and antique advertising art ever compiled. Over 6,000 illustrations, from Franklin's time to the 1890's for special effects, novelty. Valuable source, almost inexhaustible.
Pictorial Volume. Agriculture, the zodiac, animals, autos, birds, Christmas, fire engines, flowers, trees, musical instruments, ships, games and sports, much more. Arranged by subject matter and use. 237 plates. 288pp. 9 x 12.
20122-8 Clothbd. **$15.00**

Typographical Volume. Roman and Gothic faces ranging from 10 point to 300 point, "Barnum," German and Old English faces, script, logotypes, scrolls and flourishes, 1115 ornamental initials, 67 complete alphabets, more. 310 plates. 320pp. 9 x 12.   20123-6 Clothbd. **$15.00**

CALLIGRAPHY (CALLIGRAPHIA LATINA), J. G. Schwandner. High point of 18th-century ornamental calligraphy. Very ornate initials, scrolls, borders, cherubs, birds, lettered examples. 172pp. 9 x 13.
20475-8 Pa. **$7.95**

GEOMETRY, RELATIVITY AND THE FOURTH DIMENSION, Rudolf Rucker. Exposition of fourth dimension, means of visualization, concepts of relativity as Flatland characters continue adventures. Popular, easily followed yet accurate, profound. 141 illustrations. 133pp. 5⅜ x 8½.
23400-2 Pa. $2.75

THE ORIGIN OF LIFE, A. I. Oparin. Modern classic in biochemistry, the first rigorous examination of possible evolution of life from nitrocarbon compounds. Non-technical, easily followed. Total of 295pp. 5⅜ x 8½.
60213-3 Pa. $5.95

PLANETS, STARS AND GALAXIES, A. E. Fanning. Comprehensive introductory survey: the sun, solar system, stars, galaxies, universe, cosmology; quasars, radio stars, etc. 24pp. of photographs. 189pp. 5⅜ x 8½. (Available in U.S. only)
21680-2 Pa. $3.75

THE THIRTEEN BOOKS OF EUCLID'S ELEMENTS, translated with introduction and commentary by Sir Thomas L. Heath. Definitive edition. Textual and linguistic. notes, mathematical analysis, 2500 years of critical commentary. Do not confuse with abridged school editions. Total of 1414pp. 5⅜ x 8½.
60088-2, 60089-0, 60090-4 Pa., Three-vol. set $19.50